THE BOOK OF SATURN

"The wisdom and experience of several decades of teaching, practice and research are presented in Zip's excellent *Book of Saturn*. It is a must for the novice, providing a solid foundation for the delineation of Saturn in any horoscope. The clear explanations with many example charts, plus the gold mine of astrological information make *Book of Saturn* an invaluable asset to the library of both the student and professional astrologer."

Jeanne Long, astrological investor and author

The Book of Saturn by Dr. Zipporah Dobyns is a wonderfully insightful book about a traditionally grave matter: Saturn. However, unlike astrologers of olden times who portray Saturn primarily in a negative and fearful manner, Dobyns presents its correlation to human activity as neither "good" nor "bad", but rather "realistic." According to Dobyns, "Saturn symbolizes what we can do, what we can't do, and what we have to do if we want to survive in this world." Upon that basis, she sets forth to show how the principles of Saturn tend to operate psychologically (and ultimately physically) according to its natal sign and house placement, natal aspects, and as a transit, progressed, or solar arc planet to one's natal planets, angles, and even asteroids.

In one sense, this book may be used as a cookbook" - but a very, very good "cookbook." In this sense, it is very well-organized and easy to reference. But it is also infinitely more than a reference book to those who wish to develop a deeper understanding of how Dobyns views and works with astrology, particularly in relation to psychology. In one of her earliest works — *Finding the Person in the Horoscope* — Dobyns set forth her methodology for analyzing horoscopes known as the "zodiac alphabet." This brilliant "macro" or "holistic" concept of astrological application assured her role as one of the most innovative astrological thinkers of not just modern times, but all time. Now with *The Book of Saturn*, Dobyns has gone much further with elucidating her ideas on how one might apply the zodiac alphabet to understanding the psychological processes at work in individuals. Although her primary focus in this book is with Saturn, the #10 principle, she clearly lays out the formula for applying all the other letters as well. The result is a very fulfilling book, one loaded with great knowledge and wisdom.

This is not just an excellent astrology book, but one that may greatly enhance the skills of those who counsel others using astrology. Dobyns demonstrates once again why she is so highly regarded in the world of professional astrology. Highly recommended.

Raymond A. Merriman, President:
International Society of Astrological Research, Inc.

The Book of
Saturn

Zipporah
Dobyns,
Ph.D.

International Standard Book Number 0-935127-33-X

Cover Design by Daryl S. Fuller

Printed in the United States of America

Published by ACS Publications
5521 Ruffin Road
San Diego, CA 92123

First Printing, February 1997

Acknowledgments

A book is always an effort of many individuals. I want especially to thank my editors who are also my wonderful daughter and son, Maritha and Mark Pottenger. They have made many valuable suggestions which hopefully have led to increased clarity in a very complex subject. Lois Rodden's work, which sets the standards for data collectioin, was a tremendous resource. I also want to thank two friends for biographical information on the individuals whose charts were used to illustrate the principles of Saturn. Pearl Negrette and Doc Cottle have both helped immensely with library digging. I hope that they as well as many past and future students and clients will find the book helpful. We are all learning to deal with the challenges of this physical world, and the Saturn principle is one of our most valuable keys to understanding.

Contents

CHAPTER ONE

PRINCIPLES AND BACKGROUND

For thousands of years, humans have been using the sky as their clock and calendar to orient themselves in time, and as their map and compass to orient themselves in space. Neolithic hunters watched the phases of the Moon to keep track of the season when fish would come up the river to spawn. Seafarers were guided across the trackless oceans by the constellations. Modern science acknowledges the value of the sky to this extent, but modern science has accepted the basic theory of materialism, which states that the cosmos has no inherent meaning—that the ultimate reality is composed of random charges of energy ruled by the laws of chance.

Astrology demonstrates that the order in the cosmos is meaningful, not random. Information is a basic component of ultimate reality. The same principles are present in the planets, in life forms, in cultural institutions, in material objects, etc. The modern fields of research called "chaos" and "complexity" are opening the way to a scientific understanding of astrology. These studies show that information is the guiding principle which directs all forms of manifestation, rather than the material substance, the "matter/energy" being manifested. The same "set of instructions" or "information patterns" can describe physical substances at many levels: atomic, molecular, organic, etc. We can call those meaningful patterns models, maps, "archetypes," or life drives or desires, or psychological concepts or constructs. Whatever we name them, they offer insight into ourselves and our world. Materialists tend to be threatened by the implications of this new view of the world, but the leading-edge physicists are realizing that **information is a more primary reality** than the physical matter/energy perceived by our physical senses.

Over thousands of years of observations, humans have been learning to recognize and understand these basic shared principles, and that understanding is still being modified as we observe the correlations between the patterns in the sky and the events on Earth. Early humans associated the planets with the gods, and the nature and movements of the planets were believed to produce events on earth. Some of that ancient belief still lingers in modern astrology, though it is now phrased in terms of vibrations, radiations, and force fields. But when we observe the variety of manifestations which can be associated with any of the basic principles of astrology, it seems obvious to me that we are dealing with sources of information rather than material forces. We can see the same principles described by planets, by signs of the zodiac, by houses of a horoscope, by the nodes of all of the planets, by sub-divisions of the zodiac signs, etc., just as the students of chaos find the same information patterns describing molecules, organs, whole systems in the body, etc.

Knowledge is based on experience. Science does in systematic ways what everyone does in more casual ways. We analyze a variety of experiences looking for shared meaning. Is there a common principle which connects them and makes sense out of them? This is called **inductive reasoning** and is the initial stage of investigating new phenomena. Once we have formulated a theory to explain the detailed experiences with general principles, we can shift to **deductive reasoning**. We say "If this theory is accurate, given this new pattern, this new rearrangement of the basic principles, these details may result." Then, we watch the consequences to see whether our theory is supported by the results experienced. Science includes one more step where this is possible. It sets up conditions for experiments which produce the circumstances, the information pattern, and observes whether or not the predicted details do follow. Astronomy and astrology are not able to rearrange the sky, so these studies have little room for laboratory experiments.

Humans have been carrying out the first two steps in the scientific process for millennia. They watched the patterns in the sky, observed the associated details on Earth, and deduced which sky patterns were likely to be associated with similar Earth details in the future — inductive reasoning was followed by deductive. They noted that Mars was "prominent" when people were more aggressive or had accidents. They noted that Venus was "prominent" when people were more focused on pleasure. The Sun seemed connected to power and the Moon to the birth and nurturing of the young. Obviously, there was no way to set up laboratory experiments to produce different configurations of the planets to see what would happen during such periods, but many competent minds calculated the natural cycles of the planets, learned to forecast their patterns, and watched to see whether the Earth events fit their theories. Still, the results were far from consistent. Though there were some basic agreements on the nature of the planets, there were also major differences of opinion.

Culture and Mythology

Many of the differences were based on the culture of the observers. Saturn, the subject of this book, provides a good example. Most of our astrological theories originated in the Near East, were passed on by Greece and Rome, survived through the Middle Ages, had a brief flowering in the Renaissance, and were dismissed by modern science when it accepted the theory of materialism. For the most part, after astrology was written off by science as superstitious nonsense, it lacked the resources to conduct systematic research. But, in spite of its generally low status, astrology still attracted some competent students who continued to expand our understanding of its basic principles. The life experiences associated with Saturn in the ancient world of Greece, Rome, and India had some obvious differences from some of the experiences observed in the modern world when Saturn was "prominent."

In Greek mythology, Saturn (or *Kronos* to use his Greek name) was classed as a former king. By the time of the flowering of the

Greek culture, *Kronos* had been deposed by his son, *Zeus* (Jupiter, to give his more familiar Roman name). *Zeus* was clearly a god of fire, noted for his thunderbolts. He was also noted for his insatiable sexual appetites, which he indulged rather indiscriminately and which kept his wife, *Hera*, in a state of constant fury. The Greek description of *Zeus* seemed to be more Leo than Sagittarius, though *Apollo* was acknowledged as a god of the Sun. In human lives, *Kronos* (Saturn) was definitely earth, associated with **agriculture, animal husbandry, farm laborers and basically hard work**. A "prominent" Saturn in a human chart was associated with a life dominated by struggles to survive, by limits.

Modern astrology agrees that the principle of Saturn includes the "Puritan" virtues of **hard work, practicality, productivity, responsibility, care with details**, etc. But it has also been observed in association with **authority figures** who wield power in a bureaucratic structure, with **hierarchies of power and the law**, with the **disciplinary parent** in contrast to the Moon as the nurturing parent. We can make sense of this partial shift in our understanding of the Saturn principle when we analyze the cultural changes which have occurred. Astrology was codified by the ancient world during the Arian Age[1] when the supreme value was personal will — a fire principle. In such a society, Mars as the warrior was totally at home. The Sun as the King had dominion over his subjects — his will was law. Jupiter, as indicated above, was not yet clearly defined as the Priest which he became in time, as the ruler of the sign of Sagittarius. But whether he was king or priest, he expressed the fire principle: "I have the right and the power to do what I choose."

Humans who personified the fire roles had slaves to deal with the material world. The idea of an impartial Law which protected the rights of ordinary people may have been conceived by some philosophers, but it was certainly not practiced in the Arian Age. There was no place for a positive Saturn who enforced an impersonal law when the fire people were in control and making their personal wills into law. In India as well as in Greece, astrology was codified during the times of autocratic rulers under a rigid caste system which offered almost no room for personal freedom for most people. There are still many countries controlled by a small group who function "above" the law, but theoretically in democracies the law is impartial and bigger than any individual will. Obviously, this is an ideal which is often breached in human courts, but it still works in the realm of "natural law" and through character (habits) producing destiny (*Karma*).

As we follow this ancient path of inductive/deductive reasoning, it is reasonable to start with the theories and observations of humans through the past millennia, but it is important to recognize that what humans are able to conceive is limited by their culture, by the beliefs of their times. The poems of Hesiod offer us some of the earliest Greek mythology. *Ouranus* (sky) and *Ge* or *Gaia* (Earth), begat the *Titans*, but *Ouranos* would not withdraw from *Ge* to permit her to give birth. With his mother's help, the separation of the sky from the earth was achieved by the *Titan Kronos* (the original Greek name for the god called Saturn by the Romans). *Kronos* managed this feat by castrating his father with a large sickle. But *Kronos* was afraid that his own children might overthrow him as he had his father, so he swallowed his children as his wife, *Rhea*, gave birth. Eventually, *Rhea* tricked *Kronos* by hiding *Zeus* and giving *Kronos* a stone to swallow in his place. In time, *Zeus* forced *Kronos* to disgorge the previously swallowed children, the siblings of *Zeus*, and the latter was recognized as the King. The *Titans* were overthrown by *Zeus* and the other gods with the help of monsters who were also the offspring of *Ge*. In modern terms, the self-confident fire god conquered the earth god as the Arian Age superseded the Taurian Age.

Saturn Principles

Since the Arian Age ended some two to three hundred years before the birth of Jesus and of our current Piscean Age, it is not surprising that some modern cultures have revised their values, which has made it possible for them to conceive and to observe a broader meaning for Saturn. We will not become involved in the arguments over the exact timing of the astrological Ages, but no one questions that we are long past the Arian Age despite the seeming inability of humans to live together in peace. We can now at least conceive of a world in which the Law is impartial even when we see the power of great wealth to sometimes escape the consequences of personal actions. From the east, we have inherited the word "*karma*" to describe action and its consequences, and Saturn is now recognized by many as the primary symbol of the **Law of Karma**. Reincarnation is the East's explanation for the fact that some people do not seem to suffer from their destructive actions. If life is continuous, with one's character evolving through a series of bodies, some karmic consequences might be delayed to be experienced in later "lives."

Based on our current state of understanding of the principles of astrology, Saturn (and its sign, Capricorn, and its "natural" house in a horoscope — the tenth), are keys to the Law on all levels. They include "**natural laws**" like gravity and time which provide the framework in which we live in this material universe. The Saturn principle also includes **cultural regulations** such as stopping for red lights and going through green ones and driving the speed limit. It includes **authority figures** who enforce the law: parents, the police, the boss on a job, the teacher. Appropriately expressed, such power figures carry out the law — they do not make their own wills into law. The Saturn principle also includes one's **conscience**, one's inner law, and guilt when we fail to live according to its limits. Plus, it includes the consequences of how we have handled the laws in the past. In a nutshell, Saturn symbolizes **what we can do, what we can't do, and what we have to do if we want to survive in this material world**. And in its role signifying the nature and the timing of the consequences of what we have done and are doing, Saturn is our great teacher. It signals our times for feedback, for a **report card** from the world. Ignorance does not excuse us from consequences.

It is valuable to learn as much as we can through reading, listening, observing others, etc., but in the end, the only way we know what is "lawful" is to do it and to observe the consequences. Then, we can decide whether we want to do more of the action. When astrologers teach that Saturn is negative, I ask "Would you like to live in a world without law? Imagine going to bed at night wondering whether gravity might be canceled during the night and you would wake up against the ceiling." It is only the fact that the world is lawful that gives us any power. By understanding the law and working with it, we can cope with the world. We fly planes that are heavier than air by understanding and working with gravity, not by fearing it, ignoring it, or fighting it. We can learn to use time wisely. Individuals who have learned to be practical, productive, competent, realistic, etc. can cope effectively with the material world. Of course, if we only lived the earth sides of life, it would not be much fun. We all have fire and air and water as well as earth[2], and we need to find appropriate ways to satisfy each of our basic drives.

Astrology Represents 12 Sides of Life

As indicated previously, I think that the model of life offered by astrology describes twelve basic drives or desires, and that each of them is symbolized by at least one planet, by a zodiac sign, and by a horoscope house. There are also many other astronomical factors which represent the same twelve sides of life, but this book will focus on the three major forms of our "astrological alphabet."

Astrological Alphabet

Letter	Planet & Glyph		House	Sign & Glyph	
1	Mars	♂	1	Aries	♈
2	Venus	♀	2	Taurus	♉
3	Mercury	☿	3	Gemini	♊
4	Moon	☽	4	Cancer	♋
5	Sun	☉	5	Leo	♌
6	Mercury	☿	6	Virgo	♍
	Ceres	⚳			
	Vesta	⚶			
7	Venus	♀	7	Libra	♎
	Pallas	⚴			
8	Pluto	♀ or ♇	8	Scorpio	♏
	Juno	⚵			
9	Jupiter	♃	9	Sagittarius	♐
	Chiron	⚷			
10	Saturn	♄	10	Capricorn	♑
11	Uranus	♅	11	Aquarius	♒
12	Neptune	♆	12	Pisces	♓

2 See notes on page 225

When discussing the potential relationships between the different desires, it will sometimes be more convenient to talk in terms of the signs to avoid the complication of some planets ruling more than one sign. (That is, "Virgo" could be used as shorthand to represent the planet Mercury, the sign Virgo and the sixth house of the horoscope.) As we discuss the combinations of the principles in our astrological model of life, we will see where the Saturn principle is easier to blend and where there are inherent conflicts with other principles. However, it is very important to remember that the **details in our lives always depend on our handling of our desires**. Conflicting desires can be integrated with compromise, while harmonious desires which reinforce each other can lead to excesses and problems in the life.

CHAPTER TWO

THE ASTROLOGICAL ALPHABET

Cookbooks offer many combinations of a limited number of ingredients. Languages offer many more potentials for combining a limited number of basic ingredients (symbols) to create an unlimited number of products with varying degrees of complexity (words, sentences, paragraphs, chapters, etc.). The products provide a way to conceive of and to describe life. When an object has been given a name, we can discuss it when it is not present and available to let us point to it. So language lets us share information with our own species and, to a limited extent, with other species of life.

Astrology offers us a language to conceive of and to describe life. It has an alphabet which is equivalent to the letters of an alphabet offering a model of life composed of twelve basic desires or drives. Letters can be capitalized or written lower case, or turned into monograms with curls, but an "A" is recognized as carrying the same basic meaning as an "a." In astrology, we have planets, signs of the zodiac, houses of the horoscope, and other variations such as the nodes of all the planets[3] and the dwads[4] in all the signs which symbolize the same twelve basic life desires.

This does not mean that the planets and signs and houses are themselves the "same," but they symbolize the same

---

3 & 4   See notes on page 225

psychological principles. The planets are the most important, like a verb in a sentence. Everything else is metaphorically like adverbs which qualify verbs. It is oversimplified, but there is some truth in the old saying that the planets show "what" you do, the houses show "where" you do it, and the signs show "how" you do it. But the urges of life, the primary twelve desires, are potentially present in all of the different forms of the "letters" of the astrological alphabet, so information on "what" and "where" and "how" can be provided by any of the "tools."

This is a book about Saturn, so we can illustrate the preceding statements with Letter Ten of our astrological alphabet, but first we need an overview of the system. We can think of astrology's model of life as a series of stages of growth from initial self-absorption to final oneness with the Whole. We start with the drive to just be ourselves, to act immediately and spontaneously on personal impulses with **Letter One: Mars, Aries, and the first house**.

Then that fire urge to be and do is directed at a target, seeking pleasure in the physical world, our first "earth" side of life. We may make or spend money, indulge appetites, collect and enjoy possessions, create beauty, etc., with **Letter Two: Venus, Taurus, and the second house.**

Then we try to understand what is happening by developing the conscious side of the mind, the intellect. Curiosity drives us to investigate the world around us and we discover that other people are part of it. We learn to learn, to communicate, to be an equal by sharing the world with peer relationships such as siblings and neighbors. **Letter three** introduces us to air with **Mercury, Gemini, and the third house**.

Letter four completes the first cycle of the four elements. Water symbolizes the subconscious side of the mind where we absorb and assimilate the results of our experiences with the other three elements. Habits live here, and most people operate on automatic pilot most of the time. The subconscious manages the body. It digests our food, repairs damage to the body, keeps us breathing while we sleep, stores information acquired in the past, etc. Habits are great labor savers. Once we learn to do something, it takes less attention and effort to do it again, so we can satisfy the fire urge to break new ground.

Fire asks "What will I experience if I follow this impulse and do what I want to? I'll try it and find out." Earth is basically practical. This can include the ability to be logical, but the primary earth question is "Will this work? What will happen in the physical world if I do this? Do it and see." Air is basically logical, creating abstract conceptual systems, maps and models of ideas. Of course, what is considered logical depends on one's premises, so unless these are initially grounded in the practical earth, we can create castles in the air. Air asks "Is this design internally consistent and how can I communicate it?" Fire and air want to express and they normally possess a sense of humor. Earth and water want to protect, so they are normally more serious. Earth may save for practical reasons, because something could be useful. Water wants emotional security. It asks "How can I protect and preserve what is important to me?" This may simply be personal security or may include others. The water instinct is to hold on and to hold in.

At the water or subconscious level, life is connected, so water is a key to psychic ability. When water factors are combined with fire or earth factors, individuals tend to act on the inner psychic awareness, but they may not be conscious of why they are doing what they are doing and often the action is just carrying out personal habits. Water and air combinations connect the conscious and subconscious potentials of the mind. Individuals with an air-water emphasis can more readily become conscious of the knowledge stored in or accessible to the subconscious. They may or may not **do** anything with the information other than register it mentally and perhaps talk about it. Air is a spectator and commentator. Water may just feel deeply.

Fire and earth are the action elements which impact the world. At the same time, there is a natural, inherent potential for conflict between fire and earth, between the urge to keep changing and the desire for solid results in the world. The fire drive to try something new is also inherently in conflict with the water instinct to cling to the familiar past. Air can be easily combined with the other three elements and can be helpful to all of them. It provides the detachment of a broad perspective which can moderate the emotional intensity of fire and water. It offers the ability to learn vicariously through the observation of others or through visualizing possible consequences without having to knock one's own head actually doing them. It symbolizes the ability to "take things lightly."

Obviously, everyone possesses all the elements and life is a complex mixture. Everything is always potentially present but the emphasis is constantly changing. Natural conflicts need not be a problem, but we do have to find a way to satisfy all of our basic drives. Any part of our nature which is totally denied will make trouble for us. Usually, compromise works best, but we can also alternate when we want to do more of some parts of life. And, just as conflict needs attention but can be handled successfully, the consequences of harmony are not always pleasant. Harmony can lead to excesses which create problems. It is not always true that if some is good, more will be better.

The tragedy of astrology is that so much of it is presented as if it was inevitably "positive" or "negative." **Every astrological principle, every one of our basic drives/desires, can be manifested in "pleasant" or "painful" ways, in an infinite variety of details** which depend on how we try to satisfy the desires. There are always "choices" but most of the time we are not conscious of them because habits are running the show.

Remember, habits live in the subconscious side of the mind which is represented by water in astrology. **Letter four** of our astrological model of life is water and is symbolized by the **Moon, Cancer, and the fourth house**. This includes the baby/mother relationship, the home and family, our need to be nurtured and our ability to nurture others. We may care for children or pets or talk to our plants, and no matter what our age, we always retain a little of our "baby" need to feel sheltered. Properly handled, Letter Four is unconditional love. A baby is protected because it needs it, not because it has earned it.

With **Letter Five, the Sun, Leo, and the fifth house**, we move into fire again. With our initial fire, with Letter One, we simply want to be let alone to do what we please. With Letter Five, we want to do bigger things and we want an audience. We want to pour our unique, creative power out into the world and to have it acknowledged. The Sun is a star, and Letter Five needs to shine. This can include loving and being loved, procreating children, selling,

promoting, or otherwise persuading others to follow our lead, investing, speculating or gambling hoping for a bigger return, etc. Earth follows fire, and with **Letter Six** we need to function effectively in a job and in our physical bodies. **Virgo and the sixth house** symbolize the drive to do something practical and to do it well, to cope with the material world. **Mercury** traditionally is the planetary key to Letter Six, and two of the asteroids, the little planets which are mostly between Mars and Jupiter, also seem to carry similar connotations. **Ceres** is the nurturing side of Virgo with a strong maternal instinct. Work is seen as a way to help people, and Ceres is usually a key to our original mother-figure and to our ability to mother others. **Vesta** marks the need to do a good job for the sake of doing a good job! Individuals who have a prominent Vesta but who lack empathy can be so intent on the immediate goal that they ignore the effect they are having on others. When the subconscious which manages the body is overloaded with negative emotions that are being mostly ignored, it can produce bodily ailments to get our attention. Job frustrations are a common source of illness or accidents. They let us escape the job or other obligations without feeling guilty.

Once we have learned to work effectively and to maintain our health, we are ready to form lasting, adult, peer relationships with **Letters Seven** and **Eight**. **Libra and the seventh house** represent the air side of partnership which seeks pleasure with others but is less emotionally intense than **Scorpio and the eighth house** where we learn to share sensuality, possessions, and passion driven by the water urge toward fusion. **Venus** is the traditional ruler of Letter Seven but the asteroid **Pallas** also carries Libra meanings. Often, this includes potential skill in the graphic arts. Mars is the traditional ruler of Scorpio and remains a co-ruler, but **Pluto** is now recognized by most astrologers as the primary ruler. Another of the asteroids, **Juno,** provides the same message, joining the other significators of Letter Eight.

Letters Seven and Eight are polar partners of Letters One and Two. For many people, their primary challenge involves finding a balance between their own rights and pleasures and the rights and pleasures of others. The relationships may be cooperative or competitive as long as each side can win some of the time to maintain the game and, hopefully, there is mutual pleasure.

When healthy competition, which is facilitating increased abilities on both sides, turns into war and mutual destruction, it has been carried too far.

With **Letter Nine** we leave the interpersonal part of life and enter the transpersonal. Letters One and two focus on purely personal rights and needs. Letter Three is starting to become socialized to recognize the rights of others. With Letter Four we start as a baby but become an adult able to nurture others, so from three through eight we are focused on face-to-face interactions with others. As usual, each element cycle ends with water to mark closure. Letter eight seeks to probe the subconscious depths, to gain self-knowledge and self-mastery. We learn self-knowledge partly through the mirror of a mate and we achieve self-mastery partly through respect for the rights of the mate. The transpersonal Letters (Nine through Twelve) deal with social issues, humanity, abstract knowledge, laws, faith; with issues which involve masses of people and universal principles.

Letter nine marks our search for Truth with a capital "T". As usual, the new element cycle starts with fire, the urge to break new ground, to explore new potentials. **Jupiter, Sagittarius**, and the **ninth house** are all part of the picture describing where and how we search for the meaning of life, the nature of reality, for something to trust, for a way to set up a value hierarchy to make choices. Letter nine is a primary key to our ultimate goals in life, determining where we end in our life. The small planet **Chiron** (which might be a comet) carries the potentials of both sides of Jupiter, which is also a co-ruler of Pisces.

An understanding of **Letter Ten** is the central purpose of this book. **Saturn, Capricorn** and the **tenth house** show our capacity to deal with the **Law**. Letter Ten describes the "Rules of the Game," including "natural laws" like gravity and time, as well as the cultural rules of human societies. It is also a key to the authority figures who enforce the laws and to our inner authority, the conscience and guilt. In current patterns, Letter Ten marks the times when we get the consequences of how we have been handling the laws. It is the ultimate earth side of life, bringing us down to earth if we mishandle gravity.

Metaphorically, any overreach or attempt to avoid our share of the responsibility can result in some type of failure or falling short. Ignorance does not excuse us. *Karma* is just consequences which can be positive or painful. The proper handling of power brings success. We get an "A" on the report card.

Letter eleven with Uranus, Aquarius, and the eleventh house shows the drive to go beyond the laws, to resist any limits. As an air side of life, we may expand knowledge by inventing new technology. We may support democracy, equality, freedom, and human rights in general. If we have properly internalized our conscience so that we know and voluntarily accept the necessary limits, then we can be free to do what we please with Letter Eleven and we normally support the same freedom for everyone else.

Neptune, Pisces and the twelfth house symbolize Letter Twelve, the mystical search for infinite love and beauty and oneness with the Whole. In an infinite variety of ways we may be artists, saviors or victims. The latter is the person who shares a beautiful dream with the artists and saviors but has not found an effective way to move toward the vision, to make the world more ideal. Jupiter remains a co-ruler of Pisces and Chiron can also show where we may play the role of either healer or victim.

Repetition Shows Importance

Every chart includes all the twelve principles, yet each chart is a unique combination. There are many forms of the astrological alphabet, many ways to "say the same thing." Important features in the nature will be shown by repeated themes in the horoscope. As you read about Saturn in the different signs and houses and aspects to other planets, there will be a lot of repetition. It will become obvious that the same potentials are present in the related combinations. Whether we have Saturn in Aries or in the first house, or Mars in Capricorn or in the tenth house, or a Mars-Saturn conjunction, we are combining the same drives. Personal will and power have to be integrated with the limits of personal will and power, whether the limits confront us in natural law, cultural regulations, authority figures, or our individual conscience. Since the planets are the most intense form of the desire, the conjunction of two planets is the most intense form of the issue, but all combinations describe the same drives and all can be manifested in a variety of ways. Nothing in astrology is inevitably positive or negative. Every combination can be expressed in both pleasurable and painful ways. There are always choices. **Even if our current habits have been producing painful results, the potential for change is present if we are willing to make the effort to replace the old habits with new ones**. Astrology, or any other form of self-knowledge, helps us understand our desires. Then it is up to us if we want to change our habits.

When we are born, it is obvious that the world has all the power. Initially, the infant is totally dependent on others to provide basic needs. We may experience the world in the form of a protective parent who meets our physical and emotional needs, or we may have parents who are neglectful or harsh. In the latter cases, Saturn (and other forms of Letter Ten) become keys to fear of the power of the world. Even with very protective and nurturing parents, there can still be some **anxiety associated with power which is clearly outside of our control**.

As we mature and gain confidence in our capacity to cope with the world, we acquire our share of the power. Especially after we have learned to cope with the physical world through work, we can gain a sense of personal power in the realm of Saturn. **Letter ten in all its forms is a key to our careers, to how we fit into the structure of our society, our status, our roles**. Like Letter Six, Letter Ten is also a critic. To do a good job, we need to analyze the flaws and try to correct them.

This flaw-finding attitude is helpful when done with the job, but when displaced into other areas of life such as relationships, it can be a problem. Whether or not we need to work for survival, **with Saturn we need to do something to provide an outlet for the critical attitude and a sense of accomplishment and power in the world**. We will see the same potentials over and over as we analyze the placement of Saturn in the signs, in the houses, and in aspects to the other planets. We may experience the Saturn principle as fear until we have learned the rules of the game and are living with them voluntarily while manifesting our share of power in the material world.

It's Elementary

The four astrological elements represent another mental construct or "map" for observing commonalities. We note similar issues shared by planets, houses, and signs of the same element, and can observe which elements are more complementary to one another.

The **water principle** is a natural ally of earth. Water represents the desire for emotional security so it complements and reinforces the earth desire for material security. Water is willing to stay in a rut if it is safe. It indicates the subconscious side of the mind, the capacity for empathy, compassion, and intuition. It runs our bodies and stores our habits and it is our habits which primarily control our lives.

As previously stated, **earth** is the capacity to cope with the material world. Taurus accepts a rut if it is pleasant and comfortable. Virgo and Capricorn accept a rut if it provides a sense of accomplishment, of achievement.

The desires of **fire** are inherently in conflict with both earth and water. Fire symbolizes the drive to innovate, to express one's uniqueness in action. Fire is eager, dramatic, enthusiastic, exciting. It is willing to risk security in preference to being bored.

Air can blend fairly easily with each of the other three elements. Air signifies the conscious side of the mind, the ability to learn and communicate, to "take things lightly," to be a spectator, to handle peer relationships and let others do their share. Air has perspective, is able to see both positive and negative potentials, to understand them, talk about them, and accept them without having to take other action.

Of course, anything can be overdone or underdone. Excessive air can be a superficial dilettante, talk a lot but do little. Inadequate air or excessive fire and water can be a sign of too much emotional intensity. **Since all of the planets are present in every chart, no one is totally missing any principle, but each chart has a unique combination**. Life is a balancing or juggling act as we try to make room for each of our desires, to find appropriate ways to satisfy each of them.

Qualities of Life

In addition to the four elements, another useful astrological concept divides the twelve basic desires into three qualities: cardinal, fixed, and mutable. The four elements and the three qualities provide each of the twelve sides of life with a unique pair. That is, there are three fire drives and four cardinal drives but only one cardinal fire drive which is symbolized by the planet Mars, the sign Aries, and the first house of the horoscope. The twelve planet-house-sign combinations are provided in the table below.

The **cardinal quality** tends to express with overt action, action which changes the outer circumstances of the life. The action is not always consciously chosen and initiated by the individual. Aries, with its fire urge to innovate, is likely to be a self-starter, but Libra is often reacting to the action of others. Cancer and Capricorn are sometimes dragged kicking and screaming into change—Cancer when subconscious habits have been in charge

Astrological Alphabet

Letter	Planet	Glyph	House	Sign	Glyph	Quality	Element
1	Mars	♂	1	Aries	♈	Cardinal	Fire
2	Venus	♀	2	Taurus	♉	Fixed	Earth
3	Mercury	☿	3	Gemini	♊	Mutable	Air
4	Moon	☽	4	Cancer	♋	Cardinal	Water
5	Sun	☉	5	Leo	♌	Fixed	Fire
6	Mercury Ceres Vesta	☿ ⚳ ⚶	6	Virgo	♍	Mutable	Earth
7	Venus Pallas	♀ ⚴	7	Libra	♎	Cardinal	Air
8	Pluto Juno	♀ or ♇ ⚵	8	Scorpio	♏	Fixed	Water
9	Jupiter Chiron	♃ ⚷	9	Sagittarius	♐	Mutable	Fire
10	Saturn	♄	10	Capricorn	♑	Cardinal	Earth
11	Uranus	♅	11	Aquarius	♒	Fixed	Air
12	Neptune	♆	12	Pisces	♓	Mutable	Water

and we may not know consciously why our life is the way it is, and Capricorn when we are experiencing consequences from past action.

The **fixed quality** represents enduring self-will. This does not mean that individuals with an emphasis on fixity will be unchanging. Leo is highly creative. Scorpio can lead to major transformation. Aquarius is associated with inventions. But the fixed sides of life change when they are ready to change. They do not willingly let anyone else make them change.

The **mutable quality** symbolizes different mental sides of life. Gemini and Virgo both signify the conscious side of the mind and the ability to deal with the world immediately around us. But Gemini is interested in everything while Virgo wants to narrow the focus to do something useful. Sagittarius and Pisces are searching for the Absolute, for the beliefs and values which will let us find meaning in life, set up a value hierarchy, make choices, determine our goals, etc. Sagittarius represents our formal belief system whether we seek it from a traditional religion, from philosophy, science, metaphysics, or through a personal quest. Pisces seeks infinite love and beauty, the mystical experience of being one with the Whole.

The inherent conflicts between the desires symbolized in each set of the four sharing a quality lead to natural "dilemmas." The **cardinal dilemma** calls for the integration of our desire to just do what we please, our need for emotional security through being protected by or protecting others, our desire for mutual pleasure in warm, peer relationships, and our need to deal with power in the world. Obviously, we cannot be totally independent, dependent, equal, and in control at the same time. But we can make a place in our lives for some personal interests and hobbies, for a home and family, for a mate, and for a career which lets us cope with the physical world.

The **fixed dilemma** calls for the integration of our attachment to personal material possessions and pleasures, our urge to love and be loved by others, the ability to share possessions and pleasures within emotionally close relationships, and the ability to detach and remain free. We may be seeking moderation between self-indulgence versus self-mastery, or self-sufficiency versus giving, receiving and sharing with loved ones, or emotional passion versus intellectual detachment, or self-esteem versus commitment to equality.

The **mutable dilemma** calls for the integration of our capacity to understand and work effectively with the world around us while being clear about the basic beliefs, values, and goals which direct our lives. We may stay frustrated because the world never lives up to our ideals. We may have conflicts between head goals and heart goals and effectiveness in the physical world. People lacking a clear belief system have problems with priorities and may lack a sense of direction, with a tendency to get lost. Those who lack faith in a protective Higher Power may live with anxiety or depression.

Integration means making a place in our lives for each of these primary drives/desires. To be a whole person, we need them all.

Major Thirds of the Horoscope

A third useful way of combining the twelve sides of life describes them as **personal, interpersonal, and transpersonal**. With the first two sides of life (Aries and Taurus by sign), we want to meet our personal needs to be ourselves and "do our thing," and to enjoy ourselves. The third and fourth sides of life (Gemini and Cancer by sign) are initially expressed mostly as personal needs. We develop our conscious intellects by practicing on everything without taking anything very seriously. And, initially, we are babies needing a mother to take care of us. But with the Gemini (and Mercury/3rd house) principle we also start to become socialized through peer relationships with siblings or neighbors so we become aware of the needs of others. And when we mature, we become parents who can nurture others with the Cancer (Moon/4th house) principle.

The second major section is all interpersonal, where we learn to deal with face-to-face relationships with other people. With Leo (Sun/5th house) we learn to express our fire creativity through loving and being loved, including the potential of procreating children. With Virgo, the main focus is on doing a good job, but we also have to relate to our fellow workers. The Libra and Scorpio sides of life both represent our capacity to form lasting peer relationships. These may include marriage, business partnerships, counseling relationships, or good friends if we meet regularly for shared goals. In the transpersonal areas of life, we formulate our beliefs [principle 9 of the astrological alphabet], test them against the "rules of the game" (principle 10), expand our horizons with people and knowledge and make changes (principle 11), and experience the underlying connectedness of life (principle 12).

As already indicated, every horoscope has every principle, but each chart is a unique combination with its own emphasis. We can satisfy each of the twelve basic drives/desires in many different ways. **The horoscope shows the desires with which we are dealing, both the character tendencies at birth and the current issues, but our choices determine the life details**. Much of the time, our habits are running our lives. We are not making conscious choices or our conscious desires are in conflict with our subconscious desires which are ingrained in our habits, and the subconscious usually wins. When we are conscious of this conflict, we can often find a reasonable compromise so that none of our desires are totally denied. If a part of our nature is truly blocked, it will make trouble for us.

Doubtful Dignities

Many astrological traditions from the ancient world were forgotten over the years and some of them are being rediscovered and offered to modern astrologers by Project Hindsight which is translating ancient texts into English, many for the first time in history. As with any theories, the next step requires testing the ideas to see whether they are reliable and helpful. As previously indicated, I think that concepts, theories, maps, models, etc. are conceptual systems created to help us deal more effectively with the world. **The map is not the territory, and many different systems for making maps may prove useful at different times or in different situations.** Until modern science takes astrology seriously enough to conduct systematic research on its many, and often conflicting, theoretical models, **individual students need to consider that everything they read or hear in astrology is a theory to be tested, not "gospel" revealed from on high**. The conceptual system presented in this book is based on my personal experience with thousands of horoscopes, including the charts of many psychologically trained professionals. But it has not been tested by systematic research. Hopefully, during this current period of Uranus transiting its own sign, we may make a major start on such research.

The concept of astrological dignities was one of the ancient theories which survived and continues to be taught and used by many, if not most, modern astrologers. I questioned part of the concept in a book published over twenty years ago, *The Astrologer's Casebook*, and I continue to question it. I think that the association of specific planets with specific signs which they are said to "rule" is accurate. I also think that each of these "pairs" of planet and zodiacal sign are additionally associated with one of the twelve houses of the horoscope. This equivalence of meaning in a planet-sign-house set produces what I have called the "astrological alphabet," and it is the basic concept presented throughout this book.

As I have written repeatedly, planets and signs and houses are not the "same," but they symbolize the same basic life drives/desires. The planets are always the most important, like the verbs in a sentence. They are the primary keys to the action. The houses and the signs are like adverbs qualifying the action. The other primary technique in astrology, the use of **aspects**, which are the distances between the planets, provides information on **how the different desires relate to each other**. Some desires are complementary. They support and reinforce each other. But this is not a guarantee that the life results will be comfortable, since inner harmony can lead to excesses which create problems. Some desires are in conflict with each other. To integrate them, to make peace between them, we have to satisfy the desires at different times and places or find a compromise where we do less of each. With successful integration, the inherent conflict need not be a problem in the life.

The ancient concept of the dignities described the placement of a planet in the sign opposite to the one or more that it ruled as being in its **detriment** position. In the era before telescopes, astrologers had the Sun and the Moon, which ruled one sign each, and they had five visible planets which each "ruled" or were "at home" in two signs. As the ruler of Leo, the Sun was considered to be in its detriment in Aquarius. The Moon ruled Cancer and was in its detriment in Capricorn. Mercury ruled both Gemini and Virgo, so its detriment signs were Sagittarius and Pisces. Venus ruled both Taurus and Libra, so its detriment positions were Aries and Scorpio. Mars ruled both Aries and Scorpio, so its detriment signs were Libra and Taurus. Jupiter ruled both Sagittarius and Pisces, so its detriment positions were Gemini and Virgo. Saturn ruled both Capricorn and Aquarius, so it was in detriment in Cancer and Leo.

This system is tidy and logical in several ways. Mars and Venus are paired and Mercury and Jupiter are paired so the rulership signs of one member in a pair are the detriment signs of the other. **Mars and Venus** focus on the issues of self versus equal others, with **personal versus interpersonal desires**. They deal with the juggling act of defending personal rights and meeting personal needs versus sharing the world with others in lasting peer relationships with the goal of mutual pleasure. **Mercury and Jupiter deal with the mental world**: Mercury with the world immediately around us and Jupiter with ultimate beliefs, values, and goals. Saturn was the outermost planet in ancient astrology, and it was paired with both the Sun and the Moon, the two "lights" in the interchange of rulerships and detriments.

My only objection to the concept of "detriment" is the implication that placing a planet in a detriment sign is inherently and inevitably negative. I see the **six polarities** of astrology as **natural partners** which need each other and which can be readily integrated given a little awareness and effort. In fact, **quite often a harmoniously aspected planet in a sign opposite to its own rulership sign is a key to someone who is successfully integrating the polarity**. This is also often true when a planet is in the house opposed to its own "natural" house, provided the planet has mostly harmonious aspects to other factors in the chart.

The converse is also true. Omitting Mercury and Jupiter for the moment, when cardinal and/or fixed planets, including the Sun and Moon, are in other cardinal and/or fixed signs or houses with conflict aspects, they reinforce their respective cardinal or fixed dilemma*. Often, astrologers miss the full picture because

---

*See discussion of qualities on pages 18-20.

they are not taking into account the shared meanings of planets, houses, and signs. For example, astrologers may think of **Mars in Libra in the fourth house** opposite **Venus in Aries in the tenth** house as a simple opposition, and fail to realize that, actually, **each planet is a T-square in terms of the planet-sign-house combination**, and the whole configuration is a cardinal grand cross. Similarly, the Sun in Aquarius in the second house or the eighth house is actually equivalent to a fixed T-square. It is not helpful to assume that such combinations will inevitably be negative in the life, but they do call for some type of compromise for us to satisfy the different desires.

Where Mars and Venus call for us to integrate personal needs with peer relationships, the **Sun, Moon, and Saturn deal with parent-child issues, with power and dependency**. We procreate offspring (and other forms of creativity) with Letter Five and we take care of our offspring, including home and pets, with Letter Four. Letter Ten, the major focus of this book, deals with the rules of nature and of the society, with responsibility and the conscience, including whatever person or force enforces the rules. Letter eleven leads us beyond any rules or authority figures, provided we have properly internalized the necessary rules. **Power is an issue in both the cardinal and the fixed dilemmas**.

Mercury and Jupiter with their mutable dilemma are quite different. They symbolize the search for knowledge and normally just emphasize mental ability when they are placed in each others' signs or houses. This does not mean that there are never problems when they are in one of the natural homes of each other. **The most common form of the mutable dilemma is a basic conflict between the ideals of Jupiter and what is possible in the Mercury world we live in**. Lack of faith in a higher power can be a problem, or the converse, gullibility and lack of discrimination and common sense, or we can turn a fragment of life into God, making it too important, and end up disillusioned. We may stay too scattered and need to focus to be more effective, or too focused and need a broader perspective. But the fact that the mutables are in a different class from the cardinal and fixed sides of life is obvious when we realize that each of these mutable planets rules two signs which are square each other. Normally, squares are harder to integrate than oppositions, but intelligence, understanding, and conscious awareness are always potential assets with the mutables. **The most serious problems with the mutables**

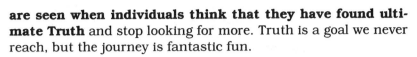

are seen when individuals think that they have found ulti-mate Truth and stop looking for more. Truth is a goal we never reach, but the journey is fantastic fun.

The concepts of exaltation and fall in the theory of the Dignities are the most indefensible. My personal theory is that these associations were chosen during the Arian Age and that they represent Arian Age ethics. I think they should have been abandoned when we entered the Piscean Age over 2,000 years ago. The male warrior hero was the supreme value during the Arian Age, so it seemed appropriate at the time to admire the Sun, the King, in the sign of the warrior. Obviously, the Mediterranean world at the time when western astrology was being developed was totally male dominated. Astrologers during the several thousand years of observation of the sky had noted that the planet showed the nature of the action while the sign colored it. **So the Sun in Aries was both King and warrior,** leading his men in battle. **Mars in Capricorn** was the warrior who could take personal power over the material world, including the laws of the society, who could **make his personal will into law.** Mercury as key to one's mental ability had its greatest breadth of vision in Aquarius.

Marriage during these early years of astrology was a fourth house matter. Women were owned like the land and the cattle. **Libra was associated with open enemies** more than with partners, so **putting Saturn, the most dreaded "malefic," in the sign of one's enemies offered the hope that the "big bad wolf" would get them.** In a wife, symbolized by the Moon, the male warrior hero wanted a woman who was **strong enough to manage the home and family, but with a pleasant disposition and fertile, to bear many children**; the Moon in Taurus. However, for a paramour on the side, the **male hero wanted a woman who was seductive but pliant, beautiful, romantic, and a bit mysterious; Venus in Pisces.** In a world full of enemies, the **only people one could really trust were those related by blood, the family, so Jupiter in Cancer was valued.** The concept of a planet being in the sign of its "fall" was simply a logical extension of the idea that if planets in some signs were especially positive, placement in the opposite signs had to be negative.

As stated above, our values have changed since the Arian Age. More often than not, I find people having problems with **Mars in**

Capricorn; sometimes trying to make the personal will into law, but, more often among those who consult astrologers, **self-critical, self-doubting, self-blocking, sometimes to the point of illness** as the fear of doing the wrong thing inhibits the natural desire of Mars to do what we please and inhibits the natural self-confidence which plays a major role in our immune systems. **Saturn in Libra initially is usually a lesson in sharing power with our lasting peer relationships**. We may choose a father figure as a mate and give him or her the power and responsibility, or we may play parent ourselves. Not uncommonly, we do first one and then the other while we are learning to share the power. Many people delay marriage out of the fear of being criticized, dominated, or hurt in some other way.

Venus in Pisces is often an indication of artistic appreciation and ability which can be in any of many fields of the arts: music, dancing, drama, painting, poetry, etc. However, it is often associated with excessive idealism in close relationships, with a tendency to expect too much from love and to be let down. Alternately, individuals with this placement may attract victims and try to play savior. Being a professional savior is fine as long as we know that we can only facilitate the growth of another person. No one can do it all for anyone else. But if we play savior in what should be peer relationships, it is usually a disaster.

With Jupiter in Cancer, we may expect too much from or overvalue food, family, home, or anything that we connect to emotional security. We may try to be a perfect parent, to produce perfect children, to keep a perfect home, etc. Turning any fragment of life into God is an idolatry which can let us down in the end.

Every combination in astrology can be positive or painful, depending on how the individual is seeking to satisfy those desires. And, obviously, we can change the way we are seeking satisfaction and change the details of our lives. Astrology will never fulfill its great potential for providing self-awareness to facilitate our achieving more effective and fulfilling lives until we outgrow the assumption that anything in astrology and life is inherently and necessarily good or bad.

Defense Mechanisms

As is clear by now, I think that astrology is a key to psychological principles, to the basic desires/drives of life. As a form of psychology, some of the latter's ideas can be helpful. Among the useful concepts in psychology are three of the "defense mechanisms:" repression, projection, and displacement. **Repression** occurs when we are not conscious of our emotions so they are buried in the subconscious. It is possible to submerge and stay unaware of any emotion, but it is the unpleasant or painful ones which create problems. Whether the emotion is fear, anger, guilt, resentment, sorrow, etc., when the feeling is not acknowledged consciously, it festers like pus in the body. In fact, infections resulting in pus are a common symptom resulting from repressed emotions. The subconscious manages the body. When it is overloaded with disturbing emotions, it tries to get our attention with body symptoms. Physical discomfort is a message from the subconscious saying "I'm not happy. Do something." Children are occasionally born without the ability to feel pain and they never live to adulthood. Pain, whether physical, emotional, mental, or spiritual, is a warning that we are on the wrong track and need to change what we are doing. The body has considerable ability to be self-healing if we can become conscious of our potentially destructive emotions and/or actions and change our life. Though most of western medicine is wedded to the materialistic belief system, an increasing amount of research is discovering the major role emotions play in illness.

Projection was originally conceptualized as individuals imagining in someone else the qualities they could not face in themselves. I think that, rather than imagining, most of us tend to attract others who will act out desires which we feel but which are in conflict with other desires. The other person, in effect, does what we will not let ourselves do because of the inner conflict. The end result is much like a seesaw. As one goes down, the other goes up. The less we do, the more the other person does, to the point of excesses and discomfort. One of the most common examples of projection in our modern western world involves the "freedom-closeness dilemma." Everyone would like to do what they please a good bit of the time, and almost everyone would like pleasant relationships with other people. But, to achieve close, continuing emotional bonds, we have to give up some of our own desires. We have to compromise. So, individuals who are consciously seeking emotional closeness are attracted to individuals who are conscious of the desire to preserve some individual freedom. Both people have the same dilemma, but the first person clutches and the second person pulls back to maintain some space. In this dance, the first person's subconscious need for space is being satisfied by the second person's action and vice versa. When both become conscious of their ambivalence, they can work out a reasonable compromise which allows some closeness and some space.

Displacement occurs when we try to satisfy one of our normal desires in a way which does not work well. A typical example of displacement is the search for the Absolute in a fragment of life. We may put our faith in money. We may look for an ideal mate. Our job may be an ultimate value, so if we lose it, we are terrified. We may never forgive our parents for not being perfect or try to be the perfect parent of perfect children. Any of these actions is a form of idolatry which will inevitably disappoint us and force us to find a bigger God.

Astrology helps us to see where we might repress, project, or displace. Once we know what is happening, we can change the way we are trying to meet the normal desires of life. Habits are not easy to change, but it can happen with patient, persistent effort. It is almost impossible to just stop a habit, but we can replace it with one which produces more satisfying consequences. Life is a juggling act. We need to become conscious of all twelve sides of life, all twelve primary desires which are driving us, and to make room for each of them in our lives. **All twelve are potentially positive, but they can be repressed, projected into other people, carried to excess, poorly done for lack of attention and effort, done in the wrong place, or we can just stay torn between two conflicting desires**. It is even possible to stay unhappy all the time by always wishing we were doing something else rather than enjoying what we are doing, and later doing something else and enjoying that. I think that most serious students of astrology are idealists. Remember to enjoy the journey toward your ideals. Don't wait until you reach them to be happy.

CHAPTER THREE

SATURN IN SIGNS

As has been indicated, there will be repetition in the descriptions of the different forms of the astrological alphabet. Since the planets are the most important form of the alphabet, the descriptions of conjunctions between planets are often the most complete picture of the principles. When looking up Saturn in a sign, it is advisable to also read the section about Saturn conjunct the ruler of that sign, and the material on Saturn in the equivalent house may provide additional useful information. For example, if your Saturn is in Taurus, also read Saturn conjunct Venus and Saturn in the second house.

Saturn in Aries forms a natural square (Saturn rules Capricorn, which squares Aries). The square calls for the integration of conflicting desires. Aries represents our feeling that we should have the right and the power to do what we please. Saturn represents the "rules of the game" which set limits on life if we want to survive in this world at this time. Failure to integrate, to make peace between these two sides of life with some sort of compromise, can result in a variety of problems.

Individuals with a dominant Letter One emphasis in their charts may feel that their will should be law. Fire-earth combinations may be steamrollers or resemble a molten lava flow. Just don't get in the way. Such individuals may live in a constant state of overdrive, trying to make the world do what they think it should. They may be dictators to the extent that they can, or they may simply be very responsible people who feel guilty if anything goes wrong. One-ten combinations can play "Atlas" and try to carry the world.

The other extreme is the feeling that the world has all the power, so we might as well not even try—we would just fail or fall short. These people may simply lack faith in their own power or they may feel that they do not have the right to be themselves or do what they please. We gain faith in our own power by doing anything successful. Of course, if our standard of success is too high, we may never feel we have achieved it. We don't know what we can do until we have done it. When the self-blocking is carried too far, when fear blocks the fire need to express actively in the world, illness is possible. Fire is the faith which fuels the immune system, the creative recuperative power of life itself. Ignoring realistic, practical physical limits can also have negative repercussions for health. To integrate our self-confidence and our limits, we need reasonable ambitions and some kind of active accomplishment in the world.

Careers for Saturn in Aries should be entrepreneurial, active, varied, and self-directed when possible. Individuals with this placement are identified with their careers, so on the one hand they tend to feel they have lost their power and identity when they are not working, yet they want to work in their own way, strictly on their own terms. Self-criticism may be a problem if they "become" the job and focus too much on their flaws.

A father or another authority figure will usually be a role model in the early life. If the father is a positive model, the individual tries to be like him, to win his approval. If the parent is a negative model, the individual tries to do the opposite. Competition with the parent is common, and frequently, individuals are not aware of how they are shaping their lives by their early experiences with authorities.

Francis Ford Coppola, the independent movie director, has Saturn in Aries.

Saturn in Taurus forms a natural trine, so individuals with this combination may be very successful in handling the material world. When driven by a small to moderate fear of the world's power or insecurity about their own power, they may make money and also hold on to it. Or they may collect possessions. Often the career may involve beauty in some way, whether they create it or sell the creations of others. Material security, pleasure, and comfort are usually important. Major conflict aspects to Saturn would suggest that there are lessons around making or handling money, possessions, or appetites. The Saturn potential for a Puritan conscience can conflict with the pleasure drives of Taurus, so individuals may swing between excesses and asceticism, between spending and saving, hoarding and generosity, etc. But the combination is normally practical and capable.

An artistic career is possible, whether as an artist or dealing with things that give pleasure to people, including home furnishings, clothing, cosmetics, jewelry, or, of course, the money that buys them. The instinct of Taurus is to conserve and to savor.

The father and other authority figures may be pleasant and comfortable, or very focused on the material world of money, possessions and pleasures, or quite artistic, or simply practical. If Saturn has conflict aspects, the father may have problems with money or sensuality or he could just be stubborn.

The conservationist David Brower had Saturn in Taurus, along with the folk singer Joan Baez.

Saturn in Gemini is a natural quincunx, the aspect which usually carries an implication of wanting to do it better. This may support the critic side of Saturn, but the air ability to see both sides of everything, to understand, and to accept, can offset the critic. With serious insecurity, this combination may try to control information and communication for a sense of security. It can be "dry," lacking in warmth, insisting on "facts" only.

This combination often illustrates the two sides of Saturn at different stages of life. Initially, children with Saturn in Gemini often doubt their mental ability, sometimes because they are comparing themselves with a parent or an older sibling. But once they have gained a sense of competence, they typically choose a mental career. This may include any form of communication, such as teaching, counseling, sales, media work, etc. Work with the hands is also possible. Gemini, like all forms of Letter Three, carries the potential for skill with eye-mind-hand coordination.

The father may have been bright and verbal and engaged in an intellectual profession. In such cases, he usually pushes the child to do well in school. Alternately, the father might have lacked education and worked with his hands. I have seen cases where such a father also pushed the child to become educated to be able to do more in life than the father could, but in other cases, the father disdained mental skills. Sometimes a sibling or other relative plays the role of parent or there is a power issue in what should be a peer relationship. Sometimes, the individual feels responsible for a sibling. Mutual criticism or power struggles can be a danger in relationships which should be accepting and cooperative.

Singer Bonnie Franklin has Saturn in Gemini. Republican Speaker of the U.S. House of Representatives Newton Gingrich also has this combination. He was a university professor before he went into politics. Theodore Kaczynski, who is accused of being the Unabomber, also has Saturn in Gemini closely conjunct his Sun and Uranus. He was considered a genius in mathematics, got college degrees at an early age, and was briefly a professor, but dropped out to live as a hermit and attack modern technology.

Saturn in Cancer is a natural opposition. The astrological drives which are opposite each other should be partners. As the opposite ends of a polarity, they have much in common, but each provides something the other needs. However, when they are not integrated, the person may express one end and have problems with the other end which can be repressed, projected, or displaced. Projection is the most common mishandling of oppositions. Typically, the individual finds someone with the same dilemma but each person consciously seeks to satisfy one end while the other person focuses on the other end. The usual result is that each person overdoes his or her end. Each is getting some vicarious satisfaction from the other person's manifestation of the other end. Unfortunately, since the desire for this end is subconscious and in conflict with the conscious desire (or the person would simply do it and not project it), the usual feeling is frustration with the other person. "If you were different, I would be happy." When both people realize that the problem is internal, when they become conscious of their own ambivalence and accept it as normal, they can work out a compromise.

The four-ten polarity symbolizes the two parents. Four should be the nurturing parent, giving unconditional love because the baby needs it. Letter ten is the disciplinary parent who teaches the rules and provides the consequences of how we handle them as part of that instruction. Obviously, real parents may not conform to the model, and the four-ten combinations in astrology point to issues which usually involve security. Neither parent may provide unconditional love or both may overprotect and "spoil" a child. Most astrology texts assume that the Saturn principle will always overpower the Moon principle, producing some variation on harsh, or dominating, or distant parents, but I have seen examples of the overprotective alternative. In the end, the child has to grow up and learn that there are rules, learn to be responsible and to cope with the world. Other variations in our divorce-prone western world include one parent playing both roles, or the parents may alternate in the roles.

Once we reach adulthood, Saturn in Cancer calls for integration between the emotional desire for a home and family and the urge for a career which provides some degree of power and accomplishment in the world. Homemaking as a career used to be an option for many women, but it is becoming less available except for women who have inherited or married wealth. Even in the latter case, the dependent spouse may feel insecure and vulnerable and may need to do some kind of volunteer work which reassures her of her power. For individuals trying to juggle both work and a family, the major Saturn issue is often time. Since no one can do everything well, we need to realistically define what is important and to be able to delegate or postpone or take less seriously what is less important. In healthy interdependence each person is able to contribute, to take his or her share of the responsibility, and also to accept help from others.

Career potentials with Saturn in Cancer can include farming and ranching, caring for the land and animals. Work in construction, interior design, and real estate are possible. Service to the public is common, including protection for families: feeding people, clothing them, or offering emotional security in some form. A family business or work in one's home are other possibilities.

Candice Bergen has Saturn in Cancer. Her role in *Murphy Brown* played out the home versus career dilemma and the single parent option.

Saturn in Leo provides another natural quincunx, and unlike Saturn in Gemini, Leo has trouble taking things lightly. Both the sign and the planet are keys to ambition. Both show the desire to be on top. Saturn symbolizes the executive who carries out laws which are bigger than personal will. Leo is the instinct to be king, to make personal will into law. So five-ten combinations can lead to major overdrive in individuals who have faith in their own power. And overdrive can lead to falls. Richard Nixon, the only U.S. President forced to resign in disgrace, had a five-ten mixture with his Sun in its own house, which is like a double Leo, but it was in Saturn's sign of Capricorn. Fire-earth mixtures need to express power in the world but to accept reasonable limits.

Career choices can include teaching or other work with young people, sales, promotion, the entertainment world, investment, etc. If possible, people with this combination need to be in charge in their work, as an entrepreneur or owner or manager of a business.

For individuals who have not developed a sense of faith in their own power and self-worth, Saturn in Leo can be manifested as a fear of failure, often in areas connected to love. Since fear normally produces the feared consequences, repeated disappointments in love relationships may eventually lead to shutting down and giving up. All of the drive may be focused into the career. Fear of failure may lead to a conscious choice not to have children, or, when the fear is subconscious, to the inability to conceive or to carry a pregnancy to term. Fear of failure may lead to reduced ambition in the career, to leaving talents undeveloped and "settling" for a job which provides survival but is unfulfilling. Saturn shows where we have to be realistic, so if a survival job is really all that is possible, individuals with Saturn in Leo need to find a hobby or avocation which lets them develop their talents and earn applause.

The father and other authority figures could be dominant and controlling, leading to power struggles as the individual tries to find his or her own strength. Or, the parent could be loving and supportive in a responsible way. The relationship with the parent is often a key to later experiences in trusting and accepting love or maintaining a guard for fear of being hurt in some way.

Comedian Phyllis Diller had Saturn in Leo.

Saturn in Virgo is a natural trine which usually indicates competence in handling the physical world. One possible danger is an excessive focus on one's work which can leave other parts of life short-changed. But major conflict aspects to Saturn may show problems in either the career or in personal health. Virgo points to our capacity to function effectively in both areas. Health problems can be caused by frustrations in a job which fails to satisfy the ambition of Saturn to reach the top and to be in control of the work, or simply to feel a sense of real accomplishment in it. If we are frustrated enough, the subconscious can produce an accident or illness which lets us leave the job without feeling guilty. Illness is a painful way to get out of a job. If we really can't find more satisfying work, we need to find something good about the job and look to a hobby or avocation to fulfill the need to do something worth doing and to do it well.

Sometimes the Saturn lesson can involve learning to be realistic about the needs of a physical body for proper nutrition, exercise, rest, etc. Painful consequences resulting from lack of "common sense" do get our attention. If the chart is "weak" in earth, the individual may be learning to work, to develop discipline and willingly deal with the dull details of an ordinary job. Saturn careers can be in any field where details and organization are important and which produce tangible results.

With Saturn in Virgo, the father may be a workaholic and rarely home for the family. He may be very critical or he may just be very competent, or he might be struggling to find satisfaction in his work. He might be very interested in health matters such as nutrition, or he might have personal health problems. As always, the horoscope shows the life issues, but the details can range from one extreme to the other.

Feminist author Betty Friedan has Saturn in Virgo.

Saturn in Libra is a natural square which calls for integration between activities as an equal and power roles. Life should be big enough for both marriage and a career, but to do justice to both, we have to make compromises. If one person in a partnership is dominant, even if acting as the responsible parent with impeccable intentions, there is no real partnership. If Saturn is still being experienced as fear of the world's power, we may marry a father-figure to protect us. If we have enough confidence in our own power to avoid doing that but not enough to deal with an equal, we may pick a partner who will let us play parent as owner of the power and the responsibility. Or, our insecurity may lead to delaying marriage for fear of being dominated, criticized, rejected, or hurt in some other way.

We only claim our share of the power of the world when we are realistically coping with the area of life symbolized by the sign and house of Saturn. When the cardinal and/or the fixed dilemmas are emphasized in a chart showing a major issue involving power and relationships it is helpful to have a place in our lives for all three of the major alternatives. We need some cooperative relationships, some competitive ones which let us develop and test our powers, and some in which we help others. The latter interactions reassure us that we have our share of the power and we use it to assist others.

Libra careers may deal with people or involve beauty in some way. The first includes counseling and consulting in many areas, law, politics, social work, arbitration, and personnel work. The second includes architecture, photography, and any area of design.

The father may be equalitarian, fair minded, artistic, pleasant, etc. if he is expressing the positive potentials of Libra. Or he may be learning to handle power in peer relationships. A close associate who had Saturn in Libra had a brutal, abusive father who was a tyrant in his home. The fact that Saturn was in the tenth house in the child's chart provided the clue that the father was a potential dictator who had not learned to respect the rights of other people, which is a Libra value. In general, other things being equal, the psychological drives of the house tend to outweigh the sign. Of course, the nature of the planet is primary. In the preceding case, Libra was far outweighed by Saturn being in its own house for a repeated message. Always watch for the repeated theme.

Ava Gardner, a movie star with a stormy romantic life, had Saturn in Libra.

Saturn in Scorpio is a natural sextile, but it can still be a challenge to integrate these two sides of life. There is often a major issue involving power, since we naturally seek it where Saturn is placed in our charts once we have developed the confidence that we can get it, or if the only way we feel safe is to be in control. But Letter Eight tends to have a power issue inherent within it, even without the complication of being mixed with other life desires. The instinct of water, as previously indicated, is to absorb or be absorbed, to seek a kind of fusion. With Cancer, the mother naturally protects the baby. Pisces can be manifested as a savior helping a victim or as God and human. But Scorpio is trying to integrate an intense will which includes a desire for self-control, and especially the avoidance of being controlled, with a passionate hunger for fusion with a mate, with the challenge of working out an equalitarian relationship. Scorpio is a double-bind in its own nature — one of the most difficult of our twelve sides of life.

So Saturn in Scorpio is often a key to lessons despite the natural sextile between the principles. As with Saturn in Libra, we may simply be learning to do justice to both career and relationships. Often, the lesson involves sharing power, especially when reinforced by conflict aspects in the cardinal and/or fixed signs or houses. Alternately, we may be learning mastery of the appetites, learning to enjoy them without being controlled by them. Any of the appetites may be involved — eating, drinking, smoking, drugs, sex, spending money, hoarding possessions, etc. Wild swings are possible as in bulimia where sufferers alternately gorge and force themselves to throw up. The Scorpio tendency is to go to the end, literally to the death, so moderation is often difficult, knowing when is enough and how to release and forgive, if not forget. Sometimes that lesson of learning to release is confronted through the death or other loss of a loved one early in life.

The father and other authority figures may be dominant, intense, but self-contained, rarely showing the deep feelings. When the emotions are over-controlled, there is always the danger of their breaking loose explosively from time to time. There may be issues around money, possessions, or sensuality. The father may be so absorbed in material security needs that he is rarely home. Or he may be fighting addictive tendencies. Sometimes there are sexual issues with a female child. He will be a role model for the child's attitudes and experiences with mates whether the child seeks a mate like the father or the opposite.

When the eight-ten combination is handled well, there is tremendous potential skill with details, ability to organize, thoroughness, a retentive memory, and the capacity to probe the inner depths whether in exploration of the mind, in history and archaeology, in work as a detective, or any area of research. Saturn in Scorpio can also point to a career handling joint resources in banking, accounting, investment, taxes, government work which uses public funds, nonprofit organizations, etc. Often in life, the bigger the challenge, the greater the results when the challenge is met and handled.

Entrepreneur John DeLorean was in the headlines for months with problems involving joint resources, including accusations of mismanaging the money others invested in his enterprises. He was also suspected of drug abuse, and could have gone to jail on both counts. He had Saturn in Scorpio.

Saturn in Sagittarius is a natural semisextile which keeps both life principles in the transpersonal area. Astrologers differ on whether the semisextile is an easy or a challenging aspect. There are major differences between adjoining signs which can make them hard to integrate, but each does tend to build on the preceding one as stages of our evolving life. Also, it is usually a little easier to integrate desires within the major areas of personal, interpersonal, and transpersonal, since each shares a basic focus.

With Saturn in Sagittarius our beliefs face the reality check of the physical world. The results can range from the skepticism of an atheist or agnostic to a gullible "true believer" who needs to question his or her basic premises about the world. But when the principles are effectively integrated, the individual can have realistic beliefs and values and higher education can contribute to career success. The choice of a Sagittarian career may include teaching, writing, work in a library or with the law or for a church, long distance travel and foreign countries, and many other variations on the search for the Absolute.

Since Sagittarius symbolizes our quest for ultimate meaning and value in our lives, there may be lessons involving ethics and morals which are determined by one's beliefs. As has been said repeatedly, astrology shows issues, not details. One individual might have unrealistically high expectations about life while another might need higher standards. The same combination can occur in the chart of a religious leader and a criminal. We determine how we manifest the principles. One hazard of Saturn in Sagittarius is the worship of power. Richard Nixon's overreach with power has been mentioned. In addition to his five-ten emphasis, he also had Jupiter in Capricorn and Saturn in the ninth house as variations on the nine-ten message.

Some individuals with Saturn in Sagittarius may overvalue authority figures, which can lead to disillusionment when they prove to be human. We might have idolized a parent or been disillusioned when he let us down. The father might be religious in a conventional way or just have high standards. He might have expected too much of the child, or he might have left the family to pursue his own personal goals.

It is also possible to place one's ultimate trust in one's job, making it an ultimate value. Then, if the job is lost or our business does not make it, it is like losing God. Others may try to do their jobs perfectly. The most reasonable alternative is to choose work which you hope will make a better world. Saturn is always about doing your share realistically.

Erma Bombeck wrote humorous columns which entertained millions with her Saturn in Sagittarius, a sign which is well known for its sense of humor.

Saturn in Capricorn is, of course, a repetition of the same principle. Its house placement and aspects provide the keys to where and how the individual will face the rules of the game and learn to use power wisely. Normally, this combination indicates a strong ambition and need for control, but until a successful role has been attained, the power will be experienced in the world, usually in the hands of authority figures. Harmony aspects may bring protection by these others, but for full satisfaction the individual has to do something which provides a sense of personal accomplishment. Conflict aspects can indicate a very difficult early life, often with the need to work and assume adult responsibilities while still a child. However, in the end, the individual who develops practical skills and learns early to cope with the material world may be light years ahead of the protected child who remains dependent on the power of others. As always with Saturn, we need to avoid the extremes of playing Atlas when we cannot allow ourselves any dependency and the failure to develop our share of the world's power and to carry our share of the responsibility.

This placement tells us that the individual's father was concerned with power, whether he had it or had problems getting it. Jim Jones, the guru who led hundreds of his followers to death in Guyana, had Saturn in Capricorn in his first house. His father was partly disabled, the family was partly supported by welfare, and the father was a racist, putting down blacks as a way to build his own self-esteem. Jim Jones took his father as a negative role model and many of his followers who died with him were blacks.

Career choices with Saturn in Capricorn include work for the government, whether federal, state, or local. Alternately, individuals may be managers in large businesses or other institutions, or they may found and run their own business, or become an independent professional.

Both the past and the current heads of Russia, Gorbachev and Yeltsin, were born in the same year as Jim Jones and have Saturn in Capricorn. Frank Gifford, famous for football and sportscasting, also has Saturn in Capricorn.

Saturn in Aquarius provides another natural semisextile with its questionable outcome. Saturn is still considered a co-ruler of Aquarius, and many astrologers think that this is its optimum sign. It is true that a successful integration of these two sides of life can produce a person able to blend the best of the past with openness to the future. The practicality of earth combined with the broad perspective and logic of air can be highly effective in the world. Both of these basic drives are transpersonal, so their focus on the world is compatible to the extent that neither is distracted by personal relationships. (Of course, the rest of the chart will almost always bring in these other desires.)

But in spite of the potential for great accomplishments when Letters Ten and Eleven are integrated, the potential for major conflicts is also present. Saturn says "there are some limits if you want to survive in this world at this time. There are some things you can do, some you can't do, and some you have to do." Aquarius says "I don't accept limits. My primary urge is to go beyond the limits. No one can tell me what to do." Saturn represents the ultimate in bureaucratic hierarchy. Aquarius wants equality.

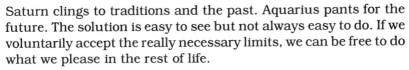

Saturn clings to traditions and the past. Aquarius pants for the future. The solution is easy to see but not always easy to do. If we voluntarily accept the really necessary limits, we can be free to do what we please in the rest of life.

With successful integration, Saturn in Aquarius shows the capacity for peer relationships with authority figures. Father may have been a friend, so the individual had no need for a teen-age rebellion. Unfortunately, when carried to excess, this combination may be manifested as a cool, distant, and/or indifferent parent, sometimes one who is too busy socializing with friends or saving humanity to be there for his family. Later, as we take on the role of parent, the same options are present. Unless we change the habits which brought us into a family which fit us, we will repeat the same patterns.

Appropriate careers for Saturn in Aquarius include all fields which advance or disseminate knowledge. Modern technology is an obvious potential, but nonconventional studies such as astrology are also good choices. Jobs may be chosen in government, whether federal, state, or local, or in large organizations dealing with public issues such as nonprofit foundations and labor unions. An effective compromise of the principles permits liberty within the law and compromise and cooperation between the executive and the legislative branches of the government.

A current political leader with Saturn in Aquarius is Dianne Feinstein, who was mayor of San Francisco for years and is now a California Senator.

Saturn in Pisces is a natural sextile, but, as with the other natural sextile in Scorpio, there can be challenges. Pisces shares the search for the Absolute with Sagittarius, but the Pisces search is more at the subconscious level, driven by the mystic's hunger for infinite love and beauty, for oneness with the Whole. Piscean professions can include many service careers as healers or in spiritual work. They can range from guarding prisoners to using the capacity for beauty in artistic fields or in persuading people that some product or activity will make their life more ideal. Work with chemicals, drugs, or fluids is possible with all of the water sides of life.

Security needs are strong in earth-water mixtures, so faith is very important. Individuals who lack faith in a Higher Power can be plagued by anxiety, fears or phobias. Though a successful career is always important and helpful wherever Saturn is placed in one's horoscope, individuals with Saturn in Pisces also need faith in Something beyond this world. Though orthodox religions can sometimes be helpful, personal mystical experiences are likely to be more so. As with Saturn in Sagittarius, Saturn in Pisces may point to lessons in faith, which can range from extreme atheism to extreme gullibility. Saturn always calls for a "reality" check. Ethics may be unrealistically high or low to the point of endangering the society.

If the faith is placed in a fragment of life, it is a kind of idolatry, and we usually lose the idol to force us to find a bigger God. In the early life, the father or other authority figures will be connected in some way with the principle of Pisces. The details can range from an adored, idealized parent to one who "should" have been god and given us a perfect life but let us down by being human. The parent could have been an artist, a savior, or a victim. A missing parent is common, whether really gone searching for his own beautiful dream or physically there but emotionally closed off. Even in Pisces, the call of Saturn remains the same. We can't do it all. God won't do it all. We have to do our share in making a more ideal world.

The long-time very liberal U.S. Congressman from Oakland, California, Ron Dellums, has Saturn in Pisces in his ninth house — a double demand for an idealistic career.

CHAPTER FOUR

PLANETARY ASPECTS TO SATURN

Aspects are angular distances between different factors in the horoscope. The distance (usually in celestial longitude) is measured between different planets including the Sun and the Moon and between these bodies in the sky and the angles of the chart which are formed by the intersections of the great circles. The latter are the circles which go through the center of the Earth and are projected against infinity. They include the **equator**, the **ecliptic** (Earth's path around the Sun), the **horizon**, the **meridian and the prime vertical of the birthplace**. The latter two circles go through the zenith and the nadir, the points which are straight up and straight down from our location. The meridian goes through the north and south points of the horizon while the prime vertical goes through the east and west points of the horizon. The intersections of the ecliptic with the other four of these great circles produce the 0 Aries-0 Libra axis (equator) and the horoscope's Ascendant-Descendant axis (horizon), its MC-IC axis (meridian), and its Antivertex-Vertex axis (prime vertical). The East Point-West Point axis is the intersection of the ecliptic with another (unnamed) great circle.

The most-used aspects in astrology are divisions of the ecliptic circle by whole numbers. Two factors within a few degrees of each other are conjunct. Division of the circle by two produces the opposition when the two factors are 180 degrees apart on opposite sides of the earth. A division by three produces a trine which is present when factors are 120 degrees apart. The square is 90 degrees, produced when the circle is divided by four. A division by six gives the sextile when the factors are separated by 60 degrees. The octile or semisquare is 45 degrees when the circle is divided by eight. The semisextile of 30 degrees is a division of the circle by twelve. The other most commonly used aspects are the trioctile or sesquisquare of 135 degrees, which is three-eighths of the circle, and the quincunx or inconjunct, which is 150 degrees or five-twelfths of the circle.

The **trine**, the **sextile**, and possibly the **semisextile** are considered harmonious aspects. Factors separated by these distances in the sky represent desires which are relatively compatible, so they support and reinforce each other. This does not guarantee positive results in the life, since it can lead to excesses.

The **square**, **octile**, and **trioctile** are considered conflict or stress aspects. Factors separated by these distances represent desires which are in some way in conflict with each other. This does not guarantee negative results in the life, since we can learn to satisfy the desires alternately or can work out a compromise which lets us have a little of each.

Oppositions are natural partnerships. The drives which are symbolized on each end by the signs and by the houses form polarities. They have much in common and need each other, but there is always the danger of projection. This can occur when we are conscious of one of the desires but not aware of our desire for its opposite. We will often be attracted to another person who has the same ambivalence but is consciously wanting the other end of the polarity. For example, someone who wants to be taken care of may be unaware of the desire for power and may find a natural "atlas" who will take on the parent role. Each person gets some vicarious satisfaction from the action of the other person, though they are usually unaware of this.

The problem with projection is that, like a seesaw, the tendency is for each person to overdo his or her own end, and sooner or later the imbalance becomes frustrating to one or both. Then the partnership is likely to break.

I call the **quincunx** the "closet-cleaning" aspect. The signs and houses which are quincunx each other are very different and not easy to integrate. Remember that integration simply means making sure there is a place in our lives for each of our basic desires, whether we do this by alternating between them or by a compromise which permits some of each of the conflicted drives. The typical feeling of a quincunx is a need to improve the situation. We may change the details to "make it better." Or we may decide we no longer want to deal with it and let it go. We may separate from a home, a job, a relationship, a belief system, or anything else. Sometimes, the action is taken by others. If we have been hating our job but afraid to quit, we may get fired. Or we may get sick enough to escape the job. Both of those are painful ways to resolve the frustrations. Relationships may be ended by the departure of others whether voluntarily or through death. The quincunx is an important aspect, and to handle it effectively we need to be conscious of our ambivalences and to look for compromises.

Conjunctions are the strongest aspects, and we do not know how they will be handled until we see the life of the person, though some combinations are obviously easier than others. With the cardinal and fixed signs, conjunctions between planets ruling signs which are square each other in the natural zodiac are usually more challenging. However, integration is always possible with insight and effort. As you will hear repeatedly, integration means finding a way to satisfy each of our desires with some kind of compromise. I consider this one of the most important principles — the understanding that **a horoscope pictures our inner emotional desires, which we can try to satisfy in a variety of ways**.

Conjunctions between planets ruling cardinal or fixed signs which are sextile or trine each other in the natural zodiac show desires which are theoretically easier to mix, but the results are not always positive since they may lead to excesses.

Conjunctions between planets ruling cardinal or fixed signs which oppose each other can be natural partners. The danger of and nature of projection has been covered above in the discussion of oppositions. Remember that a comfortable compromise is possible if both individuals become conscious of their own ambivalence and realize the partner has just been acting out a denied desire of their own.

The cardinal and fixed signs are both dealing with the issue of personal rights and needs versus the rights and needs of other people. We may be struggling to integrate personal needs versus interpersonal relationships versus transpersonal issues, but the handling of power is almost always part of the challenge.

The mutable signs, in contrast, are primarily mental. The situation is clearly different when we see that the two original mutable planets, Mercury and Jupiter, each rule signs which are square each other. Mercury deals with the world around us while Jupiter is looking for ultimate answers and values. The most common mutable conflict is between the ideals of the Jupiter sides of life and the limits of what is possible in the world around us. It is also possible to lack a clear belief system, to be uncertain of our values and goals. People for whom this is a serious problem get lost easily. They lack a sense of direction. We can also experience conflict between head goals and heart goals such as truth versus kindness. Or we may lack faith in a benign Higher Power and live anxiously a lot of the time. The mutables are not involved with power (unless they are mixed with cardinal and fixed sides of life), yet they represent the knowledge and the beliefs about the world which determine where we go in life.

Obviously, when evaluating all planetary aspects, though the planets are the most important, the signs and houses are also a very important part of the picture. There will always be mixtures. Mutable planets may be in fixed signs in cardinal houses, so there is no simple interpretation. **Rule number one is to look for themes**, for repeated messages, ways in which the chart is saying the same thing.

In the following descriptions of aspects between planets, **the most complete description is the conjunction, which describes the basic principles. Always read that first** and then check the brief statements differentiating the conflict and harmony aspects and the opposition and quincunx.

Sun-Saturn Aspects

The **Sun conjunct Saturn can be a steamroller combination** if the individual has claimed his or her share of the power in the world. Both factors represent the drive to do important things in the world. The Sun shows where we want to be the King or Queen, making the laws, unless we have profound doubts about our rights and/or our power. Saturn shows where we want to be the executive, enforcing the laws, unless we are still projecting all the power into the world. Individuals with this combination need to be in front and on top, admired by the world. If they doubt their own competence and are forced to work under others, they may be miserable. If the rest of the horoscope shows self-doubt and insecurity, the Sun-Saturn conjunction is **a clarion call to develop both the creative skills of the Sun and the practical competence of Saturn to permit the person to take his or her place as a leader in the world**. An emphasis on earth and water, whether through planets in those signs or houses or strong aspects to earth and water planets, can reinforce the caution and/or insecurity. An emphasis on air and especially on fire adds to the tiger potential.

Since **Saturn is usually a key to a father**, the individual with this aspect is likely to have had a power issue with the father and/or other authorities. This can range from a power struggle with a dominating father, to the child feeling that he or she could never live up to a famous father's accomplishments, to a truly loving father who encouraged the child's self-esteem, to a wastrel, gambler, profligate father, etc. The Sun is a key to the heart, to the ability to love and be loved, and to our sense of self-worth. It represents our creative potential, our need to be and do more than we have done before and to be admired for it. When combined with Saturn, we may choose a Leo career and become a leader or we may feel that we could never achieve our ambitions and give up. Saturn symbolizes the power of the world until we have developed our ability to cope with the world and then it becomes partly our power.

Saturn is also a key to our own ability to be a responsible parent. A conjunction with the Sun could point to people deeply invested in the parent role, whether with their own children or the world. Or it could show lessons in the area of love and/or procreation: lessons in sharing power, in practical responsibility, in trusting love, in being comfortable even when not being special, etc.

Conflict aspects between the Sun and Saturn show the need to integrate these intense desires for prominence and achievement in the world. Often, such aspects show the feeling that the personal ego-goals are being blocked by power outside of our control, whether by social restraints or by authority figures. Individuals may have had very difficult relationships with their parents or other authorities in the early life and subconsciously expect the patterns to continue. Some people take on responsibilities which interfere with their ability to achieve personal creative goals. Some just fight time, always trying to do more than is humanly possible. Integration may be managed by extending the time table, giving oneself more time to reach the goals. Or standards and expectations might be lowered in less important activities. It might be possible to delegate or postpone some obligations. Compromise can make room for some of the personal creative expressions along with the necessary practical responsibilities. You can take a chance on love.

Harmony aspects between the Sun and Saturn suggest that the individual is able to integrate the desires for prominence and power. If the balance of the chart supports these principles, they are a positive indication of success in achieving ambitions. This may include the ability to juggle love and work, creativity and practical accomplishments. Of course, it is always possible for harmony aspects to lead to excesses.

An **opposition** between the Sun and Saturn shows a need for compromise between these desires. The fire need to keep innovating has to be balanced against the earth capacity to stay with projects long enough to get tangible results. The willingness to take risks has to be balanced against caution. Depending on the signs and houses involved, there are likely to be power issues to resolve to permit successful teamwork, though the aspect could be manifested largely in vigorous competition. Projection is the main danger with oppositions, so individuals with this aspect

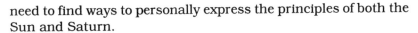

need to find ways to personally express the principles of both the Sun and Saturn.

A **quincunx** between the Sun and Saturn calls for improvement in the handling of ambitions and power. Creative urges may feel constrained by the restraints of practicality. Ego needs may be at odds with authorities. As with all aspects which indicate confrontations between somewhat incompatible desires, compromise is usually the answer.

Moon-Saturn Aspects

The **Moon conjunct Saturn connects the two parent principles** and is usually interpreted negatively in astrology. The Moon seeks unconditional love. A baby is cared for because it needs it, not because it has earned it. Saturn says you will receive the consequences of how you have handled the rules of the game, since that is how you learn what you can do, what you can't do, and what you have to do if you want to survive in this world at this time. Thus Saturn plays the role of the disciplinary parent.

Of course, in real life, either or both parents might be punitive, or irresponsible, or overprotective, or otherwise hash up the roles. Some individuals with this aspect have told me that they recognized the incapacity of their parents to handle the roles. The child felt he or she was more the parent and became a caretaker when still very young. But another person, after I had described the two alternative extremes, parents who were overdoing either the Moon or Saturn, said she had the overprotective parents. She commented that every astrologer who had interpreted her chart had told her she must have had terrible, cruel, dominating, critical parents with her Moon conjunct Saturn in Aries in the ninth house. She said that her parents gave her everything and did everything for her. She remembered that when she went away to college she was annoyed because there was no one to wash her clothes for her. Following college, she married a man who, like her parents, was providing her with everything she wanted. She did not have to work and had a maid to take care of the house. Habits create destiny. Her fire sign and house placement of Moon-Saturn shows her confidence that she has a right to what she wants in life, but it would still be risky to assume that she would get it all. The horoscope shows the psychological issues, but each principle can be manifested in many different details.

The "parental" instincts of both Moon and Saturn often lead people with this aspect into caretaking jobs, but there are still many options. We can feed people, clothe them, house them, heal them, or comfort them in many ways. Those who are confident of their ability to provide for their own needs and also care for others, will enjoy the parent role. Those who still identify with the baby side of the Moon, who still feel that the world has all the power, will often be anxious and depressed, looking for a parent to care for them. Their solution is to develop their practical skills to learn to cope with the world and to help others whenever they can, to move into the power sides of the Moon and Saturn. Some who learned young to cope effectively with the world, feeling that they had to do it all themselves, may never have learned to accept help from others. They may be deeply afraid of dependency and have to learn to let their repressed baby side be fed, to let others give to them some of the time.

The **home and family are normally very important** to people with Moon-Saturn aspects. If possible, they want to own their own home and stay connected to the family. Hereditary roots may be valued. They may look into their ancestry or collect antiques. They may be born on a farm or just love the land. They usually learn to work early, though the reasons for this may range from a farm upbringing with chores for everyone, to early poverty that called for the kids to help, to a large family that was too much for one pair of parents to handle, to illness in the home, or just parents with a strong work ethic. Except in the case of truly harsh, unloving parents, most people who have learned early to cope with the world have told me that they are grateful for the skills and confidence they developed.

Conflict aspects between the Moon and Saturn show problems connected to issues of **dependency and power**. The early life may have been very difficult, with a dysfunctional family, an unstable home, and tense relationships with one or both parents. Or the parents might have had serious problems with each other. The child might have felt he or she had to take on responsibilities which were not being handled by the parents. There may be a hunger for someone to be parent for them now or a deep fear of dependency and vulnerability. The solution will come through interdependency as they learn to trust their own competence but also to let others give to them.

Harmony aspects between the Moon and Saturn suggest that the individual can integrate some dependency with some responsibility, and can probably handle both a career and a family. They are likely to want and to attain a stable home and family connections.

An **opposition** between the Moon and Saturn shows a need for compromise if the person wants to manage both a family and a career. The individual may also be trying to integrate dependency with responsible power, trying to allow both to be part of the life.

A **quincunx** between the Moon and Saturn is calling for improvement in the home or in the career or in both. Often, individuals feel pulled between the demands of these major commitments. The underlying issue often involves dependency versus power.

Mercury-Saturn Aspects

Mercury conjunct Saturn connects the conscious intellect to realism about the world. Since Saturn may show primarily a lesson or an already developed skill, individuals with this aspect can range from genius to imbecile, from someone who doubts his or her mental ability to someone who is highly successful in a mental career.

Albert Einstein is a good example of an individual who started life with superior mental ability and was ranked as a top genius for his original theories in mathematics and physics. **Einstein had a close conjunction between Mercury and Saturn in early Aries**, which traditional astrology might consider a sign of a defective intellect, especially since Saturn was in the sign ranked as its detriment. (See the section on Dignities.) However, he entered public school at age seven, in 1886, and in that year, his mother wrote in a letter that her son was "again number one." A successful combination of Saturn's practical skill with details and willingness to work with Mercury's logic and broad perspective can produce a world-class intellect. But there are inherent conflicts between these two basic desires which can produce problems if they are not integrated. Mercury, like all air, is basically a spectator and commentator. Individuals who are unwilling to deal with the realistic details and effort which are needed to survive in a material world may end with nothing to show for their fine intellect. Alternately, individuals too stuck in the fine print and too afraid of failing or falling short to risk leaving familiar paths can remain laborers doing manual work all their lives.

Since Mercury is a **key to early peer relationships** like siblings and neighbors, there are sometimes power issues to be resolved in this area. An older sibling or other relative such as an uncle might play the role of protective parent, or, on the negative side, might be critical or dominating. Or the individual with the Mercury-Saturn conjunction might feel responsible for a sibling or other relative. Some individuals compare themselves with relatives and doubt their own ability. As always, the chart shows the issue—the need to deal with equality versus power and responsibility or the need to integrate the spectator with the practical achiever. The person creates the life details.

Conflict aspects between Mercury and Saturn show the need to pay attention and make an effort to integrate the issues of equality versus responsible power, of the spectator versus the practical achiever in the world. There are times to take life seriously, but we also need the "light" touch some of the time, the broad perspective and detachment of Mercury's air attitude.

Harmony aspects suggest that the person has already developed the ability to successfully combine the abstract with the tangible sides of life. Obviously, we need to be able to do both and also to know when each is appropriate to handle the world.

An **opposition** calls for working out a compromise, making sure that we are comfortably satisfying both our casual curiosity and peer relationships and our need to be productive and responsible, and not projecting one of them.

The **quincunx** search for something better can benefit from the capacity for both the broad awareness and logic of Mercury and the practicality and seriousness of Saturn.

Venus-Saturn Aspects

Venus conjunct Saturn, as with all conjunctions, can be manifested in an infinite variety of ways. It can be a positive sign of ability to cope successfully with the material world for those who are realistic about it, or Saturn may be pointing to a lesson in that area, especially when other planets hold conflict aspects to the conjunction. I have seen cases in which the lesson called for the person to **learn to earn a living, or to moderate the appetites** when the Venus love of pleasure was dominant, being expressed in excessive sensual indulgence and leisure. I have also seen the opposite—**workaholics buried in their work who needed to learn to slow down, relax, and enjoy life**. The whole chart is part of the picture, and themes may help to clarify the emphasis, but in the end it is up to the individual. People can and do change as they grow, learning to handle their desires in new ways to produce more satisfying results.

In the role of **Venus as a key to lasting peer relationships**, Venus conjunct Saturn can be manifested as very pleasant associations with fellow workers or bosses, or there may be issues around **equality versus control**. In the emotional peer relationships, one partner may see the other as a protective parent or as someone seeking inappropriate power. One partner may be overly focused on work and the other may feel neglected. Criticism can be an issue in the relationship. As usual, the solutions lie in learning to share the power and responsibility along with the pleasure, and keeping the criticism where it belongs in one's job.

The conjunction is often an indication of artistic talent and the **potential of a career involving the aesthetic side of life**, which can involve anything that provides comfort or pleasure to the world.

Conflict aspects between Venus and Saturn are an indication that we can't enjoy life as much as we want. We may blame the **blocking of our pleasure** on outer circumstances — a critical boss or one who makes us work too hard, an inadequate salary, time pressures, unpleasant working conditions or duties, etc. If jobs are scarce, we lack the skills to get a better one, we are responsible for others, or any other realistic fact keeps us stuck in a frustrating job, it is important to look for some kind of satisfaction in the work and to also make sure that we satisfy our pleasure needs in other ways outside of the work. At the very least, we need to stay conscious of the frustration. It is when negative emotions are buried in the subconscious that they are most likely to produce serious problems from illness to getting us fired.

When our pleasure needs in relationships are being frustrated, we can either try to work out mutually satisfying compromises with the partner or we can adjust our expectations (change our attitude). Breaking off the relationship is a typical reaction in our divorce-prone western world, but our horoscope shows our own habits. Until we change our habits, we are likely to keep reaping the same results in any relationship.

Harmony aspects between Saturn and Venus suggest that the individual has **realistic pleasure goals** and is able to realize them. The action may involve success in one's work and/or comfortable personal relationships. Artistic talent is often present and may be expressed in a job or in a hobby or just for personal satisfaction.

Venus **oppositions** to Saturn call for compromise to be able to share pleasure along with effort and responsibility, to be able to do justice to both relationships and career.

A Venus-Saturn **quincunx** shows a desire for improvement. As long as the goals are realistic, it can lead to more effective and/ or satisfying details in the situation. It is also possible for a quincunx to lead to separations. We may leave or events which are outside of our control may produce the result. As usual, individuals with an emphasis on fire and air are more likely to be conscious of the frustration and to take the action personally. Individuals with an emphasis on earth and water are more likely to be cautious, to hold back, and to have the world do it to them.

Mars-Saturn Aspects

Aspects between Mars and Saturn provide the most intense form of the confrontation between these two principles. The **conjunction** carries the same meaning as Saturn in Aries or in the first house of the horoscope, but in a more intense form. (Mars in

Capricorn and Mars in the 10th house are alternate forms of the same issue.) **Our personal will and power (as symbolized by Mars) must come to terms with the limits of our power**. The limits may exist in the form of natural laws such as time and gravity. These are basically the way this world works. When we understand the laws and work with them, there is no problem. We fly planes that are heavier than air by working with gravity. We do not ignore it, fight it, or try to run away from it.

The laws may be cultural regulations like stopping for red lights and going through green ones. As long as we obey the rules, there is no problem. But if we try to drive on the right side of a two-way street in England or the left side of a two-way street in the U.S., we will have a problem.

The Saturn principle is also manifested by **authority figures** who enforce the laws. When the laws are fair and enforced with justice, they protect the rights of all members of society. Since neither humans nor the laws they create are perfect, there will be many occasions when we need to change the laws or replace the enforcers. But "lawful" ways to do this are usually more effective than revolution and war. The latter are measures of "last resort," and mundane astrology notes that wars and revolutions are typically signaled by conflict aspects between Mars and Saturn.

At the inner level, the Saturn principle symbolizes one's **conscience and guilt**. We punish ourselves when we have transgressed what we consider legitimate laws of conduct. The appropriate handling of guilt calls for making restitution if we can and then resolving not to repeat the action. Then it is vital that we forgive ourselves! Persistent guilt is like holding a grudge against ourselves, and it is highly destructive, often leading to illness. It is also possible to feel unrealistic guilt if we exaggerate our power and responsibility and think we should be able to do more than we can. However, what is obviously unrealistic guilt may sometimes be a "screen" covering some genuine guilt in another area which we are not facing. Persisting negative emotions call for some serious self-analysis.

Mars represents our basic identity, including our right and power to be ourselves, protect ourselves, assert ourselves. An overdeveloped personal will expressed at the expense of others and/or in conflict with the law in other ways will eventually produce disaster. The **law is bigger than any individual**. (It is true that a few powerful individuals seem to escape the consequences in this life, but occult tradition asserts that karma gets them eventually.)

More commonly, certainly among the students of astrology and their clients, the **Mars principle may be repressed**. We may overrate the power of the world (Saturn) or underrate our own (Mars). When our faith in our own rights and power is severely blocked, it can literally shut down the immune system and lead to a variety of illnesses. When our anger is blocked and turned in against ourselves, it invites accidents or attacks from the world. Any of our basic desires/drives which is denied will make trouble for us, but blocking our fire is especially destructive. Fire represents the life force. If what we want to do is really not possible, we have to find something else which we want to do and can do, and then do it!

A successful integration between our personal power and the rules of the game can lead to major success in the world. One of my favorite examples is a former astrology student who was about to start a period of **twenty years when his secondary progressed Mars would hold a conjunction with Saturn in his sixth house**. The extended time was due to progressed Mars making a station and changing direction while in the one-degree orb permitted in progressions. Tom had read the typical doom and gloom material in most astrology books and **was anticipating the worst** — the death of his father, poverty, illness, maybe his own death.

We discussed the principles. Both Saturn and the sixth house called for realistic work. Tom had been living on the fringe, getting by without a real profession or even a regular job. He went back to trade school, became a licensed plumber, electrician, and contractor, and managed an increasing number of apartment complexes. **He now owns property in two states and has more money than he ever dreamed of**. None of this was given to him. He worked long hours, working days and studying at night. He has not been ill and his father did not die. He continues to work effectively with the Saturn principle.

Conflict aspects between Mars and Saturn show that the individual needs to pay extra attention or to make an extra effort to integrate the different desires. The individual needs to make sure he or she has a realistic outlet for the personal power, trying to avoid either overdrive which attempts the impossible and leads to failure or self-blocking which denies legitimate needs which could be attained. One negative form is constant personal battles with authority figures (beginning with father), but we can also struggle with an overactive conscience, with self-criticism, or other variations on the theme of personal will versus limits.

Harmony aspects between Mars and Saturn suggest that the individual has already learned to integrate these two sides of life by voluntarily living within the limits. This ability can lead to success if supported by the balance of the chart.

As with all potentially challenging Mars-Saturn aspects, **oppositions call for teamwork between personal power and power outside of our control,** whether in the form of other individuals or in organizations or social regulations. The Mars instinct is to either fight or leave and neither works well when Saturn is involved. Compromise is the name of the game.

The **quincunx** between Mars and Saturn usually lives up to its reputation for wanting to do it better. If the rest of the chart mostly supports Saturn, the individual may stay put and keep improving the details in his or her life. If the rest of the chart mostly supports Mars, the individual may keep leaving one job or home or relationship after another, hoping the next one will be better. Compromise remains the goal.

Jupiter-Saturn Aspects

Jupiter conjunct Saturn combines our beliefs about the world with the reality of how it actually works. One ancient tradition held that **world teachers** could be born at such times, which occur at about twenty-year intervals. Theoretically, some souls coming in then had already acquired an understanding of the laws of the universe and could therefore share that knowledge with others. However, as has been said repeatedly, Saturn also shows where we may need to learn about the limits which are part of the world, so the Jupiter-Saturn conjunction may point to lessons connected to one's belief system and the ethics, values, and goals which are determined by it. One end of the lesson continuum is atheism or agnosticism, the view of modern science that physical matter/energy is the only reality, the denial of any Higher Power. The other end of the continuum is the "true believer" in any of many religions which claim to possess final truth and demand that their followers accept it without question.

The reality may be that "truth" is a goal which we never reach, but the journey can be enormously exciting. It seems likely that the Absolute is far bigger than our present level of consciousness, that we can experience glimpses but are not able to fully comprehend it. Astrology demonstrates the nonsense of the materialistic beliefs which deny any inherent meaning in the world, claiming that chance rules all in a random world. The pervasive reality of psychic experiences also demonstrate the limited perspective of materialism.

But we may have needed materialistic science to break the domination of traditional religion in the west, which was even more dogmatic than science in the denial of any reality beyond the dogma of each particular sect. Jupiter symbolizes one of our "freedom" drives. Unlike Mars, which simply wants personal freedom to act on the desire of the moment, the Jupiter drive seeks the freedom to pursue the Absolute wherever it takes us. Thus it is associated with long trips and foreign countries. As a key to the search for truth with a capital "T," it is also connected to churches, libraries, universities and law courts. It includes the desire to disseminate the knowledge once gained, so it is also connected to publishing, writing, teaching, etc.

A **Jupiter-Saturn conjunction can point to a career in any of these areas**. There is no guarantee that the person playing "guru" in some way has actually "got" it, but as a fire side of life, Jupiter is usually associated with both confidence and the urge to let it hang out. Since the Saturn urge is to be safe rather than sorry, and especially to stay in control, there can be a real conflict between these two drives. If the earth and water are stronger, the person may bite his tongue and keep looking for more evidence before sounding off. But he may also try to reassure himself that he is right by forcing others to agree with him. From such instincts we have inquisitions and religious wars. In most areas I try to use neutral language in referring to the sexes, but in this area, the perpetrators have mostly been males and the victims have often been females.

Individuals with this conjunction have **a parent, most often the father, connected to faith.** They may have idealized the parent or been disillusioned when he was human and did not provide them with a perfect life. They may have expected too much from the father or he may have expected too much of them. The father might have been religious or just had high standards. He might have tried to be a perfect father, or he might have been gone, off looking for his own ideals. The Saturn lesson might involve learning not to overrate authorities or not to worship power or a career. When any part of life is turned into an idol, we may lose it to force us to find a bigger God. When we can value our work in the world and use it to make the world more ideal but also maintain perspective which provides room to enjoy all twelve sides of life, we have it together.

Conflict aspects between Jupiter and Saturn call for us to test our beliefs against our world. If they "work," if they produce desirable consequences, great! If we keep getting painful consequences, we need to widen our horizons, to check out new ideas. We may just be expecting too much, always wanting more than is possible. Or we may lack faith and be afraid to try things for fear of failure. When in doubt, it is best to try things in a small way that does not court disaster.

Astrology offers us a marvelous tool for conceptualizing ideas about the world and then testing them. You don't have to watch the passing aspects in transits and progressions for very long before you will see that most of the "doom and gloom" predicted details from specific aspects do not happen. Guessing details is not astrology's greatest gift. It helps us understand the driving desires in our own nature and then we can often produce better details.

Harmony aspects between Jupiter and Saturn suggest that our goals and values are in harmony with the rules of the game and thus can be attained. That does not mean that no effort is required! Saturn always points to the puritan virtues of realistic work for success in this world.

An **opposition** between Jupiter and Saturn calls for checking to make sure we are manifesting both ends of the polarity ourselves and not totally delegating one end to other people. With awareness and compromise, we can work out an **effective partnership between faith and realism**, between being Atlas trying to do it all and waiting for God to do it all.

A **quincunx** between Jupiter and Saturn reinforces the urge to "do it better" since the sides of life represented by these two planets are the two sides of perfectionism. Jupiter is looking for ideals and Saturn is looking for the flaws in order to do it right. Remember the value of moderation when you deal with perfectionism. As usual, compromise helps.

Saturn-Saturn Aspects

Saturn aspects to its own natal position can occur in a variety of systems which describe current issues or project into the future. **Transits** are the most universally used system, with transiting Saturn forming major aspects to one's natal Saturn approximately every seven years. These will be the conjunction, the separating square, the opposition, and the applying square, after which the cycle repeats with a new conjunction.

Solar Arc Directions[5] reach a semisextile at around the age of thirty, an octile at around age forty-five, a sextile at around age sixty, and a square for those who reach ninety. Few astrologers place much emphasis on the interval when **Secondary Progressed**[6] Saturn remains within one degree of its natal position, but if it leaves the one-degree orb and then changes its direction and returns to a conjunction, it can be meaningful. Of course, if progressed Saturn is still very close to its natal position, when another planet aspects either one it may aspect both to intensify the issue. More commonly, the aspect from the other planet will simply last longer as it contacts both the natal and progressed positions of Saturn in turn.

Any aspect of Saturn to itself marks a **feedback time** when we get a **report card** from the world, which lets us know how we are doing in handling the "rules of the game." Obviously, the whole chart will be relevant, describing the psychological issues being faced at the time. The important emotional issues will be repeated by a variety of planet-house-sign combinations. Always **look for the repeated themes in the chart**.

Since the conjunction is the strongest aspect, **Saturn conjunct Saturn may be the most intense form of this feedback**. But Saturn aspects to planets to which it has natal conflict aspects may be more challenging since the natal chart shows the basic habits which are directing our lives. As readers know by now, Saturn is a key to what we **can** do, what we **can't** do, and what we **have** to do to survive in this physical world. Its harmonious aspects to other factors in the chart show issues which we have probably already learned to handle, talents and skills which can be helpful in coping with the world. Its conflict aspects show areas which need attention, where we need to work out compromises between the desires symbolized by the other factors and the realistic limits which exist in this world and in our particular culture and time.

When we are analyzing **consequences** which take the form of situations and events in our lives, the basic Saturn questions include: "What subconscious emotional habits in me, or what past actions and reactions, could have invited these consequences in my life?" We can follow up with "What is the most effective way to handle these consequences? What will happen if I do this or that?" We only find out what will happen by actually doing it and observing the results, but in cases of major uncertainty, it is realistic to test the limits in ways that do not risk too much. To find out if something is really a wall, we can feel it with a finger rather than knocking our head against it.

Saturn aspects will often mark **confrontations with authority figures** in the life, which could be a father, a teacher, a boss, a police officer, etc. Alternately, we could be dealing with **"natural" law**, including the needs of a physical body for proper nutrition, exercise, rest, shelter, plus the consequences of emotional habits. Many intelligent and idealistic individuals will be confronting **time pressures**, being forced to curtail the effort to be Atlas and carry more than their share of responsibility for the world. Good intentions are not enough to turn us into supermen or superwomen. It is vitally important that we do our share, which will usually be through our career, our role in the society. Whether we are a mother/homemaker or a major power in the world, earning a living or offering voluntary assistance to the community, managing our personal survival or a big business or a country, we are all dealing with the same basic issue with Saturn. We are learning to **mesh our personal skills and other assets with our personal desires and goals and with the laws of our world**.

Conflict aspects from Saturn to Saturn show the times we need to be especially **vigilant in our analysis of feedback from the world**. If we are experiencing painful consequences such as the failure to achieve our goals despite major efforts, we need to either change the techniques we have been using, or change our goals. Sometimes, a series of small, "bite-sized" goals will work for us, permitting us to keep moving toward the bigger goal. Sometimes, we just need to extend our time-table, to allow more time to reach the goal. Sometimes, what we want is truly unrealistic, whether really impossible or needing assistance from others, or a new approach. It is also possible to achieve success at times of conflict aspects if we have learned the Saturn lesson of realism. Our consequences tell us how we are doing. However, at such times, we need to keep a wary eye out for the danger that the **successful results might have been attained at the cost of serious neglect of other important parts of our nature**. For example, career success might be achieved by neglecting one's family. Life remains a juggling act as we try to make places for all parts of our nature. We can take comfort from the fact that we do our major growing by meeting and learning to handle challenges. When we do something right the first time, we already knew how to do it, though we might not have been conscious of it. When we do something poorly, but try again and do it better, we have learned and grown.

Harmony aspects from Saturn to Saturn should be a time for **successful accomplishments**. These are often related to career success, but might bring the resolution of issues with authority figures or of our ability to handle personal responsibility and power. Since the whole chart is always part of the picture, a single harmonious aspect could be counteracted by major conflict aspects between other factors in the chart. Almost always, there will be a mixture of harmonious and conflict aspects at the same time. The positive aspects involving Saturn point to the capacity to cope realistically with the situation, even when it offers challenges.

Saturn opposition Saturn by transit (first occuring around age 14-15) marks the midpoint of the Saturn cycle of around twenty-eight years. If we have been learning to cope effectively with our world, this can be a time of fulfillment as we enter adolescence, deal with school and may begin a part-time job. If we have not learned to handle limits realistically, adolescence is often a time of rebellion against authority in any form. Oppositions should be partnerships. We need to **increase our personal power at this time, but recognize and accept voluntarily its limits.**

The second transiting Saturn opposition to natal Saturn comes in the early forties and often coincides with other major aspects, in both transits and other systems. These include transiting Uranus opposite natal Uranus at about age forty-two, and all of the Directed planets octile their natal positions, which comes around age forty-five. Psychology has recognized this period as a common time for a "mid-life" crisis. Individuals who have been living conventional lives focused on job and family may suddenly rebel, make radical changes, and shock their associates. Where the "rules" are being effectively handled, the early forties may be a time for major achievement and success, a fulfillment phase in the Saturn cycle.

The third transiting Saturn opposition to natal Saturn usually comes early in the seventh decade of life. Many individuals will have retired by this time, and if they have not continued activities which maintain their ability to cope with the world, this decade can start a downhill slide into impotence and illness. The couch potatoes who have retired to the TV will be losing muscle tone. The lack of self-confidence may be shutting down the immune system. The lack of a sense of accomplishment can lead to depression. Medically prescribed drugs often contribute to problems with memory and balance. Obviously, the antidote is to **do something** which restores the sense of personal power and self-worth, something which produces a sense of accomplishment. Individuals who do that can be successful "late bloomers," sometimes in careers that they had wanted to try but been unable to when they were younger, due to limiting responsibilities.

Saturn quincunx Saturn calls for analysis with the usual goal of improving the situation. The bottom line with Saturn is always "what will work?" or, "what will happen if I do this?" Depending on the stage of the life, we might study something to advance job prospects, or parenting skills, or to develop a rewarding hobby if retirement has provided extra time. If we are dealing with problems in any area of life and our own analysis has not provided reasonable solutions, it is appropriate to look for additional information from a specialist (authority figure) in the area of the problem. The quincunx invites us to look outside the "standard" grooves of our thinking and our life.

Saturn-Uranus Aspects

Saturn conjunct Uranus can be a challenge as we try to mix tradition with innovation, bureaucratic hierarchy with equality, rules and limits with the drive to defy all rules and transcend all limits. Successful integration can produce great success in the world through bringing new information into effective production to meet the practical needs of the world. Can you row a boat and rock it at the same time? If so, the world needs you.

As usual, integration is easier said than done. When the Uranus rebel overwhelms the common sense of Saturn, the revolution may be exciting at first but end up destructive. When the caution or outright fear of Saturn overwhelms the Promethean instincts of Uranus, people try to turn the clock back. The Epimetheans can range from religious extremists to Luddites like the Unabomber. But these two sides of life are such a terrific team when they work together, we have to keep trying even if we don't personally have the aspect in our charts.

Of course I am biased, but I see the psychological understanding of astrology as just such a combination. The new awareness of how our emotions control our bodies and our lives is being combined with the ancient knowledge that the sky is a key to life on earth. When we stop thinking that the sky is doing something to us, when we realize that it is a mirror showing what we are doing, **when we grasp precisely how our emotional habits** produce our destiny and how they can be changed to create a more satisfying destiny, we are on the way to combining **Uranus and Saturn in a synthesis** that is both exciting and effective.

The knowledge is Saturnian since we can test it and watch the consequences. What happens in my body and the affairs of my life when I focus on this emotion? What happens when I look at life with a different perspective and different emotions? Uranus is the willingness to experiment with new perspectives.

For those who have Saturn conjunct Uranus, it brings with it a **father with Uranian qualities**. He might have been open, accepting, original, articulate, and treated you like a friend. Or he might have been cool, distant, indifferent, weird, or even insistent that his way was the only way since Saturn can always do the dictator number when driven by insecurity or an overblown sense of responsibility. I have seen cases where the father was totally accepting when the child was young but went into power-struggle mode when the child was old enough to have his or her own ideas. Obviously, we would expect such a father to have less air in his own chart, hence more emphasis on the other elements. He would be working on the lesson of air, the ability to be equalitarian, understanding, and accepting.

A Uranian career can obviously include any field which expands or disseminates knowledge. Work with the public is common. Saturn is a key to the executive branch of government and Uranus is a key to the legislature in a democracy. Social issues and values can be important along with anything connected to the future.

Conflict aspects between Uranus and Saturn show the need to make peace between the past and the future, between total freedom and reasonable limits, between authority and equality, between intellectual castles in the air and what is possible in this physical world. Success is worth the effort and certainly possible if one integrates the potential skills of the intellect with common sense.

Harmony aspects between Uranus and Saturn suggest that these very different life urges have been reconciled so we can draw on the assets of each of them. In theory, we should be able to make all of our desires complementary in order to be a whole person.

An **opposition** between Uranus and Saturn calls for us to find opportunities to satisfy both the old and the new, conventional and unconventional, free-wheeling and structured, theoretical and concrete, etc. Hopefully, we can work out a partnership between them within ourselves rather than attracting others in our lives who are overdoing the one we are neglecting.

A **quincunx** between Uranus and Saturn needs compromise as usual, which should be attainable with the help of the Uranian broad perspective. There is always some danger of the Uranian urge to escape limits and try something new leading to repeated separations rather than hanging in and working out a compromise.

Neptune-Saturn Aspects

Neptune conjunct Saturn unites our need to cope with the physical world with the mystical potential for oneness with the Whole. Where Jupiter represents a conscious search for the Absolute in the form of a set of beliefs which will determine our ethics, values, and goals, Neptune symbolizes the subconscious search for infinite love and beauty. The desires represented by both Jupiter and Neptune are for perfection, but, of course, different individuals can have very different ideas about what is perfect. Theoretically, Neptune's realm is totally inclusive, but just as humans may think they have found truth and stop far short of the ultimate potential, humans may form small enclaves which they call heaven, each presided over by its local god created in the image of man, with the vast majority of their fellow humans excluded. There are many ways to discover that there is more outside their dream worlds. Maybe some people just get bored eventually and peek through the curtain of their visions.

Since Saturn is always calling for a reality check, people with it conjunct Neptune are rarely allowed to stay for long in their visionary cocoon. The world keeps breaking through the walls, often starting in early life with a father who had the same issue, who was trying to make peace between a beautiful dream of a perfect world and the rude reality we live in. The parent might be idealistic or artistic or psychic, playing a savior role in the world. Or he might be a victim running away from the world through drugs, alcohol, illness, psychosis, etc. Or he might just be unhappy because his life, other people, and the world never lived up to his ideals. Obviously, the **child is likely to be working on the same issues as the parent** to which he was drawn. Hopefully, he or she can learn from the parent's example what **to do** or what **not** to do.

Sometimes the Saturn lesson involves a **lack of faith** in a benign Higher Power, in help beyond human understanding if we can open to it. The urgent drive to conquer the natural world, the focus on knowledge for power in materialistic, atheistic science may be partly due to such a lack of faith. People without such faith can be anxious and depressed since no one can be in control of their lives all the time. We have to do what is within our power and then let go and trust.

Sometimes the Saturn lesson involves the **limited beliefs** mentioned above — little, human-created gods with little exclusive heavens. Most of these are really religions of fear rather than faith. Many so-called "new age" gurus are cut from the same cloth. "Their" followers will be saved when the immanent catastrophe arrives. Follow them, and contribute to their material comfort, if you want to be saved. Over and over the prophets predict the disaster and when it fails to materialize, the followers look for a new guru and repeat the pattern. The end of the world as we know it keeps being postponed.

However, the world is constantly changing. Some traditional religions are building higher walls and buying guns, but some are reaching across sectarian boundaries to communicate and cooperate, to become more inclusive, allowing women and gays to be priests, opening to mystical, psychic experiences and to spiritual healing, questioning the rigid dogmas handed down from the past.

Neptunian careers can include any type of service which helps the world. The jobs can be totally mundane like work with fluids, chemicals, drugs, the ocean. It is possible to work with the aesthetic side of life or to persuade people that if they buy your product or your service their life will be more beautiful. Neptune's potential includes a highly creative imagination which can lead to a career in the entertainment world or in advertising and public relations, producing artists and con artists. Healing, including self-healing, can be part of the gift of Neptunian faith.

Conflict aspects between Neptune and Saturn are often experienced as a confrontation between faith and fear. A variation on the same principles is faith versus realism. But what we define as realistic depends on our beliefs about the nature of ultimate reality. We know the materialists are wrong, but who can say with certainty what is right? As long as we live in a physical world, we have to respect the rules of the place. Too extreme flouting of the rules gets us thrown out of it. But life encompasses much more than this physical realm, and the urges symbolized by both Uranus and Neptune call us to look farther. Life is a balancing act. We need all twelve of our basic drives to be a whole person.

Harmony aspects between Neptune and Saturn suggest that our faith and our fear have been reconciled, that our dreams are realistic and we are capable of moving toward them, of bringing them into this world.

An **opposition** between Neptune and Saturn is a call for a partnership between our ideals and our capacity to cope with the physical world. They are magnificent when they work together, bringing the ideals into manifestation in the physical world.

A **quincunx** between Neptune and Saturn holds the hope of a similar result if we can give a little on both sides while calling on the talents of both sides to find a way to make things better.

Pluto-Saturn Aspects

Pluto conjunct Saturn is another combination of desires with a major issue involving power. Pluto symbolizes a part of life where we need to learn to share power and pleasure with close, lasting peer relationships. This may be with marriage or business partners or in counseling or consulting interactions. It also includes competitive activity, whether in sports or games or business. Saturn represents the power of the world and it should include our ability to have a share of the power and the responsibility.

As usual, it is possible to express these principles in either of two opposite extremes which are both destructive. **Those who have not learned to share the power with peers or with the world will seek total control**. They may be playing Atlas out of a sense of personal responsibility. "If I don't make it right, I will be guilty." Or they may try to be dictator because that is the only way they feel safe. **The opposite extreme produces dependent and helpless people who feel they have virtually no personal power**. They may hope for a parent-partner who will take care of them. They may make sporadic efforts to claim some power to protect their own rights and engage in power struggles. Or they may use their helplessness to manipulate others to protect themselves. They may simply retreat from any close relationships to avoid being hurt.

The obvious solution calls for sharing the power and the responsibility along with the pleasures and possessions which are part of the Pluto side of life. As with all major growth challenges, this is easy to say, but not easy to do. The weak person has to develop more self-confidence and the strong person has to be willing to give up some of the control. We develop self-confidence by doing things successfully, which means that we have to have reasonable standards for what we consider success.

A **successful integration of the Pluto and Saturn drives can lead to major success in the world**. Both of these sides of life are associated with a strong will and a good memory, with patience, thoroughness, precision with details, the urge to go beyond surface appearances and to follow projects through to completion. Both are cautious and deliberate. They are two of the three sides of life which are sometimes called "obsessive-compulsive." (The third is Letter Six in our alphabet.)

Pluto careers can include any activities involving joint resources such as bookkeeping, accounting, banking, investment, pensions and taxes. Government work is possible using public funds, or work with non-profit foundations. Any type of research is appropriate. There could be interest in history, archaeology, genealogy, antiques or other reusable objects. Depth psychologists and detectives and undertakers are Pluto professionals.

Pluto-type fathers may have been so busy working that they had little time for their families. Security issues are almost always important, but the parent might have struggled for financial survival or gained enough wealth to leave a comfortable inheritance to their heirs. Often, they are deeply emotional but have problems showing the feelings, and the individual with this aspect is likely to share that tendency, to keep a "stiff upper lip." Depending on their level of personal security, such fathers may have been dictators or dependent and vulnerable or both, bluffing to cover feelings of inadequacy. With both the Pluto principle and the Saturn principle concerned with the ability to share power, one dealing with equals and the other with power greater than their own, security is usually a major issue.

Power struggles are normal with Pluto-Saturn aspects, and can be helpful as long as they can be defined as a game where we can win sometimes and gain confidence but can also gain if, when we lose, we realize we are not destroyed, that we can play again and may win next time. Muscles and other forms of personal strength which build self-confidence are developed by resistance. When the struggle risks life or death consequences, it has gone too far. **One of the major dangers of Pluto is going too far, not knowing when to quit and how to let go.** Water in general seeks completion, closure, and Pluto as a fixed planet with enduring self-will may find it difficult to be moderate. One possible remedy is to remember the other sides of life, which are also important and which will be denied if we carry one too far. Life is a juggling act,

Conflict aspects between Pluto and Saturn show the need to integrate these two sides of life. With any two basic drives, there will be some similarities and some differences. The sides of life which are naturally sextile or trine are more compatible with more in common between them, so they tend to reinforce or complement each other. Scorpio and Capricorn, the signs of Pluto and Saturn, are sextile and have much in common as described above, so the primary challenge of conflict aspects between them is often some kind of excess. **The potential talents of caution, precision, thoroughness, etc. can become obsessive-compulsive, leading to over-control and fear of the unfamiliar.** Too much emphasis on earth and water can be like wading through a swamp.

Of course the opposite is also possible. Any conflict aspect involving Saturn may be calling for realism. When connected to

Pluto, **the target about which we need to be practical, to recognize limits, can be joint resources, possessions, appetites, and/or power**. The individual may be trying to be Atlas or not carrying his or her share of the responsibility in a relationship. A common Pluto issue is learning to master the appetites, to enjoy the sensual world without being a slave to it. Or there could be lessons in making sure that relationships are mutually pleasurable. As always, compromise is the answer.

Harmony aspects between Pluto and Saturn suggest that we have learned to handle both of these parts of life with relative ease and success. We may be able to do justice to both partners and career, to share the power and the pleasures.

An **opposition** between Pluto and Saturn shows the need to compromise to be able to satisfy both of these basic desires. As described already, this may require making time for both love and work and making sure that our needs and the needs of the emotionally important "others" in our life are being recognized.

A **quincunx** between Saturn and Pluto also usually can be handled with some compromise. The drives symbolized by both Pluto and Saturn tend to be analytical, supporting the natural inclination of the quincunx, and understanding issues can usually help us find ways to improve them.

CHAPTER FIVE

SATURN ASPECTS TO ANGLES, ASTEROIDS AND NODES

Saturn Aspects to the Midheaven

In the astrological alphabet, the Midheaven (MC) carries the same meaning as Saturn, so an MC-Saturn conjunction is like a double Saturn. (The Midheaven or *Midi Coeli* [middle of the sky] is the above-the-horizon intersection of the ecliptic with the meridian of the birthplace, the great circle which goes through the zenith and nadir and the north and south points of the horizon. Most astrologers use the Midheaven or MC as the beginning of the tenth house in the horoscope.) Individuals with this aspect in their natal charts will usually seek a power role in the world unless they are extremely insecure, feeling that the world has all the power. (In such people, there is a real danger of illness which relieves them of at least some of the guilt they would otherwise feel for their lack of accomplishment.) Several of the examples in this book describe political leaders with natal or progressed Saturn conjunct the MC.

When Saturn comes to the MC in transits, which happens at about 28-year intervals, the individual will be dealing with power in some way. The timing of Saturn's first MC conjunction depends on its house position at birth. Depending on one's age at such times, individuals may move into a position of power, become an entrepreneur, start a new business, be promoted to a higher level in a larger business, etc. They may choose or be forced to take on new family responsibilities, or "play parent" in other ways in the society. They also may be put down in some way if they have overreached and taken on more than they could handle.

Few people will have progressed Saturn reach their MC in their lifetime since it moves very slowly and would have to be in the ninth house close to the MC at birth to reach the aspect. If Saturn is retrograde in secondary progressions, these house positions will be reversed, since the planet will be moving into earlier degrees of the zodiac as it is viewed from Earth. A tenth house Saturn can retrograde to the Midheaven, but a retrograde Saturn in the ninth house will move away from the MC and never conjunct it. Solar Arc Directed Saturn moves about one degree a year, so a slightly larger number of individuals, those who were born with Saturn in the seventh to the ninth house, will experience that aspect. This will still be a minority of the people in the world. The progressed or directed MC also is moved about one degree a year, so it will form a conjunction with Saturn for a different minority of people, those who have Saturn in the tenth to the twelfth house. Of course, the arcs of direction (including solar arc) are never retrograde.

Some traditional works on Saturn assume that the planet is negative and always brings suffering, while the MC is positive and always brings success and prominence, but a little observation will easily show the fallacy of the assumption that any astrological factor is inherently and always negative or positive.

President John F. Kennedy offers a good example of the dual potential of the MC. He was born with Saturn in the tenth house, the natural house of Saturn, and he was pushed by his father into running for president of the U.S. after his older brother died. When Kennedy's progressed Sun reached his local MC in his chart calculated for Washington D.C., the locality of the presidency, he was elected President. Three years later when Kennedy's progressed Sun reached his birthplace MC he was assassinated. **The Saturn principle, whether signaled by the planet or by the MC, can show our potential for achieving power and also the danger of a fall if we overreach.**

Conflict aspects between Saturn and the MC show the tendency toward power struggles in some form. This may be constructive competition in sports, games, politics, business, fighting for causes, etc. It remains constructive if we compete within the rules of nature and of our society. Both sides can gain strength and skill in the contest. If it turns into a life-and-death war, it has gone too far. It is also less constructive if we end up fighting members of our own team. But not using, blocking one's power, can also be destructive. It can lead to illness or can unconsciously invite attacks from others who will take our unused power and turn it against us, e.g., the legendary "boss from hell" would be a projection of Saturn or the MC or other keys to Letter Ten. Any part of our nature which is denied and not allowed expression will make trouble for us.

Harmony aspects between Saturn and the MC suggest that the individual has learned to deal with laws, limits, and power in realistic ways. This ability should facilitate success in the world.

An **opposition** of Saturn and the MC shows a need to integrate dominance and dependency, since Saturn would be on the IC, which carries the meaning of the Moon. The individual would need to be realistic about power and responsibility, able to wield his or her share but also to accept help from others. A former client offered an example of this aspect. He had gone through about twenty jobs in the preceding five years. He hated taking orders but was too insecure to quit a job, so he would come late until the boss fired him. Shortly before I did his chart, he had finally recognized the repetitive pattern and become conscious of what he was doing.

A **quincunx** between Saturn and the MC is usually experienced as the need to improve the world. If we manage to do this in realistic ways, it can be quite constructive. If we keep leaving the scene when we feel restricted or can't make the world conform to the way we think it should be, we need to do some analysis of our motives and look for realistic ways to deal with the situation.

Saturn Aspects to the Ascendant

The horoscope Ascendant, which is the degree of the ecliptic on the eastern horizon at birth, carries the same meaning as the planet Mars. It symbolizes what we do naturally when we are just being ourselves. The zodiacal sign of the Ascendant, the placement of its planetary ruler, and any planets in the first house are also part of the picture of our natural self-expression, our sense of personal identity, including the degree to which we feel we have the right and the power to be ourselves. I also find two additional angles, intersections of great circles, to be useful keys to one's sense of identity: the East Point and the Antivertex. The following discussion of aspects between Saturn and the Ascendant can also be read for its aspects to these auxiliary Ascendants. They are less important than the primary Ascendant, but can be meaningful and helpful when they have aspects to the traditional astrological factors.

An emphasis on fire (through planets and/or signs) in the first house will tend toward self-confidence and spontaneous self-expression. Earth signs and planets there will usually be more practical. Air will be curious and verbal. Water will be sensitive and self-protective.

Saturn conjunct the Ascendant carries the same meaning as Saturn conjunct Mars, though the planetary forms are the most intense expression of the principles. There is always the potential for conflict between fire and earth, between spontaneous desire carried into action to go after what we want and the practicality that weighs the possible results of such action. Individuals who are confident about their ability to cope with the world may be steam-rollers, trying to make their personal will into law, to make the world be the way they think it should be. Individuals who feel that the world has all the power may doubt their own rights and block their own power. If this inhibition is carried too far, it can shut down the immune system and lead to illness. If the person feels he or she has rights but no power, the normal response is frustrated anger which can lead to either illness or accidents. Surgery is one variation on such blocking of the Mars principle, in this case being symbolized by the Ascendant.

Saturn conjunct the Ascendant is almost always a key to an **important father-figure** who was a personal role model. The child may have wanted to be like the father or the opposite or a little of both, but there was usually an intense effect. A grandfather or a stepfather or other person could have played the role. Though Saturn can be a protective and responsible parent, it represents limits, and, especially if it has conflict aspects to other factors in the chart, it can indicate a very difficult early life. Possibilities include poverty, working when very young, being responsible for family members, harsh parents, etc. Among other variations, I have seen charts where the impact was due to the father being missing. Since Saturn's meaning is not limited to authority figures, it can also indicate other types of limits on personal freedom and power such as birth with a physical disability or handicap. Integration of the two principles calls for being realistic about what we can do, what we can't do, and what we have to do, and continuing to develop personal confidence and power to whatever extent we can.

Conflict aspects between Saturn and the Ascendant show the need to make peace between the personal will and power and the limits of our power. No one can do everything that he or she would like to do, but we had better do something! Giving up is apt to lead to a quick and unpleasant exit. Compromise remains the name of the game.

Harmony aspects suggest that the person has learned to live within the limits, avoiding the extremes of overdrive and self-blocking. The realistic use of personal energy will usually lead to success in the world.

An **opposition** of Saturn to the Ascendant puts the planet on the Descendant where it is connected to partners. This is likely to indicate lessons in the area of lasting peer relationships, primarily in the handling of power. Insecure individuals may choose a father-figure as mate, looking for protection. Unfortunately, they may find they have acquired a boss rather than a partner. Alternately, they may pick someone who will let them be father, but that is not conducive to mutual respect and they may get tired of carrying most of the responsibility. It is also possible to delay marriage for fear of being criticized, dominated, rejected, or hurt in other ways when the power of the world is being projected into other people. An original parent may be a positive or negative role model for what is being sought in a mate, or we can maintain a peer relationship with a parent after we are adults. It is possible to pick a workaholic partner, to attract others who are critical or to perceive others as judgmental, even when they are not— if flaw-finding is displaced from the job into relationships. The solution is the same for any of these variations: learning to share the power and responsibility so each person has something to give which the partner values and can receive.

Saturn on the Descendant can be expressed constructively by working with other people, through a career involving team-work or beauty or balance. In all relationships connected to Saturn, it is important to keep the tendency to look for flaws focused on the job rather than on the other people. A family business is possible, working with parents or partners. One of my clients who had Saturn in the seventh house was an artist who appreciated his wife's willingness to pay the bills and manage the home, leaving him free to focus on his creative work.

Saturn **quincunx** the Ascendant carries the danger of fre-quent separations, of difficulty in maintaining long-term commit-ments. This may occur in the work when Saturn is in the sixth house or in partnerships when Saturn is in the seventh or eighth house. It is also possible to stay in a situation in a chronic state of dissatisfaction which is obviously not a comfortable solution. With the quincunx, we need to do what we can to improve things but also to be able to experience satisfaction from the positive facets, not limit our focus to the problems.

Saturn Aspects to the Nodes of the Moon

The nodes of the Moon are derived from the intersection of the Moon's orbit with the plane of the Earth's orbit, which is visualized as an imaginary floor reaching to infinity. Where the Moon crosses that imaginary surface to move into the northern hemisphere we locate the north node. At its south node, the Moon moves back into the southern hemisphere.

In traditional astrology, the north lunar node was described as similar to Jupiter, where things came easily to us. The south lunar node was said to be more like Saturn, a key to a part of life where we had something to learn. Also like Saturn, once we learned it, we had something to give to the world. Recent astrologers have almost reversed this interpretation, calling the south node the "path of least resistance," something we already know and should avoid while pursuing the area of the north node.

I consider this appallingly bad advice. Any part of our nature which is denied and blocked will become a problem. **Oppositions are natural partnerships**. Each end needs the other, and we have to express them as a team working together. The lunar nodes are produced by the Moon's orbit, and I consider them similar to auxiliary moons in the chart. They show where we seek emotional security, which, for most people, means through personal relationships. Though the south node is often a bit more of a challenge, both nodes are water in their basic nature, like the Moon, so both are connected to the past. Both are keys to the subconscious habits we bring in with us at birth.

When Saturn is conjunct either node it is simultaneously opposite the other one, so integration is needed in the areas of dominance and dependency to allow us some of each. We may be struggling with time, trying to handle a career and a family, and need to realize that we can't do everything well. We will also have to deal with the polarity issues of the signs and houses in which the nodes are placed.

Conflict aspects, which include Saturn square both nodes or octile one and trioctile the other, pose the same issues and have the same solution — interdependency.

Harmony aspects include Saturn sextile one node and trine the other, suggesting that these parts of life can be successfully handled.

A Saturn **semisextile to one node produces a quincunx to the other node** and a more questionable outcome. The individual is likely to be feeling the need to improve their handling of home/family and/or career, to be trying to "do it better." **Success is possible by combining the empathy of the Moon and the practical responsibility of Saturn.**

Saturn Aspects to Asteroids

Starting in 1801, following the invention of telescopes, astronomers began to discover **small planets, mostly orbiting the Sun between Mars and Jupiter**. The new objects were called asteroids, though "planetoids" would be a more accurate name. They are not little stars. The total which have been discovered and named is now over 5,000 and climbing. The astronomer who discovers a new asteroid has the right to name it, and the names range from mythical figures to celebrities in many fields to geographical regions to the personal names of friends or patrons of astronomy, etc. The amazing experience for astrologers who work with these small planets is the realization that they carry the meaning of the name they were originally given. If we needed any further proof that this world is meaningful, not random, ruled by chance, the asteroids provide it. Somehow, the astronomer who will give an asteroid its "right" name is the one who discovers it, or the discoverer accepts an appropriate name suggested by someone else.

The first four asteroids to be discovered were Ceres, Pallas, Juno, and Vesta. An ephemeris providing their positions was initially published by Eleanor Bach in 1972, and some astrologers have been working with them since then. ACS was able to publish a more accurate ephemeris shortly after Ellie Bach's, giving daily positions for the first four asteroids. I worked with them from the time they were first available, and wrote the introduction for the ACS ephemeris.

Based on experiences to date, **Ceres** symbolizes a blend of Cancer and Virgo. It is usually a good key to one's mother-figure and to the ability to be a nurturing parent. But it is less emotional than the Moon, with the Virgo practicality, the urge to do a good job. I see it as the service side of Virgo, the attitude that the purpose of work is to help people.

Saturn aspects to Ceres intensify parental issues. Harmony aspects strengthen the capacity to be a "good" parent, whether we do this with a personal family or in a service occupation. Conflict aspects show problems needing to be resolved, which may be job-related or connected to the family. Conjunctions can be manifested either easily or with difficulty, depending on the level of integration of the person. Both oppositions and quincunxes are often a key to tension from trying to handle both a family and a career. With any combination which includes both Virgo and Capricorn overtones, it is important to have reasonable standards. No one can do everything well! Possible dangers include a critical parent or being critical of one's own children, heavy work obligations which limit the time and energy available for the family, health problems which are often due to work pressures, etc. Budgeting time to make sure there is some time for pleasure may help.

On the positive side, Saturn-Ceres aspects may indicate high-level skill in handling the physical world. Any service profession is possible, especially some type of healing work. Parents may have been very competent and responsible, with a strong work ethic. Since these factors represent keys to the two parents, a conjunction can indicate similarities between the parents or one parent playing both roles.

Pallas (Athena) carries the meanings associated with Libra with possible overtones of either Sagittarius or Aquarius. It is usually prominent in the charts of all varieties of counselors and consultants, including social workers, psychologists, astrologers, lawyers, politicians, business consultants, etc. Part of the drive it symbolizes includes the Libra sense of fair play and social justice and a strong intellectual component is part of its possible connection with Sagittarius or Aquarius. It can also show talent or interest in the graphic arts, the Libra attraction to form and balance and harmony.

Saturn aspects to Pallas can point to a career as a consultant or in the arts. As a key to one's father, Pallas may point to a pleasant relationship, but power struggles are also possible. The desire for equality and fair play which Pallas symbolizes can lead to involvement in social causes like "women's liberation" or to personal battles against domination. The shoe can also be on the other foot. Any aspects between Saturn and Pallas except for sextiles and trines may point to a lesson in treating others as equals, a call to avoid playing Atlas or boss.

Juno is the smallest of these first four asteroids, but it can be mighty important in a horoscope. It is the "marriage" asteroid, signaling the Pluto passion for an intense, committed, lasting, close relationship with a mate. In more than 20 years of work with these little planets, I have never seen anyone get married or unmarried without a progressed aspect involving Juno. Plus, Juno conjunctions between charts have "explained" strong attractions between people whose charts were otherwise not particularly compatible. Juno signals both the positive and difficult potentials of Pluto: emotional intensity, persistence, depth, sensitivity, along with the hazards of jealousy and possessiveness.

Juno aspects to Saturn may indicate an intense relationship with the father, which can range from love to power struggles to either or both individuals having to learn to let go. Occasionally, conflict aspects to Juno may be a key to the death of a father-figure. With a **conjunction**, the father may be a role model for the choice of mate, either positive or negative, or the two may stay involved after the child is grown. If a mate is chosen to play a father role, power struggles are likely later when the "child" in the relationship wants to become more equal. Alternately, the more dependent partner may use manipulation for self-protection and to meet personal needs. Fire and air are usually openly expressive. Earth and especially water may hide their feelings for security reasons.

Juno careers can include the large range listed for Pluto. The section of Pluto should be read for additional information on Juno potentials, which can include interest in depth psychology, occultism, research, the past, joint resources, and issues with sensuality and appetites. In Saturn's role as indicator of possible lessons, any of these areas could be a place for growth.

Vesta has been associated with more dramatic events in the lives of clients than any others of the first four asteroids. It seems to be the "ultimate" Virgo. With Ceres, the goal of the job is usually to help people. People with a prominent Vesta sometimes seem to be driven to "do a good job for the sake of doing a good job." The accomplishment is the reward. The hazard in this attitude is that sometimes the focus on the job is so total that the effect on people is ignored. This tunnel-vision focus on a single goal can also occur with Saturn and with Pluto and Juno, so aspects between any of the preceding and Vesta can signal the ultimate in a compulsive one-pointedness. When there is a lack of empathy and compassion, the result can be ruthless. A slightly more benign form of this compulsiveness produces a workaholic.

On the positive side, this commitment to doing something worth doing and doing it well can indicate an enormously capable person. When combined with empathy and compassion, Vesta often signals the capacity for healing. Unfortunately, it can also show a danger of illness. Individuals driven by the need to do something really well who have not found a satisfying vocation are in danger of illness which will let them escape from unfulfilling work without guilt.

I have seen Vesta-Saturn conjunctions in world leaders and in moral monsters. The latter include Jim Jones, who is blamed for the mass suicide of hundreds of people in Jonestown, and Jeffrey Dahmer, who murdered several young people in particularly gruesome ways. Leaders who had this aspect in their progressions during major portions of their lives include Gorbachev and Yeltsin, the two men most responsible for bridging the gap between Russia and the western world. Neil Michelsen, the founder of ACS who was noted for his strong work ethic and focus on health and nutrition, also had the aspect. I have also had a variety of clients with the pattern and tried to encourage them to set reasonable standards for themselves, to do the best they could, but then to try to relax and enjoy the journey.

Chiron

Chiron was discovered in 1977 in an orbit between Saturn and Uranus, where it takes about 50 years to go around the Sun. Astronomers think that it may be a nearly-burned out comet since they have seen it change in brightness as comets do from time to time. Many more astrologers started including Chiron in their charts soon after its discovery than were including the initial four asteroids. This may have been partly because an ephemeris of its positions was made available almost immediately, and partly because Zane Stein wrote a book about it soon after its discovery.

Although astrologers working with the small planets have been universally impressed with the way their apparent meaning matches their names, and Chiron was named for a figure in Greek mythology, there are still differences of opinion about the precise meaning of Chiron. Part of this is probably due to the individual astrologers who are working with him. We each see in the world what fits our own nature and experience.

In Chiron's myth, he was a teacher and healer who was incurably wounded. He was immortal so he could not die. The gods took pity on his suffering and transformed him into the constellation of Sagittarius. From this range of possibilities, some astrologers have focused on the issue of healing and illness and associated Chiron with Virgo. Some have emphasized his uniqueness and called him a maverick. I have found Chiron prominent in people who have a passion for knowledge, who love to learn and to teach, fitting the Sagittarius connection. But I have also found Chiron prominent in healers and sometimes individuals who needed healing, fitting Jupiter's other sign, Pisces. I have also seen the Jupiterian optimism and ideals. I have rarely seen the inescapable "wounding" which some astrologers made a major theme for Chiron. I basically think that Chiron is a kind of "little brother" of Jupiter with many of the same potentials.

Aspects between Saturn and Chiron can point to Jupiterian careers such as teaching, preaching, traveling, etc. When studying charts connected to the murder trial of O.J. Simpson, I found Chiron consistently prominent in the lawyers and in charts for the different stages of the trial. Lawyers, along with issues of morality and truth, are obviously Sagittarian. As is always possible with Saturn, it can first indicate a lesson in coping with the world, and once learned, a skill to help the world.

Fathers connected to Chiron seem to also have the Jupiter range of possibilities. They may be intelligent, educated professionals, or idealistic, or remote, looking for their own goals, or struggling with faith and too high expectations. Since work with Chiron and the asteroids is so new, we will have to continue to observe them in many charts before we can feel certain about their full meanings.

CHAPTER SIX

SATURN IN THE TWELVE HOUSES

Since the planets are the most important form of our astrological alphabet, generally the most complete statement of the meaning of the twelve sides of life is presented in the aspects between the planets, especially in the discussions of conjunctions, the strongest aspect. Though there will be a lot of repetition, when looking up the interpretations of planets in the zodiacal signs and in the twelve houses, you are encouraged to also read the sections on Saturn conjunctions with the ruler of the relevant sign and the related house in the natural zodiac. For example, read Saturn conjunct Mars when investigating Saturn in Aries and Saturn in the first house, the "natural" house of Mars.

Aspects provide important clues on the ease or difficulty of handling the various combinations of planets in signs and in houses. Even when a planet is in a sign or house which is potentially in conflict with its principle, if it has mostly harmonious aspects the desires it represents will usually be easier to integrate. On the other side, the desires symbolized by a planet in a harmonious sign and house will still need attention and care if there are difficult aspects to the planet.

Try not to overrate any single factor in a chart. It is essential to consider the whole chart and to always **look for themes**, for repeated statements of the same principles.

Saturn in the First House

Saturn in the first house is less intense than Saturn conjunct Mars, but it represents the same issue. **Personal will must be integrated with the limits of personal will**. There is an inherent potential for conflict between our first house sense of our own identity, our right and power to do what we please, and the Saturn principle which represents the "rules of the game." The "rules" include "natural law," cultural regulations. authority figures, and the conscience. **We may resist any limits on our will and fight the world, trying to make our own will into law. Or we may doubt our own power and rights and give up, convinced that if we tried to do what we wanted to we would just fail or be put down by the world**. To integrate the conflict we need to compromise so that there is a place in our lives for each of these sides of life. We need to find some things which we want to do and can do which are not in conflict with the rules, so that we have our share of the power of the world.

Saturn is a key to authority figures, and our first exposure to them is usually a father-figure, which could be a grandfather, stepfather, etc. In the first house, the **parent is a personal role model** for the child, who may want to be like the father or may want to do the opposite. I have seen both extremes—individuals with brutal fathers they feared and individuals who adored their fathers. Endless variations are possible.

One example of a first house Saturn was a woman whose self-esteem was damaged because her father obviously preferred her sister. Years after the death of her father, this woman was still having recurrent dreams. She would hear her father calling "wait. I'm trying to catch up to you." She would turn in the dream, thinking "at last, my father wants to be with me." Her father would see her face, say "Oh, I thought you were your sister," and disappear.

If we doubt our own worth and power and feel that all the power is outside of our control, we may not attempt many things we could otherwise do. In extreme self-blocking, we can shut down our immune system and become ill. No one can do everything they want, but we had better do something.

Saturn in the first house also shows an identification with a career. Once we have learned the rules which let us survive in this physical world, our skills permit us to cope with the world. They define our role in the society, our status, our share of the power if we develop practical skills. When something is part of our identity, we have to do it or feel wiped out, so people with Saturn in the first house have to feel powerful through some sort of accomplishment. But at the same time, the first house is demanding that our work be active, independent, varied, and under our own control This can produce an entrepreneur, a self-employed professional or business person, etc. Mechanical skills are possible, which can lead to work with machines or tools, including modern technology, military, or medical fields, etc.

The current U.S. Vice President has a first house Saturn combined with Pluto and Mars and all of them in Leo, calling for a position of power and leadership. His father was in the government and Al Gore has also served in a variety of government jobs.

The identification with power and accomplishment may cause problems if such people retire. But a recent client who had been a highly successful business executive has managed it successfully by substituting control over his investments for his former job managing employees.

Part of the Saturn principle is a critical attitude, since to work effectively we have to look for the flaws and correct them. It is possible to so identify with this attitude that we are critical about everything in our lives, or we may just be too self-critical. In trying to handle any combination of two or more of the basic life desires, compromise is almost always the best solution. We have to learn to be ourselves, defend ourselves, and assert ourselves in the first house, but Saturn always reminds us to live within the limits. Jim Jones, who led hundreds of followers to suicide in the jungles of Guyana, is a tragic example of a first house Saturn man who did not learn to live within the limits. He despised his father and took him as a negative role model. Fred Astaire (rhythm and timing of dance) lived a disciplined and productive life. Percy Shelley faced the health challenges that are possible with Saturn in the first, but was a productive poet. Robert McNamara and George Patton had personal confrontations with power.

Saturn in the Second House

Saturn in the second house can show first a lesson and later skills in handling the material world. This can include many variations on making money, collecting possessions, indulging appetites, or creating beauty. The more common reaction is to be careful with money and possessions, to always have some put away for a rainy day since Saturn shows where we are conscious of the power of the world. But, since Saturn can be a lesson, there will be some individuals with this position who are learning to earn a living, or to conserve resources, or to moderate the appetites. I have also seen some who were workaholics and needed to learn to relax and enjoy the flowers. The chart shows the issues in the nature. The individual habits determine the details, and they can be changed if we are willing to make an effort.

Fathers described by the second house may be pleasant, indulgent of themselves or others, intent on making money, artistic, or many other variations. The individual's choice of career is also likely to be somewhat Venusian. This may simply mean the person wants to enjoy the work, or the salary may be the main focus, or aesthetics may be important. Usually, security is sought and there is enough practicality to achieve it.

Newt Gingrich, who became Republican Speaker of the House of Representatives in the U.S. Congress in the election of 1994, has Saturn in his second house if the birth time of 3 AM given by his family is accurate. He has been highly successful in raising funds for Republican causes despite his Gemini tendency toward periodic foot-in-mouth bloopers. Prince Charles has Saturn here with his inherited money carrying a great responsibility. Arnold Schwarzenegger of movie fame and Republican politics also has Saturn here.

Saturn in the Third House

Saturn in the third house may be originally experienced as doubts about one's mental ability, but once the individual has learned to cope with the world, he or she will often work in a mental career. The father or siblings may play a role in the mental development.

One female client with a grand trine to Saturn in Libra in the third house was told by her father that she was stupid. Where Saturn is placed, we have to prove to ourselves that we can cope by doing it. This woman got a BA in mathematics, an MD degree, became a successful psychiatrist, and still said "I don't have a very good mind." Where Saturn is concerned, we just have to keep doing it till we know we can. Setting realistic standards may be part of the lesson.

Other individuals with a third house Saturn might have fathers who are equalitarian and accepting, encouraging a sibling relationship, or there could be older siblings who played parent or younger ones for whom the person felt responsible. The third house Saturn lessons involve developing skill with the intellect and the ability to handle peer relationships. Growth may come through learning to handle a basic part of life which has been neglected, or it may just call for knowing "when to do which." When should we be equalitarian and let others do their share and when should we take responsibility?

Other third house careers may involve dexterity leading to work with the hands. Letter three in our alphabet can indicate skill with eye-mind-hand coordination. A recent client has just opened her own hair-care salon so she is now the boss, but she is recognizing that she can't do everything and looking for associates who can handle some of the routine details which are less satisfying to her Pisces' love of beauty. Peter Sellers and Ellen Burstyn, both drawn to communicate through movies, have Saturn here. So did writer Hermann Hesse.

Saturn in the Fourth House

Saturn in the fourth house emphasizes the early home and parents. Children with this position usually learn to work early, though this can be for many different reasons. Life on a farm is possible, with chores for everyone. Help from the children may be needed because of poverty, illness, or just a large family. There might be a single parent playing both parental roles. Guessing details is a futile effort in astrology. When we understand the principles, we can often change the details.

The main issues for Saturn in the natural house of the Moon involve dependency versus power and responsibility. Some people are struggling to do justice to both a family and a career in the world, and they have to accept the fact that we can't do everything well. The answer to dominance/dependency is interdependency — each person able to give something that others value and can receive. As small children, the power is all outside and sometimes Saturn in the fourth house shows a truly difficult early life, but as we gain skills we can create the secure home and family we want.

Fourth house careers can include "mothering" our own family or the world. We can feed, clothe, house, or comfort the public. An office or business in the home is possible, or a family business which follows in the footsteps of the parents. Family roots, genealogies, antiques, could be treasured. Security is very important, but concerns can range from self-absorption in an insecure person to the urge to protect all of life including mother earth. Some individuals might not have children of their own for fear of "not doing it right," but they might substitute pets or a garden to satisfy the parental instinct.

In her book *Profiles of Women*, Lois Rodden gives an interesting example of an author with Saturn in her fourth house. Sidonie Gabrielle wrote under the name of Collette, began writing as a child, and said that it was "as easy as frying eggs." Her chart fits the theory that the natural water houses, four, eight, and twelve, are especially important keys to habits brought in from past lives. The water element represents the subconscious side of the mind. Collette's Saturn is in its own sign, Capricorn, conjunct Mercury within just over two degrees. The pattern is appropriate for a career writer working in her home and affecting masses of the public. Letter four primarily signifies our need for emotional security for which we look to our home and family, but it can be extended to apply to one's homeland and its people in general. Apparently, Collette did not go through the initial doubt of her mental ability which is so common with Mercury conjunct Saturn and/or Mercury in Capricorn. In her case, she seems to have brought in an already developed career talent.

But Collette also had the need for closeness which is indicated by a strong fourth house. Hers included a Sun-Moon conjunction in Aquarius in addition to Saturn-Mercury. Collette was married three times, each time to a man in a related profession: a collaborating writer, her Editor-in-Chief, and a journalist. She wrote fiction, drama, criticism, and literary correspondence for a newspaper, but was best-known for her stories of girls and women in love. Her specialty certainly fits her Libra rising and Mars in Scorpio, which show her identification with a mate, and her Venus in Pisces, Neptune in the seventh house of partnership, and Jupiter in Leo, which show the tendency to idealize love and relationships.

An astrological colleague with Saturn in the 4th house says she did not have harsh, punitive parents or a difficult childhood. She and her siblings didn't have to do any work, though their single parent worked hard. Saturn ruled her seventh house and her grandparent did some parenting. She was aware of "poverty" in that depression-era messages were received from both her mother and grandmother, so she felt "poor" sometimes even though she wasn't. She worked from the home, followed parental footsteps in career, and works in a field involving emotional support of people. She also chose not to have children. Others with a fourth-house Saturn include Glen Campbell, Ernest Hemingway, and Omar Sharif.

Saturn in the Fifth House

Saturn in the fifth house shows the need to deal with love and self-esteem. Fire and earth can be natural antagonists and need to be integrated. If the fire wins, the individual keeps changing, looking for new excitement and thrills and applause, but is likely to have twinges of guilt because at the end there is little to show for the energy expenditure. If the earth wins, the individual persists until something has been accomplished, preferably with tangible results, but feels frustrated at being tied down, not able to keep moving. Compromise is needed to allow some variety and some achievement.

Fathers described by a fifth house Saturn can range from loving and responsible to too involved in personal ego to notice the needs of others. They may be dominating or easily manipulated with flattery. They want to be heroes. They need an audience.

Since the fifth house is a key to the person's own ability to love and accept love and to procreate children, there are likely to be lessons somewhere in that area. The example of the father can point to growth potentials whether the father was a positive or a negative model. Some individuals with this placement may not have their own children because of the responsibility and fear of failing in some way. Some produce children but separate from the partner and have to learn to share the responsibility. Single parents may be carrying too much and separated parents too little. Some people choose a career involving the children of others.

The fifth house shows a need to create something unique and to have it acknowledged by others. Possible careers can range from the entertainment field to teaching, from selling and promoting to investment. If possible, the individual needs to be in charge of the work rather than have to take orders. There may be intense ambition, but also the danger of giving up if the goals seem impossible to achieve, or too much work, or taking too long. Saturn reminds us that reaching the top is a long journey, that it requires time and effort, so we need to keep going.

Another example from Lois Rodden's book, *Profiles of Women,* was Barbara Rooney, who had Saturn in her fifth house in a close conjunction with Venus in Pisces. One of the traditional keynotes for the fifth house associates it with the entertainment world, and Barbara Rooney chose careers in that area moving from beauty queen to model to starlet. Shortly before she was twenty-two years old, Barbara became the fifth wife of Mickey Rooney and switched to a career of producing children, one of the many potentials for the creativity of the fifth side of life. Barbara and Mickey had four children in the next five years, to the dismay of traditional astrologers who often suggest that Saturn in the fifth will deny children.

But Mickey got into financial trouble while he was siring offspring rather than successful movies, and he filed for bankruptcy in 1962, shortly before the birth of their last child in 1963. On January 24, 1966, Barbara Rooney filed for separate maintenance and Mickey counter-filed for divorce. A week later, on the morning of January 31, Barbara and her lover were found shot to death in the bathroom. She was shot in the jaw and he was shot

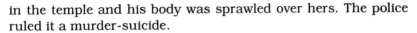

in the temple and his body was sprawled over hers. The police ruled it a murder-suicide.

Saturn calls for realism. It is hardly realistic to continue to have children while going a half million dollars into debt and sustaining an affair with a potentially violent lover. Many aspects in Barbara's chart showed the potential for tension. Progressed Saturn formed a T-square to the lunar nodes in the second-eighth houses for many years, showing a lesson in handling finances and passions. The second house includes our personal resources and the eighth house covers shared resources among many other meanings. The handling of debt and joint money, possessions, sensuality, etc. is a Letter Eight issue. The midpoint of Saturn/south lunar node can be a special key to lessons since both of these factors point to growth areas in the nature. Barbara's Saturn/South Node midpoint was on Uranus, square the Sun, and opposite the midpoint of Ascendant/Mars. This configuration in fixed signs and cardinal houses reinforced the tendency toward power struggles already described by cardinal factors (Saturn and the lunar nodes) in fixed houses. If we lack an outlet for "healthy" (game-playing) competition, the power struggles can be manifested in very uncomfortable ways, displaced into relationships which should be cooperative or with the power projected into others who may use it against us. Barbara was expressing her competitive nature appropriately while working in the entertainment field, but when she tried to satisfy all her potentials through relationships, she became vulnerable, with her power displaced and projected.

Others with Saturn in the fifth house include Winston Churchill, Merv Griffin, Dean Martin, Bruce Lee, and Henry Kissinger.

Saturn in the Sixth House

Saturn in the sixth house intensifies the work ethic, the need to do something worth doing and to do it well. This may be a key to major success, but the individual might sacrifice other important parts of life to achieve the success. Or, since Saturn is usually a lesson, we might have to learn to work effectively at the start of life.

The Saturn desire for power will normally push toward owning one's own business or having a professional career in contrast to the sixth house willingness to work for others, but both of these life drives want the job done right. This may lead to feeling that we have to do it ourselves — no one else will do it right.

One client business owner with Saturn in the sixth house complained of his inability to find responsible employees. His need to oversee every detail could not let anyone else have a share of the power which is part of responsibility.

It is also possible to set such high standards that they are impossible to attain and one never feels the sense of satisfaction in the accomplishments which both Saturn and the sixth house crave. If the frustrations become too strong, especially if they are repressed so the individual is not aware of them, illness is a danger. An illness or accident can get us out of a job without guilt. Guilt is a health hazard if we feel responsible for something that is outside of our control or can't be changed. Part of Saturn's lesson involves doing what we can and then accepting the limits of being human.

It is possible to be born with health problems so that a major life lesson involves learning to function effectively with the body. If we accept some type of life continuity, which is usually called reincarnation, our habits at the start of life are brought in from past existence and we keep revising them as we learn and grow. The horoscope at birth shows our habitual desires, skills, and conflicts. We act on the habits, get the consequences, and change the habits which bring undesirable consequences. The horoscope and any other tool for self-awareness helps us understand the principles and change before life gets painful.

A father described by Saturn in the sixth house will be dealing with Virgo issues. He may have been a workaholic, or just very capable, or unable to function effectively in the world, or very critical with "puritan" ethics, or ill. Astrology shows issues. We do not know whether they are being handled well or badly until we observe the life.

Appropriate work for an individual with this placement includes all types of service or craftsmanship, taking things apart and/or putting them together. Usually there will be skill with details, patience, thoroughness, and a desire for tangible results. Individuals with this placement include Jimi Hendrix, Nelson Rockefeller, Alfred, Lord Tennyson, and Simon Wiesenthal.

Saturn in the Seventh House

Saturn in the seventh house indicates the need to learn when to be an equal and when to wield responsible power and when to accept limits. The latter will usually be connected to the rights and power of other people. With integration, we can cooperate with others in marriage and in teamwork in a job, sharing the power and the responsibility.

A seventh house father may be a partner or may be gone in light of the potential for separations in the opposition aspect and the natural opposition of the seventh house to the first house of our own identity. The father may be artistic and pleasant or argumentative and combative. If we learn compromise and cooperation early in life with both authority figures and peers, we will be prepared to enjoy our adult equalitarian relationships.

Often Saturn in the seventh house calls for recognition that a variety of types of interactions can be appropriate, including cooperation, competition, and helping others. We just need to have a place in our lives for each and to know when to do which.

I was initially puzzled by a male client whose chart was dominated by air signs, which are normally equalitarian, but he had both major lesson factors, Saturn and the south lunar node, in air signs. But Saturn was in the seventh house and the south node was in the tenth house, pointing to lessons somewhere in the area of equality and responsible power. I described the issue to the client, and he was able to understand it. He said that he was a manager in his job, responsible for seeing that employees worked properly. He recognized that his tenth house Aquarius was leading him to be too equalitarian with the employees and they were taking advantage of his leniency. But in his seventh house, which was calling for equality, he "had his thumb on his wife" to quote his phrase.

Seventh house careers can involve all kinds of teamwork, especially counseling or consulting in some way. Fields involving arbitration and law and politics are common choices. Litigation is part of the potential, or other forms of competition. Power struggles are "healthy" and can contribute to both sides gaining skills if they "play by the rules," are able to win sometimes and lose sometimes, and keep in mind that it is a game. Remember that until we are exercising our share of the world's power, we still feel that it is in the hands of others. Other seventh house careers can use its potential artistic talent for jobs in the graphic arts such as design, photography, architecture, city planning, and landscape gardening.

Individuals with Saturn in the seventh house include Prince Albert (whose work was being partner to Queen Victoria), Henry Cabot Lodge (diplomat, negotiator and politician), Michelangelo (artist), and Jerry Rubin (confrontational politics).

Saturn in the Eighth House

Saturn in the eighth house is, like Saturn in the seventh, usually working on issues of power versus equality. As part of our desire for deep lasting peer relationships, but with the added intensity of water, the eighth house can be more challenging than the seventh, where we are usually more consciously aware of both sides of situations and more willing to compromise. Water instinctively seeks fusion, but in the eighth house, as with Scorpio and Pluto, we also want control. It is not easy to be passionately involved with a mate but able to release to allow equality, to control ourselves but not anyone else, to realize we cannot possess another person. Complicating the situation is the water need for dependency and the Letter Eight fear of loss of control. The prize for success is shared power and shared pleasure with possessions and appetites. We learn self-knowledge partly through the mirror of the mate and self-mastery partly out of respect for the rights of the mate.

In an interview with a female client who had Saturn in the eighth house I was delicately trying to get across the issue of sharing power with her husband without suggesting that there was something "wrong" with her. She just looked at me and said "Yes, my husband and I do fight a lot. We enjoy it. Then we kiss and make up." So I said "Fine." Usually I advise competing with members of the other team rather than our own. But if you are doing it consciously as a game, it is not a problem. When something is happening in our lives which disturbs us and we are not sure why it is there or how to deal with it, then we need to do some analysis.

An eighth house father may be possessive and dominating if his family is his main or only place where he can feel in control. Or he may be so busy seeking security in the material world that he is rarely home. This combination can also indicate the death of a parent or other important authority figure in the early life, teaching us how to let go. Unless the father is unusually secure, he may feel deeply but seldom express his emotions. Emotional manipulation is a sign of too much insecurity to seek what we want openly. There may be sexual issues, especially if the relationship between the parents is poor. If the father tends to repress his emotions, they may periodically come out explosively or they may lead to illness. He is likely to be trying to learn moderation, when is enough, and how to let go. If the child can learn from the father's example, he or she will be ahead of the game.

We can direct the Saturn drive for power in the world into a career with teamwork. It could deal with joint resources in banking, investment, taxes, insurance, or public funds in government work. Or it could deal with the search for hidden answers through depth psychology, archaeology, detective work, or any type of research. Saturn and the eighth house bring together two of the "obsessive-compulsive" sides of life, so individuals with this combination are often very good at detail and organization, with phenomenal memories and a strong will. If they possibly can, such people keep on going until they get there.

Jerry Garcia demonstrates how one can handle one of the possible Saturn lessons but still be struggling with another one. Jerry had Saturn in the eighth house, where the most common forms of the Saturn lesson involve mastering appetites or learning to share power, possessions, and pleasures with close peer relationships, to handle joint resources. Jerry was tremendously successful in the area of joint resources. His band, The Grateful Dead, was one of the top earners of royalties. For years, their concerts were consistently sold out, and they made a lot of money selling records and CDs and many other spin-off products such as T-shirts. Plus, Jerry was enormously generous with his earnings, giving much to charity, including supporting other musicians who were less successful. Unfortunately, he did not manage his appetites as well. His early death was partly blamed on his unhealthy diet and his addictions to tobacco and a variety of drugs. He ended with diabetes and blockages in the arteries to the heart.

Bob Packwood, the Oregon Senator who was forced to resign after many women accused him of sexual harassment, has Saturn in the eighth house in Capricorn. The position fits his long career in the Federal Government, but warns against the abuse of power. Other individuals with Saturn in the eighth house include Jacques Cousteau (emphasizing the shared resources of our water planet), Sigmund Freud, Jean Houston and R.D. Laing. The last three were all involved in psychology and/or psychiatry.

Saturn in the Ninth House

Saturn in the ninth house connects our beliefs about the world with the physical reality of its laws and limits. Beliefs can range from the materialistic atheism of western science, which can only maintain its dogma by ignoring most of human experience, to the equally dogmatic and equally narrow beliefs of a variety of fundamentalist religions with small gods presiding over small and exclusive heavens. To stay in good standing, you have to follow the rules: "don't look, don't question."

It does not take much knowledge of astrology to demolish both of these extremes. Astrology shows that we live in a world that is inherently meaningful, not a world of random chance. It is not chance when a newly discovered minor planet (asteroid) is given a name which describes its meaning when you observe it in horoscopes. It defies logic to claim that a single universal God can have chosen one group of people or one leader or one holy book to favor, while everyone else is condemned.

An effective synthesis of the principles of Saturn in the ninth house calls for a realization that Truth is a goal we never reach but the journey can be a marvelous career. Plus, with Saturn, we can and should test every new idea, note the consequences, and keep enlarging our understanding. We don't even have to totally deny the ideas which don't "work" as we thought they would. They can be put on the shelf. They might work at a different time under different circumstances. The Cosmos is almost certainly bigger than our current mental capacity.

A ninth house father may be a searcher, whether a highly educated professional sharing his knowledge with the world, or a vagrant wandering the world looking for an unattainable ideal. We could have a father from another country, a conventionally religious father or an independent thinker with high standards, a wastrel and irresponsible father who assumed that god would provide, or many other variations. The father might have expected too much of the child or vice versa or he might have had an outrageous sense of humor and been an eternal optimist. From him or his surrogate, we learn not to expect perfection of authorities or life. We can learn whether he showed us how **to** do it or how **not** to do it. We can learn to keep questioning and not close off our options, but to test them and watch the consequences.

The ninth house consequences can include confrontations with human laws and judgment as well as cosmic. Former U.S. President Richard Nixon had Saturn in the ninth house. He thought he was above the law and was forced to resign after the scandal known as Watergate.

Astrological research by Françoise and Michel Gauquelin analyzed the horoscopes of thousands of famous professionals and found that Saturn was in the ninth house (or early in the tenth house) significantly often for scientists. As previously noted, scientists tend to be materialists. Ninth house careers often involve public service, including fields which profit from higher education or which deal with long-range areas. Common choices are teaching, preaching, writing, the law, publishing, libraries, traveling, foreign countries, etc., etc. Bon Voyage.

Richard Nixon's Vice President, Spiro Agnew, also had Saturn in the ninth house, and he was forced to resign due to infractions of the law. Steve Allen did a show which involved meeting the great minds of history, Edmund G. Brown, former Jesuit and former governor of California, and writer Albert Camus all had ninth-house Saturns.

Saturn in the Tenth House

Saturn in the tenth house is "at home," producing a double statement of the same principle, which is still stronger if Saturn is close to the MC. Several of the individuals we will examine in more depth were born with Saturn conjunct the MC, and most are functioning in power positions. However, it is also possible to have Saturn in its own house and still feel that the world has all the power. We only know we have it when we have used it and proved it to ourselves. There are major hazards in having the potential for power and not using it, including health problems or having the world use power against one. Any part of us which is denied and blocked, is not allowed to express, will make trouble for us.

On the other hand, we can't do it all. Atlas people may end with back problems or just find they can't do what they feel they should be able to do. One client with a very conflicted tenth house Saturn was carrying three jobs simultaneously; a regular job to earn a living, a second job to earn money to buy material to build a house, and the third job was building the house. He was keeping himself under incredible pressure with hardly time to sleep. He asked about back problems and I explained that they often stemmed from such pressures, but were not predictable, that he could have also had problems with his hearing or his teeth since they were also associated with the Saturn principle. He commented that he had those problems as well. I urged him to extend his time table, to give himself more time to accomplish his jobs.

A tenth house father can exemplify either of the extremes of feeling responsible for the world or feeling powerless and anxious or depressed. Guilt can be a pervasive issue if we think we should be doing more than we can do. A recent mother of grown children who has Saturn in Pisces in the tenth house kept saying she wasn't doing enough, while her grown daughter kept insisting the mother was doing too much for others and asked me what her children could do to help her. I suggested they just tell the mother she was great and encourage her to enjoy life. But with that placement of Saturn, it is true the mother could not live with herself if she just sat in front of the TV or played bingo. She has to feel she is accomplishing something for the cosmos.

In general, tenth house careers are most satisfying if the individual sees tangible results from the efforts, and, of course, if they are in charge of what they are doing. Some people with a tenth house Saturn have to learn to take orders and some have to learn to give them, or at least to delegate the duties some of the time. An emphasis on earth, especially if water is also strong, can show an overly serious nature. If the burden is getting heavier, we may need to broaden our perspective and cultivate a sense of humor.

Individuals with Saturn in the tenth house include Muhammad Ali, Albert Einstein, Zsa Zsa Gabor and Daniel Berrigan.

Saturn in the Eleventh House

Like Saturn in the tenth house, Saturn in the eleventh house is another common pattern in the charts of people who seek careers in public service. The eleventh house deals with more equalitarian organizations and with the expansion of knowledge, with humanitarian issues including equality and freedom, with casual friends and the legislature in a democracy. Where Saturn describes the limits, the eleventh house seeks to go beyond the limits. Where Saturn is the epitome of hierarchy, the eleventh house demands equality. Where Saturn insists on staying grounded, the eleventh house builds rockets to go to Mars and beyond. Saturn is the law and the eleventh house rebels against it.

Obviously, Saturn in the eleventh house calls for integration if we want to avoid constant inner conflict. But what a great team they are when they work together. It takes the innovation and the willingness to take risks of the eleventh house to build rockets, but it also takes the understanding of gravity and other forces in our physical universe. The practicality of earth and the abstract intellectual skills of air are magnificent when they work together. Once we accept the necessary limits which let us survive in and cope with a material world, we can be free to do what we please. We can choose any career which expands or disseminates knowledge, and, if possible, lets us be our own boss working with peers.

Eleventh house fathers can be Aquarian in many ways, from intellectually brilliant and verbal to defiantly different, from being a friend with their children to being cool, indifferent, and sometimes just physically gone or emotionally unavailable. The father may be theoretically learning to be equalitarian, understanding, and accepting, the air principles, but may actually still be dogmatic or controlling. He might also just be unpredictable or rather strange. Whatever his version of the principle, the child has a chance to learn what to do or what not to do.

Sybil Leek is an interesting example of a person with Saturn in the eleventh house. Her data is given in Lois Rodden's book *Profiles of Women*. She has been called "The Billy Graham of Witchcraft" and her autobiography *Diary of a Witch* is probably a primary key to the current fame of modern witchcraft as a nature religion. Sybil was involved in the occult from childhood, and she parlayed her unconventional interests and her psychic talents into a variety of careers. These included being the subject of a BBC documentary, running an antique shop, being president of several companies, worldwide lectures, participation in parapsychology research, raising two children, writing as a journalist and poet, explorations into astrology, and homes in her native England and adopted U.S. Saturn in the eleventh house fits many changes of job or a job with great variety and/or unconventional jobs. Sybil managed to integrate the Saturn demand for realism with her strong eleventh house and Mercury in Aquarius which pushed her to go beyond the usual limits, and with the mysticism of her Sun-Venus-Uranus closely conjunct in Pisces in her fourth house.

Other individuals with Saturn in the eleventh house include several varieties of rebels: Marlon Brando, Lenny Bruce, Adolf Eichmann, and Vincent Van Gogh.

Saturn in the Twelfth House

Saturn in the twelfth house connects the ultimate creation of structure with the final dissolution of structure. Twelfth house careers include artists, saviors, and victims: the prisoner and the jailer, the patient and the doctor, the homeless person and the social worker. We can work within the society's rules or fight them or give up. Saturn demands realism, but the twelfth house needs faith in a Power beyond humans. When that faith is present at the subconscious level, we are totally protected. We still have to do our share of the practical effort, but then we can let go and trust, knowing it will be ok. The Gauquelin research was mentioned in connection with the ninth house. In addition to Saturn in the ninth house for scientists, they also found Saturn significantly often in both the ninth and the twelfth houses of famous doctors. Doctors are both highly educated and playing a savior role, but the emphasis on the physical world in their training may make it harder for some of them to maintain faith is a Power beyond the physical world. The burden of personal responsibility which results when we lack such faith may be one of the reasons many doctors die young.

A twelfth house father can manifest any of the variations already mentioned, and many more. He may be an artist, a savior, or a victim in innumerable ways. He may be missing, having gone looking for his beautiful dream. He may be too busy saving the world to be there for his family. Or he may adore his family and be idealized in return. Or he may expect too much of himself and his family and vice versa. As with Saturn in the ninth house, sometimes we have to learn not to turn human authority figures into gods. When we put our faith in a fragment of life, it is an idolatry and we may have to lose it to force us to find a bigger god.

One of the hazards of Saturn in the ninth or the twelfth house is the worship of power. Nixon was a ninth house example. O.J. Simpson is a twelfth house example, with Saturn and Pluto conjunct in Leo in the twelfth house. The evidence presented at his trial and since strongly suggests that he did murder his estranged wife and her friend, Ron Goldman, though the jury in the murder trial acquitted him. Up to the deaths of Nicole and Ron, O.J. had gotten what he wanted most of his life. He was a football star, acquired wealth from commercial ads, had some roles in movies, and mingled with the Hollywood elite. He had power and money and fame. If he did murder Nicole, what he lacked was the twelfth house capacity for empathy and compassion, for morality and faith in a Higher Power. His own ego desires had replaced a bigger god. He spent over a year in jail during the trial, one of the painful possibilities for Saturn in the twelfth house, and he has since been rejected by many of his former friends, so his ego is suffering. He is also reported to be having nightmares of Nicole's death, which suggests that his inner Saturn, his conscience, is still alive.

Other individuals with Saturn in the twelfth house include Larry Flynt (a pornographic publisher who was shot and partially paralyzed), Ira Progoff (a depth psychologist who is expressing the ideals of the twelfth house), Robert Redford (who is into environmental causes) and Walt Whitman (a famous poet, who created beauty in the world).

Astrology shows our psychological issues and potentials. We create the details of our lives.

CHAPTER SEVEN

SATURN CYCLES

Astronomy and Calendars

The ancient world knew Saturn as the most distant planet which symbolized its association with limits or boundaries. Saturn marked the end of the region of the "wanderers," the seven visible lights which moved against the backdrop of the stars which were grouped in relatively stable constellations. This realm beyond Saturn belonged to the "fixed stars." With the advent of the telescope, Saturn's rings were clearly visible and offered an additional symbolic representation of limits. As astronomers have acquired more powerful telescopes and in this century have been able to send rockets into space which could relay closer photographs back to Earth, they have discovered more tenuous rings around all of the four big gaseous planets: Jupiter, Saturn, Uranus, and Neptune. No one knows whether space is boundless, whether the expanding galaxies we see will continue to move out in all directions forever or will someday collapse in upon themselves. The more we increase our ability to probe farther, the more worlds we discover.

The tenuous rings around the other three big planets hint that nothing in this physical world is totally without limits. The four giant planets symbolize the transpersonal sides of life which reach beyond everyday personal needs and interpersonal relationships.

Three of them deal with the ultimate beliefs, values, and goals of life, always seeking to transcend limits. Saturn (which has more massive rings) reminds us to keep our aspirations grounded, to look for ways to bring our visions into form in a physical world.

Astronomers have also found additional moons orbiting the planets. By August 1995, 18 had been discovered for Saturn. Later reports of additional moons were said to be mistaken. Though Saturn is not the largest planet in the solar system, its moon Titan is the largest moon. Astrology is not able to use these moons since, when we observe their positions from Earth, they are too close to their respective planets to be differentiated. We can use the asteroids, the small planets which are mostly orbiting our Sun between Mars and Jupiter, but that is another story for another book.

Saturn was the slowest of the seven "wanderers" which were visible to the ancient world without telescopes. The Sun, Moon, and five visible planets moved relatively rapidly against the backdrop of the "fixed" stars whose movement in relation to each other was imperceptible in a human lifetime. Saturn was sometimes called the "chronocrator" or time-keeper, but the Sun and Moon were the primary sources of calendars. Known as the "lights," the Sun ruled the day and the Moon ruled the night. Many cultures had two calendars, a solar year of the seasons when the Sun moved in front of the visible groups of stars called constellations, and lunar months based on the Moon's orbit of the constellations in about 28 days. Since the movements of the Sun and Moon were incommensurable, that is, they did not come out even, different cultures tried different ways to make the calendars mesh. One common technique was to have 12 months of 30 days each and to make the extra five days of the solar calendar a special time of religious rituals. Since the solar year is not exactly 365 days, that would still produce a problem in time as the seasons gradually moved out of synchronization with the calendar.

The seasons were highly important, especially to agriculturists who needed to know when to plant their crops. Early astrologers searched for reliable patterns in the cycles of the sky. The Egyptians used the heliacal rising of the star Sirius, the day when it rose just before the Sun, as the key to their time to plant. They had discovered that the annual flooding of the Nile river would follow, providing water to germinate their seeds in a semi-desert region with very little rainfall. The Moon's period from one new moon to another was divided into four weeks of seven days each, and the days were named for the five planets and the Sun and Moon. The correlations are easy to see in English for Sunday, Monday, and Saturday. The names of the other days come from the equivalent Norse gods. *Tyr* or *Tiw* in Anglo-Saxon was the war god, so Tuesday is the day of Mars. Wednesday was given to *Woden*, the closest match with Mercury. Thursday belonged to Jupiter, so *Thor*, the Norse god of thunder, was the source of the name in English. Venus owned Friday, with the English name coming from *Frig*, the Norse goddess of domestic fertility. The French words for the days of the week are a closer fit to the Roman names of the gods for the different days. They are *Mardi* for Tuesday, *Mercredi* for Wednesday, *Jeudi* for Thursday, and *Vendredi* for Friday.

Planetary Cycles
in Mundane Astrology

In addition to Saturn, Jupiter, the next slowest planet known to the ancient world, was also an important timer for longer periods. Saturn's cycle through the zodiac takes about 29.46 years while Jupiter's is just under 12 years. Jupiter and Saturn are conjunct, in the same degree in the sky, approximately every twenty years. The general patterns in the sky at these conjunctions were interpreted as clues to the nature of the next twenty years for the society. Early astrologers were interested in the general situation in their immediate world. They wanted to forecast the weather, the possibility of wars or plagues or famine, and the well-being of the ruler. This part of astrology is currently called "mundane" astrology, and few modern astrologers devote much time to it. Most modern astrology students are interested in the horoscopes of individuals, which reportedly came into wider use in Greece a few hundred years before the Christian era.

Current mundane astrologers still watch horoscopes calculated at Jupiter-Saturn conjunctions as keys to the world scene. The conjunctions occur in each of the elements for approximately

200 years, so they cycle through the four elements in about 800 years. Astrologers have noted that each of the U.S. Presidents who was elected close to a Jupiter-Saturn conjunction, after they moved permanently into earth signs in 1840, has died in office. Their conjunction in 1802 was in an earth sign and was not followed by the death in office of President Jefferson who was elected in 1800. Jefferson's protection may be due to the fact that the following conjunction in 1822 was in a fire sign, so the earth element had not yet been established. Our first presidential death in office followed the earth conjunction in 1840. Some of the deaths were from natural causes and some from assassinations. Franklin Delano Roosevelt was elected for his third term as president in 1940, but survived to be reelected once more in 1944. He died in 1945, so he did not leave the office alive. The 1980 Jupiter-Saturn conjunction was the first in the present 800 year cycle to occur in an air sign. Reagan was elected as U.S. President that year, and was shot just two months after his inauguration. In a previous century, he would have died, but he was saved by modern medicine. We will have one more Jupiter-Saturn conjunction in an earth sign, in Taurus in 2000. We will see what happens to the president elected that year. After 2000, the conjunctions continue to occur in air, followed by water, until a new major cycle starts in fire.

Conjunctions between Saturn and Uranus occur at approximately 44 to 45 year intervals. The U.S. has managed to be at war around the time of the last three, but in light of the frequency of wars, the correspondence may not be very helpful. During the three 1897 conjunctions we were starting the propaganda which would propel us into the Spanish-American war. In 1898 we invaded Cuba, Puerto Rico, and the Philippine Islands. This was really the start of our role as an imperial power in the world. World War II was spreading and we were helping England when Pearl Harbor in December 1941 precipitated our full participation in the war just before the Saturn-Uranus conjunction in 1942. There were three conjunctions again in 1988 when we were gearing up for the Gulf War against Iraq in January-February 1989.

A clearly meaningful Saturn cycle has involved its conjunctions with Neptune, which occur at approximately 35 year intervals. Since the middle of the last century, these conjunctions have marked important stages in the evolution of communism. During the three 1846 conjunctions, Karl Marx was writing *Das Kapital*, which became the "bible" of communism. Three conjunctions can occur if the faster planet passes the slower one, then retrogrades to go over it again, and finally passes it for the third time.

The 1882 conjunction followed widespread unrest among ordinary citizens in several countries in 1881. Russia's Czar Alexander II was assassinated, leading to a period of persecution of both Jews and Roman Catholics and helping to set the stage for the Russian revolution. U.S. President Garfield was also assassinated, and protests increased in the U.S. over the treatment of Jews, Blacks, and American Indians. Irish tenant farmers also protested their treatment while their leader was sent to jail.

The Russian Revolution followed the 1917 Saturn-Neptune conjunction. Within four months after the August conjunction, the Bolsheviks were in power. There were three conjunctions in 1952-3. Stalin had held absolute power in Russia since 1928. His death in 1953 marked a change in the government, which began making tentative steps toward more openness and individual freedom.

Three conjunctions came again in 1989, and most of our readers will remember that the Berlin Wall came down that fall and within an incredibly short time all of the eastern European countries freed themselves from the dominance of the Soviet Union.

Three Saturn-Pluto conjunctions in 1914-1915 marked the beginning of World War I. By the 1947 conjunction, we were starting the "Cold War" between former allies: the U.S. and western Europe against the Soviet Union and its satellites in eastern Europe. 1982 had a fairly "normal" number of small wars, including the ongoing one between Iraq and Iran, Israel versus Lebanon, and England against Argentina, which invaded the Falkland Islands.

Much of history is a list of wars, so to find a more meaningful thread in the conjunctions of Saturn-Uranus and Saturn-Pluto, we would have to extend our series of dates and look more deeply. Saturn is the primary key to bureaucratic structures and the power people who run them, so it should have meaningful patterns when governments are involved. We also expect it to be involved at times of natural disasters such as earthquakes or avalanches, but so far, we have not found a reliable formula to forecast such events. We can always find something appropriate looking hindsight, but attempts to predict disasters produce too many "false positives," to use a medical term. That is, there are often aspects which would fit a disaster when nothing major occurs. Astrology is a "work in progress." With computers and sophisticated programs now being applied to it, we may see major breakthroughs in the coming years.

The Saturn-Mars conjunction in February 1962 provides a good example of the hazards of predicting detailed events and of the use of these conjunction charts in Mundane Astrology. A major stellium was present in the sign of Aquarius, including the Sun, Moon, Mercury, Venus, Jupiter and the south lunar node in the middle degrees of Aquarius, while Mars and Saturn were conjunct in the early degrees of the sign. Many astrologers predicted drastic events during that period. Hindu astrologers and others using sidereal zodiacs were especially convinced that there would be catastrophes, since their zodiacs put the mass of planets in Capricorn, the sign of Saturn. However, nothing major happened in the world at the time.

Planetary conjunctions mark the beginning of new cycles, and sometimes there are no major events at the beginning but later aspects to the conjunction chart mark important stages in the cycle. Saturn, as previously stated, represents governments, bureaucratic structures, the people who run them, and the consequences of past actions. Mars symbolizes our feeling that we have the right and the power to do what we want, so Mars is always involved in wars and other forms of violence when people are fighting for personal rights or overdoing personal power. Conflict aspects between Mars and Saturn are typically present in wars, revolutions, riots, etc., when individual wills are challenging power structures and people or governments are confronting each other.

In the fall of 1962, when Mars had moved halfway around the zodiac to form an opposition to the degree of the Saturn-Mars conjunction in the preceding February, the U.S. nearly went to war against Russia. In the Cuban missile crisis, the U.S. and

Russia confronted each other over missiles Russia was putting in Cuba. Russia agreed to withdraw the missiles and we settled back into the more normal "cold" war state. Though we now have three planets beyond Saturn, it remains an important key to the Law and limits of all kinds; to natural law, cultural regulations, and authority figures who enforce the law. It also symbolizes one's internal law, the conscience and guilt.

Saturn for Individuals

One of the best known of the planetary cycles in the charts of individuals is the "Saturn Return." Since Saturn circles the zodiac in about 29 years, it will transit over its natal position in individual charts around the ages of 28 to 30, 56 to 58, and 84 to 86 for those who make it to that age. In view of its promise of "feedback" on how we are doing, these periods are important times when we get a report card from life. Depending on the degree to which we have worked effectively with the laws of life and of our society, we may move into power positions, achieve major goals, and produce lasting results in the world. Both scientists and artists often do some of their most creative work in their twenties. At the opposite end of the spectrum, we may fail if our efforts have been unrealistic or overly ambitious. Or we may be pressured by life to take on responsibilties we have been evading. Individuals who have been reluctant to grow up may finally settle down in a profession or in their personal relationships. Life learns through the consequences of actions. Saturn signals a time to pay attention to consequences.

The well-known astrologer, Grant Lewi, suggested two other Saturn cycles in individual charts which can be important. Its first transit over one's Sun and one's MC can come at any time up to age 29, depending on the distance in the natal chart between Saturn and the other two factors. Lewi considered the MC cycle especially important. He offered examples of famous individuals who moved into power positions in the world as transiting Saturn moved up to the MC. Lewi wrote that they tended to retain power as Saturn continued through the last three houses of the chart, but that they often went into a position of greater obscurity or more inwardness as Saturn transited the lower half of the horoscope. When it passed the IC, the fourth house cusp, they might start a new climb back toward a more prominent and public life. Saturn's cycle with the Sun is described as similar, a rise to a peak of power and recognition followed by a later reduction in both.

In my personal experience, we need to be wary of overrating a single factor in a chart. I have not seen many charts in which these Saturn cycles worked in this simplistic way. Saturn's passage through the horoscope signs and houses is clearly meaningful, but the details vary widely depending on the individual's situation. For example, a woman who had been working in her home as Saturn transited through the top of her chart opened her own business outside her home when it was passing through her first house. This is an appropriate action as she took personal power (first house) over her career (Saturn), but her life was much more public following this action than it had been before. Lewi's formula is most likely to occur when the Sun and the MC are close together so the two cycles reinforce each other. When the Sun is in the lower part of the chart, they tend to cancel each other. As in all work with astrology, it is important to look for repeated messages. Anything important in the life will be symbolized in the chart in a variety of ways.

CHAPTER EIGHT

EXAMPLE CHARTS

Humans have studied the relationship between the Earth and the sky for thousands of years, but there are still many uncertainties and areas of disagreement in the subject. Humans, life, and astrology are enormously complex. There are many different medical systems for diagnosing and treating the physical health: allopathy, chiropractic, homeopathy, naturopathy, etc. There are many different schools of psychology which diagnose and treat the psychological health: operant conditioning, psychoanalysis, cognitive, humanistic, transpersonal, etc. Similarly, there are many astrological systems. Hopefully, in time we will have systematic research which will answer some of the questions. It seems logical that different systems are more helpful in different circumstances and/or with different people. Psychological insight will obviously be more helpful to individuals who are willing and able to work on changing personal habits. Many people will prefer traditional "good day/bad day" astrology, hoping to manipulate the world without having to change themselves.

Planets are ranked as prominent or important in a chart when they have many aspects to other factors and the aspects have tight orbs, that is, they are nearly exact. There is a wide range of opinion among astrologers on the issue of orbs. How far can the angular distance between two planets be from 90 degrees for one to consider that the planets are still square each other? The only agreement is that the closer the distance is to 90 degrees, the more important the square is thought to be.

Conjunctions, when the planets are very close to each other, are the most important of the aspects. Among the most important conjunctions are the ones between a planet and an "angle" of the chart such as the Midheaven or the Ascendant. The section on planetary aspects discussed the source of these angles, which are the intersections of great circles that have been projected against infinity. The intersections come in pairs which are opposite each other as we look out at the sky from Earth. The most important pairs are the Ascendant-Descendant, which are basically the eastern and western horizons at birth, and the MC-IC, which lie on the circle that goes through the zenith and nadir. The charts I have chosen as examples are individuals who were born with Saturn conjunct one of these angles. These are people dealing with power in the world, with the "rules of the game."

There are many astrological systems which offer information about one's continuing life after birth. They show the psychological state of the individual, which can produce a variety of life details depending on personal habits and choices. The most commonly used system is transits, which calculates the actual positions of the planets at the time being investigated. Two other systems which are also widely used in astrology are clearly symbolic. In Secondary Progressions, the patterns in the sky are analyzed one day after birth for each year of age. To understand the psychological state at age 40, one looks at the sky 40 days after birth. In Solar Arc Directions, the distance the progressed Sun has moved is added to every factor in the chart. The whole chart is turned like a wheel with everything moving at a constant speed. Since the Earth orbits the Sun at a rate of about one degree a day, from our point of view the transiting Sun is moving about one degree a day. Since one day equals a year in the Secondary Progressions, that approximate movement of one degree is the annual increment added to everything in the chart in Solar Arc Directions.

These systems of progressions and directions and many more ways to manipulate the sky are obviously symbolic, and my personal opinion is that transits are equally symbolic. I think that we are born where we "fit" the state of the cosmos, and the many changing patterns picture the natural stages of growth of the character with which we started. Just as planets and signs and houses symbolize the same twelve psychological desires/drives, so we can "say the same thing" in many ways in the natal chart, the different systems which let us understand our current life and look ahead will provide the same basic information in a variety of ways.

This is a book about Saturn, not a general textbook on astrology, so if more than this brief explanation is desired, a list of references is provided in the appendices. The individual discussions which follow will also be brief, with examples from the three principal systems which help us understand our ongoing lives and help us handle them more effectively. Since our focus is on Saturn, we will be looking at events which involved power issues and changes of marital or career status, part of Saturn's realm.

People can and do change their attitudes and actions in their personal lives, and when we change our habits we change our destiny. However, we cannot change anyone else. We can only set a good example and encourage others. I think that the future is less easy to change when more people are involved, so the major events which involve masses of people may be largely predestined. If this is true, one's personal character may have a very small role in producing the events, but it attracts us where we "fit" to experience the events and learn from them. Human minds do not produce earthquakes unless we are prepared to grant a lot of power to the minds of fish, since there are many more earthquakes in the ocean than on land. Human character can lead us to live where we will experience earthquakes or war or whatever will bring about growth.

Life seems to be a mixture of fate and free will. The "big" events may be largely predestined as consequences set in motion in the past, while at the same time individuals have choices and can act in unpredictable ways. If this is true, astrology with its predictable cycles should be able to predict the major events which involve masses of people. One of the reasons astrologers keep experimenting with new factors, new techniques, new systems, is this feeling that they might help make more precise predictions.

Third Party Candidate

John Anderson was born in Rockford, IL on February 15, 1922 at 8:55 PM CST. Saturn was rising at his birth, within one degree of his Ascendant but retrograding. That means that in the following days it was appearing against earlier degrees of the zodiac as it was seen from Earth, so it moved away from the Ascendant into the twelfth house.

Anderson was an Illinois lawyer elected to the U.S. House of Representatives as a Republican. Though originally very conservative, he became more uncomfortable with his Party during his years of government service, and in 1980 he declared himself an Independent and ran for the Presidency.

The major emphasis in Anderson's chart is in air signs in fire houses, which are not normally associated with conservatism. Earth and water are the elements which usually cling to the status

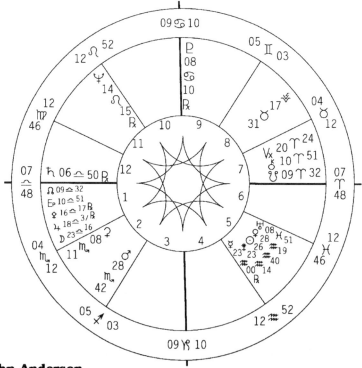

John Anderson
Source: Birth Certificate
Gauquelin Book of American Charts

quo. But knowing that the planets are the most important factors in the horoscope, we can note that the water planet Pluto in a water sign is closely conjunct the MC, which is equivalent to Saturn. At the same time, Saturn itself and a lunar node (as an equivalent to the Moon) are conjunct the Ascendant and the East Point, two keys to one's instinctive identity at the start of life. The other auxiliary Ascendant, the Antivertex, is conjunct the Moon. (The chart shows the Vertex at 20 Aries 24; the Antivertex is directly opposite.) Mars, which is always a key to identity, is in the water sign of Scorpio and in the natural house of Taurus for earth. Thus, in spite of the air signs and fire houses, Anderson's chart shows an underlying identification with water and earth.

However, we start to grow after an initial emphasis on the first and the fourth and tenth areas of the chart, the latter two being the keys to the heredity and family we come into. We tend to develop toward the fifth, ninth, and eleventh sides of life as we evolve. With Anderson's stellium in Aquarius in the fifth house, including his Sun in the sign, it is not surprising that he moved away from the focus on tradition suggested by his dominant Saturn and Pluto on the major angles, and toward more independence.

Anderson declared himself a candidate for the Presidency as an Independent on April 24, 1980. The Democratic candidate was Jimmy Carter, with Walter Mondale as Vice Presidential candidate. Ronald Reagan and George Bush were the Republican candidates and they won. Anderson got 7% of the vote in the November 4, 1980 election.

Transiting (T) Saturn was retrograding in 20 Virgo when Anderson announced his candidacy. It was trine his Vesta, a good augury for job success, semisextile the first house Libra group of Jupiter, Antivertex, and Moon, and it was quincunx Mercury and Juno in Aquarius. The semisextile is considered weak but potentially harmonious. The quincunx points to changes, either in the details of what we are doing or by moving into new activities.

If we limited our analysis to T Saturn's aspects to Anderson's natal chart (and ignored the historical odds against third party candidates), we might have thought he had a shot at winning. But aspects with transiting planets are used with all of the other systems, applied to progressions and directions as well as to the

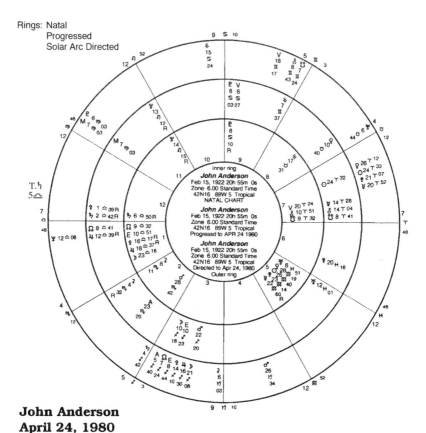

Rings: Natal
    Progressed
    Solar Arc Directed

John Anderson
April 24, 1980

natal chart. So we note that T Saturn was square to Progressed (P) Mars, a suggestion that Anderson's personal will and power (Mars) were in conflict with the limits of his power. Squares do not guarantee failure, because the person may get what he wants but have a hard time dealing with it after he gets it, but in this case it did foreshadow Anderson's defeat.

T Saturn was also aspecting two progressed asteroids, P Juno and P Ceres. Both of these asteroids were connected to work and to joint resources in Anderson's chart. P Juno was in his sixth (Virgo) house and Ceres is partly Virgo in nature. Juno is associated with Scorpio and P Ceres was in the sign of Scorpio. It was also in the second house of personal resources. T Saturn's opposition to P Juno and octile (or semi-square) to P Ceres fit his inability to get the job he wanted, and the connection to resources fits the shortage of funds which hampered his campaign.

Progressed aspects when Anderson announced his candidacy included P MC, which carries the Saturn meaning, square P Vesta, the asteroid most connected to the actual details of one's job. P Vesta in Gemini in the ninth house speaks of problems in getting media coverage, which is obviously connected to the lack of funds to buy ads. P Ascendant in 23 Scorpio was square Mercury and Juno and octile or trioctile the Ascendant, the P lunar nodes, Pluto, and the MC, a much stronger statement than the transits of the odds against Anderson.

Directed (D) Saturn was in 4 Sagittarius on the third house cusp and octile Jupiter and the Antivertex. The third house repeats the emphasis on media activity which is strongly shown in both the progressions and the directions by planets occupying the third house. The current positions of the P and D MCs are the same, but the D Ascendant is moved at the same speed as the rest of the chart factors, so it was on the third house cusp with Saturn.

By the time of the election on November 4, 1980, T Saturn had reached five Libra, so it was approaching a conjunction with natal Saturn, Anderson's second Saturn Return. The return of Saturn to its natal place can be a time of very meaningful feedback from the cosmos telling us how we are doing in handling the "rules of the game." We will see cases which did not fit Grant Lewi's theory of Saturn's movement through the houses, but Anderson's life did follow the script. Since this campaign, he has mostly been off the political stage. There were, of course, many other aspects in all three of the systems described above, but our primary interest is in the way in which Saturn can help us understand how we are doing in the world.

Peanut Farmer and President

Jimmy Carter was also defeated in the presidential race in 1980. He was born in Plains, GA on October 1, 1924 at 7 AM, CST. Instead of being born with Saturn on the Ascendant, it was on the East Point, which is actually the Ascendant at the Equator.

Though it is not as important as the birthplace Ascendant, the East Point carries the same meaning, and, when it has close aspects, it is quite meaningful. Carter not only was born with Saturn within one degree of the East Point, but it was also just one degree from Juno, and the trio were in Scorpio, the sign of Pluto and Juno. Carter was noted for his close relationship with his wife, and they have continued to work together in a variety of projects since he left the presidency.

Carter's identification with power was not only shown by Saturn in the first house and intensified by being on the East Point. He also had the Moon, which ruled his Cancer MC, in the first house, and Venus, which ruled his Libra Ascendant, in the

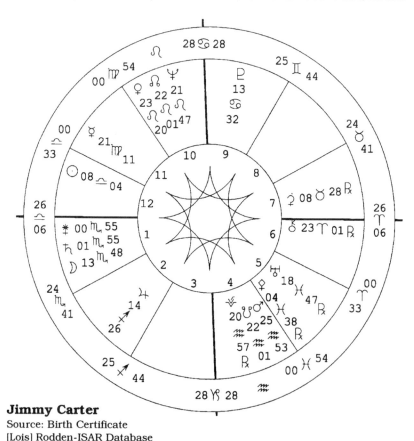

Jimmy Carter
Source: Birth Certificate
[Lois] Rodden-ISAR Database

tenth house, giving a repeated message. He was also identified with idealism with Pluto, ruler of the Scorpio in the first house, placed in the ninth house, plus he had the Antivertex, another auxiliary Ascendant, in Sagittarius conjunct Jupiter, the planetary form of Letter Nine. His life since leaving the presidency has demonstrated this idealism combined with the responsibility of Saturn more than almost any president in our history. He founded an academy devoted to peace, he has worked as an arbitrator repeatedly to try to reconcile warring groups in many countries, he is involved with supporting the Atlanta Project which strives to provide positive options for people on welfare and at risk for drug use, and he has been actively involved in Habitat for Humanity which builds homes for poor people.

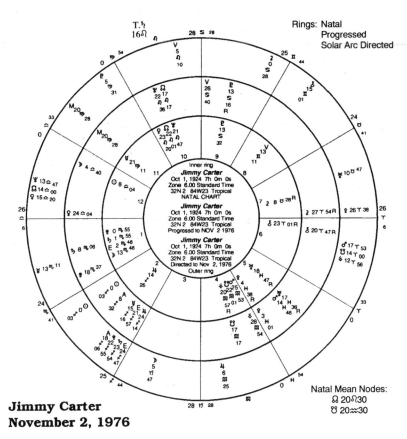

Jimmy Carter
November 2, 1976

Carter won the presidency in November 1976 with T Saturn in 16 Leo conjunct his progressed North Node in the 10th house, trine his natal Jupiter and progressed Mercury, quincunx progressed Mars and progressed Uranus, and opposite the progressed South Node. The conflict aspects did not deny the victory but foreshadowed problems in the office. The tenth house placement of transiting Saturn was appropriate for executive power. The trines between planets in fire signs were appropriate for success in getting what Carter wanted, while the opposition to the Node in the fourth house (and quincunx to Mars, which was originally in the fourth house) fit his separation from his home to go to Washington D.C. for his new career.

P Saturn in 1976 was in 8 Scorpio, holding a semisextile to the Sun which lasted for years. Such long-term progressed aspects are important keys to basic character. The Saturn-Sun semisextile shows Carter's ability to handle constructively the personal power drive symbolized by the Sun and the rules of the world which are always bigger than any individual. By the time he was inaugurated on January 20, 1977, Carter's P Moon had reached a conjunction with his Sun and a semisextile to P Saturn to signal his move to a position of fame and power. P MC was conjunct Mercury for both events, and its quincunx to the (mean or average) South lunar Node (at 20° Aquarius) and Vesta was appropriate for his change of residence and work. P Ascendant in 8 Sagittarius was sextile the Sun and semisextile Saturn to reinforce the potential for increased power. Many other aspects could be mentioned, but our focus is on Saturn and its surrogate, the MC.

D Saturn for Carter's election was in 23 Sagittarius trine his tenth house Venus and Chiron in his sixth house, a very positive configuration for success in work with fire signs (personal desire) in earth houses (coping with the physical world).

When he lost the election in November 1980, T Saturn was in 5 Libra holding octile-trioctile aspects to the (mean) lunar nodes and Vesta. P Saturn had moved only a few minutes, but P MC had moved into an octile to it along with a square to P Jupiter. D Saturn was in 28 Sagittarius octile the Moon.

United We Stand

H. Ross Perot has been in the news in recent years as he attacked the two primary political parties in the U.S. and tried to found a third party. Perot was born on June 27, 1930 at 5:34 AM CST in Texarkana, TX. Saturn was setting at his birth, within one degree of his Descendant and retrograding into his sixth house. In addition to the Ascendant, Saturn opposed the Sun and Jupiter in Cancer in Perot's twelfth house. The Moon, Pluto, and Ceres were also in Cancer but in the first house while Mercury, Pallas, and the East Point were in Gemini in the twelfth house.

The combination shows a strong identification with the role of parent, which is repeated by the presence of Aries in the tenth house. An identification with idealism is indicated by the Sun

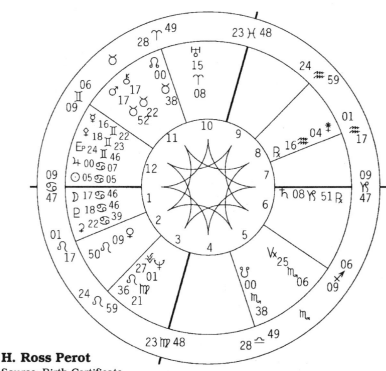

H. Ross Perot
Source: Birth Certificate
Gauquelin Book of American Charts

which rules the bit of Leo in the first house being in the twelfth house and on Jupiter, and by Mars closely conjunct Chiron, which is like Jupiter. Perot may have good intentions similar to those demonstrated by Jimmy Carter, but I am less confident that his desire to be parent and god of our country will always be handled as wisely. His squares and oppositions in both cardinal and fixed signs and houses show a strong power-struggle nature. So far, this seems to have been mostly constructively handled in his competitive business and in politics, but handling power wisely remains a lesson for him.

When Perot ran for the U.S. presidency in November 1992, T Saturn was in 12 Aquarius sextile his local MC in Washington D.C., the power center which was the goal of his effort. It was also widely sextile his tenth house Uranus, opposite Venus, and

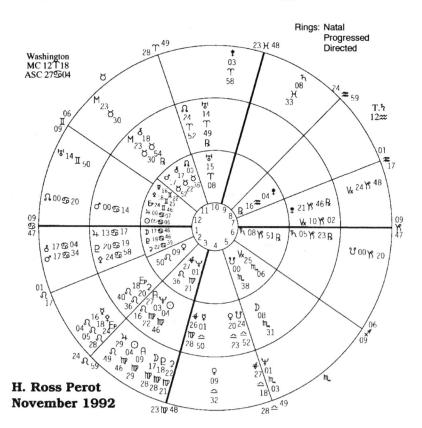

H. Ross Perot
November 1992

quincunx the Ascendant. The latter two aspects can indicate a separation from one's goal, though Perot did better than most third party candidates in our history.

On the positive side, Perot's P Sun was trine his P Saturn and sextile natal Sun. P MC was sextile natal MC at the same time, since it progresses the same distance as the P Sun. P Moon in 8 Scorpio was sextile Saturn and P Mars was conjunct Jupiter, so Perot was feeling considerable confidence in his ability to get what he wanted. However, other progressed aspects showed a mixed bag, with enough conflict patterns to show that success would be difficult. Some of the squares included P East Point square Mars and P Chiron and P Venus square P Pluto, and P MC was trioctile Saturn.

Perot's D Saturn at the time was in 8 Pisces, sextile its natal position and just starting a trine to the Ascendant as well as a quincunx to Venus. However, there is a cautionary note to remember when working with current patterns. Unless the individual has changed, the current aspects show the timing of an issue in the life but the natal aspects show the way the person will tend to handle the issue. P Saturn was natally opposite the Ascendant, so, despite a current trine, the nature of the opposition, the hazard of problems with power, was still potentially present in Perot's nature.

Perot is currently spending some of his billions to found a third political party, and he may well run for president again in the fall of 1996 before this book is in print. T Saturn at that time will be in 1 Aries square his Jupiter, quincunx Neptune and the south lunar node to form a double quincunx or yod, and it will also be octile Mars and Chiron. This is not an encouraging combination of aspects for success. The yod is often an indication of a major new direction in an individual's life. While this could conceivably point to Perot being elected to a political office for the first time, the odds are against it.

P Sun will trine natal Saturn in the fall of 1996 instead of P Saturn as in 1992, and P Moon will be sextile-trine its own nodes, but the rest of the picture is more conflicted. P Ascendant on Neptune shows the danger of seeing one's hopes rather than what is really there. P Venus will be on the south lunar node, signaling a lesson. P Mercury will square the Sun, suggesting problems with the media and Perot's reputation. P MC will square Vesta, showing conflict involving two keys to work, though it is also sextile Pallas, our political asteroid.

D Saturn is in 12 Pisces, so it is semisextile Perot's MC calculated for Washington D.C. but trioctile his local Ascendant there. His odds are not good for winning the gold ring in 1996.

Alphonse D'Amato

Another person who is very much in the limelight as this book is being written in the spring of 1996 has spent his life in government work. Al D'Amato was born on August 1, 1937 at 10:15 AM EDT in Brooklyn, NY. He earned his law degree in 1961, passed the New York Bar exam in 1962, and has worked for the government in

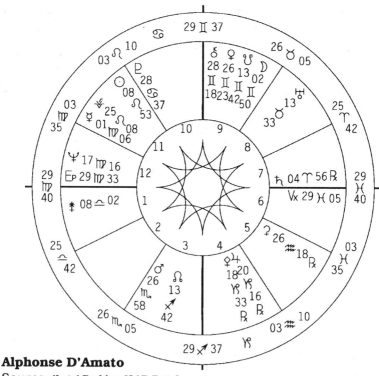

Alphonse D'Amato
Source: [Lois] Rodden-ISAR Database
          quotes mother

some capacity ever since. He was elected to the U.S. Senate as a Republican in November 1980 and reelected twice since then. He is currently head of the committee which is investigating the Clintons' involvement in Whitewater and Arkansas Savings and Loans.

Like Perot, D'Amato was born with Saturn conjunct his Descendant and retrograde, but in D'Amato's case it was farther into the seventh house so it has not yet progressed back to the Descendant. When he was first elected to the Senate and moved beyond work at the state level, T Saturn was in 5 Libra opposite its natal position. This aspect fits the astrological theory of planetary cycles, which describes the conjunction (in this case a Saturn return) as a new beginning, the first square as a turning point, the opposition as the start of a fulfillment phase for the area

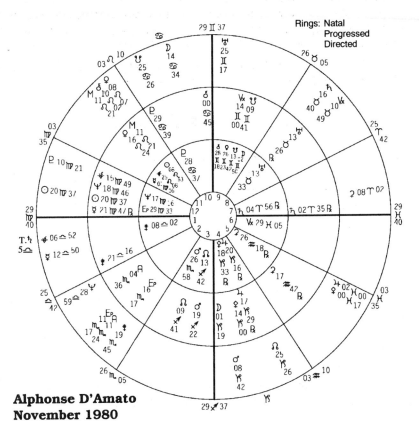

Alphonse D'Amato
November 1980

of life symbolized by the planet, and the last square as the start of completing the activity of the cycle preparing for a new beginning at the next conjunction. In the case of Saturn, each of these quarters of the 28 year cycle would be about seven years.

D'Amato's entry into national prominence in 1980 does not fit the Grant Lewi theory that we go into a period of obscurity when Saturn crosses the Ascendant going into the first house of the chart. Obviously, we always have to look at the whole chart, and in the end, the details depend on the person. In D'Amato's case, as in many others I have seen, Saturn in the first house marked a time of attaining personal power in the world.

D'Amato also had aspects from two of his progressed angles to Saturn when he won his election to the Senate. P Ascendant was quincunx Saturn and P East Point started a trioctile to P Saturn in early 1981. Neither aspect is considered easily harmonious, but D'Amato had some aspects for harmony, including P MC sextile-trine the lunar nodes and P Moon trine Mercury.

D Saturn was in late 16 Taurus, forming a grand trine to Neptune and (almost to) Pallas, a strong suggestion of success.

Bogey and Bacall

The power issues of Saturn can be lived out in arenas other than politics. Lauren Bacall was born on September 16, 1924 at 3 AM EDT in New York City. She was a successful actress in a Broadway play in 1942 and a hit in Hollywood in 1944, where she starred with Humphrey Bogart. She married her co-star on May 21, 1945 and they had a happy marriage until he died of cancer in 1957. As we would suspect from the fire and fixed emphasis in her chart, Bacall was a strong-minded and very dramatic lady. Though she made many films, her tenth house Aries and Saturn opposite the MC were manifested in frequent power struggles with her bosses at Warner Brothers in Hollywood. In fact, she was suspended twelve times and finally bought out her contract from the studio in 1950. Her greatest successes in her later years were on Broadway, where she received a Tony award in 1970.

Saturn was widely conjunct Juno, the marriage asteroid, when Bacall was born, and P Juno was on P Saturn when she met, starred with, and married Humphrey Bogart. The Juno connection to Saturn points to some kind of lesson involving relationships, which could have called for learning to share power and pleasure or for working out an obvious "freedom-closeness dilemma" which is shown by the oppositions in Leo-Aquarius and both the signs and houses of Aries-Libra. Hindsight, in light of Bogey's death after only twelve years of marriage, we can see that the latter was a primary issue. Saturn is often found in either water signs and/or houses, especially Letter Eight, when we are learning "when is enough" and how to let go. Water and earth tend to hold on while fire and air tend to move on. One potential of the "freedom-closeness" dilemma is the choice of a mate who will leave, whether voluntarily with conscious awareness or through death under the control of the subconscious. Obviously, no one chooses such a mate consciously. At the time of Bacall's marriage,

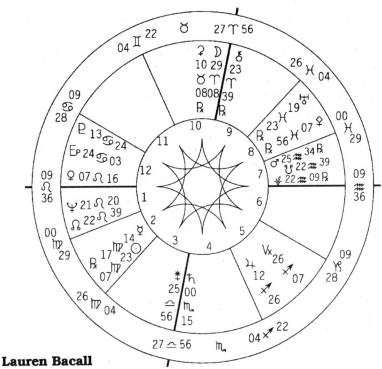

Lauren Bacall
Source: *Profiles of Women* and
R.I.D. Autobiography and quote from her

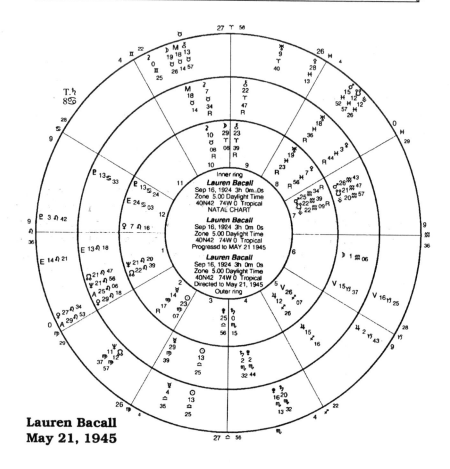

Lauren Bacall
May 21, 1945

P Moon in early Aquarius was square N Saturn to repeat the issue of holding on versus moving on.

Other Saturn aspects at Bacall's marriage included Solar Arc Saturn in 20 Scorpio 33 square her mean lunar nodes, pointing to the freedom-closeness issue. Both the sign and house polarities of her nodes call for resolution of the inherent tension between the urges for freedom versus closeness. T Saturn was in 8 Cancer 35 on the twelfth house cusp, suggesting that her subconscious faith was highly important. As the Gauquelin research demonstrated, twelfth house planets are often keys to highly successful individuals. My interpretation is that a positive subconscious faith leads to success, while a lack of faith invites anxiety, depression, and a variety of problems. T Saturn also was trine Pallas in the eighth house, which is part of the partnership area, but it formed octiles or trioctiles to the Leo-Aquarius polarity to add to the theme given by the other systems. No matter how we manipulate the sky, it keeps giving us the same information.

Pushing the Limits

Janis Joplin was another star in the entertainment world who was born with Saturn opposite the MC, the cusp of its own natural house. Joplin was born on January 19, 1943 at 9:45 AM CWT in Port Arthur, TX. Like Lauren Bacall, Joplin resisted the "establishment," but she was far more rebellious than Bacall. Joplin's chart is dominated by Aquarius, with Mercury, Venus, Ascendant, south lunar node, and Pallas in the sign and Uranus, its ruler, conjunct Saturn. The emphasis on Letter Eleven shows that it is a major component of her nature, but Saturn's conjunction with Uranus shows that it remains a lesson. In such cases, the challenge is often the danger of excesses.

Joplin was also strongly Piscean, with the Sun, Mercury, and Venus in the twelfth house and Vesta plus the two auxiliary Ascendants, the East Point and Antivertex, in the sign of Pisces in her first house. The primary urge of Letter Eleven is to go beyond any limits, while Letter Ten reminds us that there are limits if we want to survive in this physical world. The conjunction of Saturn with Uranus and the placement of Capricorn in the natural house of Uranus repeat the need to integrate these two very different drives. We do this by voluntarily accepting the necessary limits, and then we can do what we please.

Joplin did not accept any limits. Though she had her Sun in Capricorn and Mars in the natural house of Capricorn, the nature of the planets is always paramount and these two planets of self-will were expressed as "my will is law" (the one-ten and five-ten combinations) and as "my will is god" (the one-nine and five-twelve combinations). Once you have a clear understanding of the twelve primary drives of astrology, the subject is quite logical. You understand what is driving the person, though you do not know

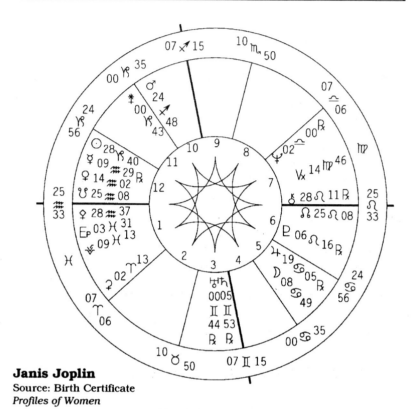

Janis Joplin
Source: Birth Certificate
Profiles of Women

how the person will handle those desires, and it is always possible
to change the ways we are trying to satisfy the desires and
consequently to change the details of our lives. Joplin's first house
Aquarius showed she identified with the rejection of any limits.
Her Pisces search for infinite love and beauty was expressed
positively through her musical talent and destructively through
drugs. Joplin died of a heroin overdose on October 3, 1970 in
Hollywood, CA. She had said "Man, I'd rather have ten years of
superhypermost than live to be seventy sitting in some GD chair
watching TV."

The defiance of any practical limits is clear in both Joplin's
natal chart and in her progressed aspects when she died. As has
often been mentioned, the south lunar node points initially to an
area of life where we have something to learn, and then, after we
have learned whatever it is, something to give the world. Joplin

had her P mean south node conjunct her Ascendant for her whole short life, and her P Sun was going over it for the last two plus years of her life. The Sun symbolizes our growth potential. Maybe her early departure taught Joplin something. Her P nodes stayed sextile-trine her Mars for most of her life, encouraging her feeling that she had the right and the power to do what she pleased. She also had several aspects for shorter periods of time which added to the overconfidence that led to her excesses. Remember, harmony aspects show inner harmony between our different desires. They show that we know what we want and think we should have it. If what we want is not realistically possible, as will be shown by other conflict aspects, usually to earth planets, houses, or signs, we may keep over-reaching and hitting walls.

Joplin's progressed chart included three grand trines, among the strongest statements provided in astrology of the feelings that we should be able to do what we want. Her P East Point was in a grand trine to her MC and Pluto. In this case, the fire signs outweighed the earth houses. An air grand trine included P Uranus to P Mercury and P Neptune. A water grand trine linked P Moon, the natal Antivertex , and the local MC in Hollywood. P Moon was also trine P eighth house cusp, which had been crossing the local MC for the preceding two years while Joplin was increasing her drug habit.

Karma arrived on October 3, 1970, as indicated above. P MC was in Saturn's sign with a quincunx to Saturn and to P Pluto - a yod which often signals major change and new directions in the life. She had failed to accept the physical limits symbolized by Saturn and to learn the Pluto lesson of moderation, mastery of the appetites, and "when is enough." But Uranus was the star in Joplin's flight from the limits of the physical world. In addition to the grand trine mentioned above, Joplin's P local Ascendant in 0 Pisces 7 was square Uranus. P Jupiter was octile it and P Mars was trioctile. Plus, Joplin's local P Part of Death had been conjunct Uranus for nearly two months. It is pretty clear that she wanted out.

The other forms of Saturn were less dramatic, though T Saturn, which was retrograding just under 22 Taurus, was within two degrees of Joplin's natal Part of Death in 23 Taurus. (Though progressions and arcs of direction are limited to one-degree orbs, for transits to provide appropriate information, it is often necessary to stretch the orbs to two or three degrees.) The Arabic Part of Death is derived by adding the Ascendant to the eighth house cusp and subtracting the Moon. It can be calculated for both natal and progressed positions. Of course, it can point to many types of "endings," not just physical death. Also, since astrology pictures one's state of mind, many aspects will be functioning on the mental-emotional level without any expression in events.

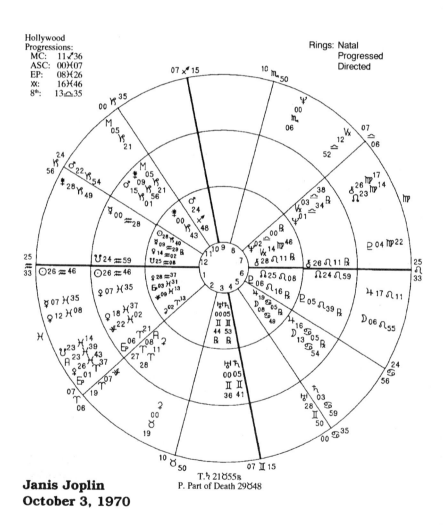

Hollywood
Progressions:
MC: 11✗36
ASC: 00)(07
EP: 08)(26
XX: 16)(46
8th: 13≏35

Rings: Natal
Progressed
Directed

T.♄ 21♉55ʀ
P. Part of Death 29♉48

Janis Joplin
October 3, 1970

Joplin's Solar Arc Saturn was just coming to four Cancer and quite unimpressive with just a trine to the East Point, though we could find other aspects if we looked to midpoints, planetary nodes, Arabic Parts, etc. Arc Saturn had spent two years passing over what I call the Arabic Part of Saturn (Ascendant plus Saturn minus the Sun), and the aspect had ended just over two months before Joplin's death. We could interpret that aspect as a call to recognize the Saturn limits which are necessary if we want to stay here. As already indicated, it is pretty clear that Joplin did not want to do that.

Helping Humanity

Rosalynn Carter's original claim to fame was as the wife of U.S. President Jimmy Carter, but she earned recognition for her personal ability through her work for the mentally ill and as an author both of her own books and of a book written jointly with her husband. Carter was born on August 18, 1927 at 6 AM CST in Plains, Georgia. Her chart shows intense idealism, with four factors in Leo in the twelfth house, including Mercury which rules the Ascendant, two more factors in the ninth house including Chiron closely conjunct her Moon, and Saturn, Ceres, and the south lunar node in Sagittarius. But Carter also is very identified with earth with her Ascendant, Mars, and Venus all in Virgo in the first house.

Her life demonstrates a successful blend of the earth practicality and the idealism of Letters Nine and Twelve. Her inherent talent for this integration is shown repeatedly in her chart. Chiron is similar to Jupiter, so its placement in the ninth house reinforces the idealism. But it is in the practical sign of Taurus and closely conjunct the Moon, which symbolizes our need for emotional security and/or our capacity to help to provide it for others. Where security is at stake, we tend to be more cautious. Additionally, Chiron and the Moon are closely trine the Virgo Ascendant. In fact, P Chiron held the trine within one degree from her birth to Carter's taking on the role of First Lady when her husband was elected U.S. President.

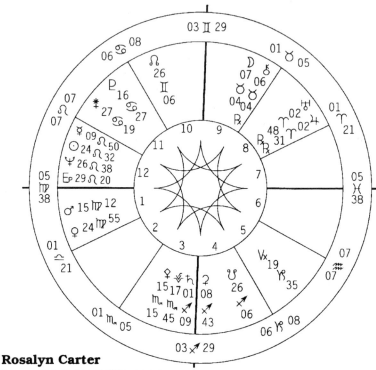

Rosalyn Carter
Source: Printed in *Dell Horoscope*
"from her mother"
Profiles of Women

Carter also had Saturn, our primary earth planet, in the
Jupiter sign of Sagittarius. and it was trine Jupiter and Uranus in
Aries for many years in her early life, while P Uranus is still holding
a trine to Saturn. These aspects show Carter's ability to harmonize
her Aries personal will and power with her idealism in "lawful"
(realistically possible) Saturn ways. The potential for integration
does not mean that it was achieved without challenges and effort.
Saturn is opposite the MC, trioctile Pluto, and widely square the
Ascendant. When Carter became First Lady, P Saturn had held an
exact opposition to the MC for years and P Antivertex and P Pallas,
(our most political asteroid) were conjunct N Saturn. P Saturn was
also quincunx P Chiron while P Mercury (her Ascendant ruler) was
opposite P Chiron, as she had to face the reality that she did not
have the personal power to completely realize all of her ideals.

Solar Arc Saturn at the time was in 19 Capricorn 3 conjunct Carter's Vertex (which is like an auxiliary Descendant) and trioctile her MC. In Washington, she had to confront a power system and powerful individuals. T Saturn was in 16 Leo conjunct her local (Washington D.C.) Antivertex and semisextile natal Mars while sextile progressed Mars, both suggesting an increase in her personal power, but it was also square Pallas and Vesta and widely opposite her P Moon for the difficulties she would face in her attempts to work for political justice for the public and especially for the mentally handicapped. In Carter's natal chart, Pallas, as a key to social justice, on Vesta, a key to one's job, plus Saturn, a key to career in the larger sense, were all in the third house, pointing to her concern for educational opportunities for every-

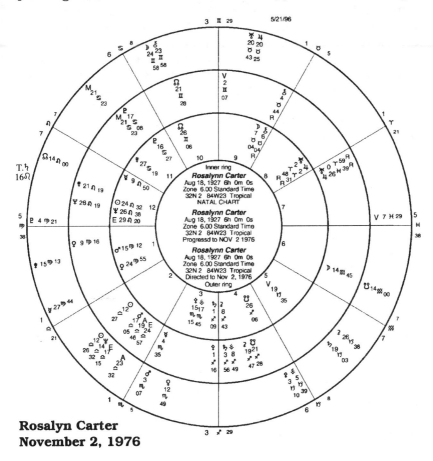

Rosalyn Carter
November 2, 1976

one. Since leaving Washington, both Jimmy and Rosalynn Carter have dedicated their lives to promoting peace in the world, and they have also worked for Habitat for Humanity, not just fund-raising, but literally helping to build houses for low-income people who would otherwise have remained in very substandard home conditions.

Equal Rights

Illustrating another variation on how individuals can handle a natal Saturn opposite the MC, Gloria Steinem expressed her Aquarian Saturn in a writing career devoted to supporting equal rights and freedom for women. Despite her Scorpio Ascendant, which usually indicates an inner conflict between the freedom drive of the first house and the Scorpio desire for a mate, Steinem was definitely tilted toward freedom. Pluto, her Ascendant ruler, was in the ninth house, adding to the freedom drive and to the conflict over closeness with its placement in Cancer. Mars, co-ruler of her Ascendant, was conjunct the Sun in Aries to repeat the issue. The Sun and its house show where we want love or at least admiration, while Aries says "on my terms."

Steinem was born on March 25, 1934 at 10 PM EST in Toledo, Ohio. In her case, Saturn in Aquarius became a remote father who left the family when Steinem was twelve years old. Her P MC at the time was quincunx her Aries Sun. Character (habits) create destiny. When we want independence more than dependence, the universe is likely to say "OK" and give it to us. In high school, Steinem was able to leave a home in the Toledo slums and live with an older sister. Her strong Aquarius, including Jupiter in the eleventh house, and additional emphasis in the third, sixth, and ninth houses, plus her Antivertex in Sagittarius, all point to high level intelligence. Steinem graduated from Smith College *magna cum laude* and received two years of graduate training in India afterwards. She started her career as a writer in New York in 1960.

Steinem has been a leader in many civil rights organizations and campaigns over the years and has received many awards for her public work. She was a co-founder of *MS Magazine* in July 1972, and one of thirty-three well-known women who signed an ad in the magazine in 1973 announcing that they had had

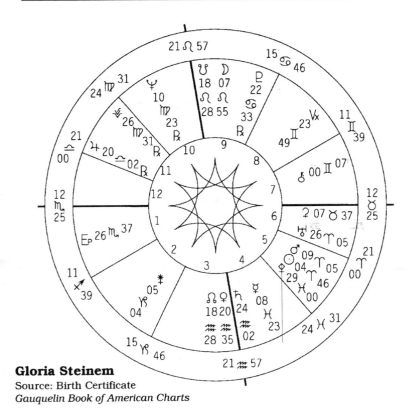

Gloria Steinem
Source: Birth Certificate
Gauquelin Book of American Charts

abortions. Steinem's progressed chart when she took on the job as editor of the new magazine pointed to her new public role with P Sun crossing the Descendant. P MC opposed Pallas, the asteroid of politics and social justice, and P East Point squared Pallas as the new magazine became a bellweather in the women's liberation movement. P Pallas was quincunx her Ascendant for this new public activity. It was also octile P Saturn, while the latter had been quincunx Vesta for years as Steinem explored a variety of jobs in her quest to improve the world.

Solar Arc Saturn was in the first degree of Aries for this shift in her career, and it had an octile-trioctile to the lunar nodes in the houses of the mind and writing. T Saturn in the middle of Gemini was sextile-trine the nodes. The placement of the nodal axis in the Gemini-Sagittarius houses and the Leo-Aquarius signs is classic for perpetual students and natural teachers and writers. Steinem has certainly used her talents.

Gloria Steinem
July 15, 1972

Life as Theater

Shifting to two examples of women with Saturn conjunct the Descendant, I chose one whose P Saturn retrograded back to stay in the sixth house and one whose P Saturn crossed into the seventh house.

Ethel Barrymore was born on August 15, 1879 at 10:00 AM LMT in Philadelphia, Pennsylvania. Her famous theatrical family traced their roots in the theater back for nine generations. At the age of 13, Barrymore and her two brothers, Lionel and John, put on a performance of *Camille* in a local barn. She had already had a real stage role at age twelve with her P MC sextile Venus. The twelfth house Venus in Libra combines the major keys to artistic talent: Venus and its signs for pleasure in the "ordinary" world and Letter Twelve for the quest for infinite pleasure and beauty. Barrymore made her first movie in 1900 and was a star in the theater by 1906. She was still a star at age sixty-five when she won an Oscar as best supporting actress in *None but the Lonely Heart* March 15, 1945 in Hollywood.

Barrymore's chart when she won the Oscar is a good illustration of the importance of local houses, which are calculated for a current residence or the location of an event. Both natal and progressed house cusps can provide useful information with the local chart calculated as if the person was born in the new area.

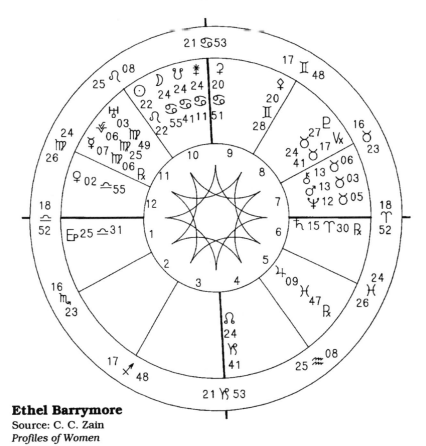

Ethel Barrymore
Source: C. C. Zain
Profiles of Women

In Hollywood, the site of the Oscar ceremony, several of Barrymore's angles were aspecting Saturn. P Saturn held a long sextile to her MC there while her P MC was on P Ceres and trine N Saturn. Her P Ascendant was quincunx P Saturn and her natal local MC, trine Jupiter, and opposite Neptune and P Chiron. This produced a dramatic network of aspects. The yod from Barrymore's local P Ascendant to the natal MC (equivalent to Saturn) and P Saturn connected personal action to career changes, while her local P Ascendant was also in aspect to all three planetary keys to ultimate values: Jupiter, Neptune, and Chiron. The configuration fits the realization of long-range goals. T Saturn was in early

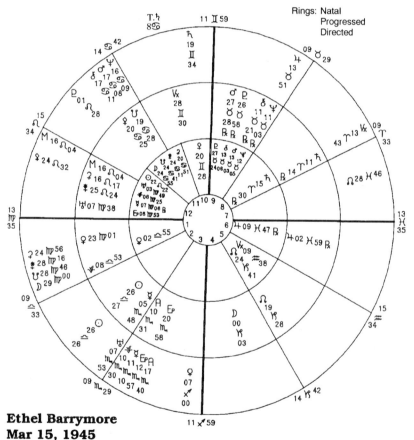

Ethel Barrymore
Mar 15, 1945
Relocated to Hollywood, CA

Cancer trine Barrymore's P Jupiter and sextile her early Virgo planets. Solar Arc Saturn was conjunct Pallas and trine her natal Ascendant.

Barrymore was married long enough to have three children, as we would expect with her Sun in Leo and her Cancer stellium, which included the Moon in its own sign, one of its nodes, Ceres, an asteroid associated with mothering, and Juno, the marriage asteroid. But though her family was highly important to her, her work was the center of her life with her loaded tenth house and her sixth house Saturn, and she left her husband in 1923. Psychologists have recognized the period of the mid-forties as a typical time for a mid-life crisis, when many people become dissatisfied with their lives and make major changes. Around the age of forty-five, the P Sun is octile the natal Sun and, for those who progress the MC by the solar arc, the distance moved by the P Sun, the P MC will octile the natal MC during the same two-year interval. Solar Arc Directions move every factor in the chart the same distance as the P Sun, so in this system. every factor (planets, angles, nodes, etc.) is octile its natal position for two years around the age of forty-five. Many people at this age are asking "Is this all there is?"

Beauty in Motion

Margot Fonteyn was also a star in the entertainment world. Like Barrymore, she started young and continued to perform into the years when most people have retired to the sidelines. Fonteyn was born on May 18, 1919 at 2:15 AM UT in Reigate, England.

She started dancing at age four, studied at the famous Sadler Wells Ballet school at age fourteen, and was a professional dancer a year later. By 1940, she was the prima ballerina, and in 1956, she was given the Order of the British Empire, which made her a part of the minor nobility with the title of Dame. Through the 1970s, Fonteyn was featured in a BBC series, appeared in films, wrote two books, and received awards from several countries. Her meeting in 1962 with Rudolph Nureyev, a ballet star from Russia, led to what amounted to a second career as his dancing partner.

Fonteyn had met her future husband at Cambridge in 1936, and almost twenty years later they met again when he was the

Panamanian Ambassador to England. This time, the relationship led to marriage in 1955. Fonteyn's husband, Roberto Arias, was shot in June 1964 in a political fracas in Panama, and the spinal injury left him partially paralyzed. Fonteyn's encouragement helped him to keep going. At the time, her P Vesta was on Saturn and octile Venus and P Pluto, while P Venus was on P Saturn square Mars and octile P Sun. P Saturn had been square Mars for years but had ended that aspect and moved into a square to Fonteyn's Sun. The combination fits her husband (Venus) becoming a major career (Saturn). P Moon had recently entered Virgo in the seventh house to repeat the idea of work and/or health issues connected to peer relationships.

Adding to the squares between factors in Taurus and in Leo, Fonteyn's P Ascendant in late Taurus was square her rising Pallas which can signify partners as well as politics and "causes." P Juno,

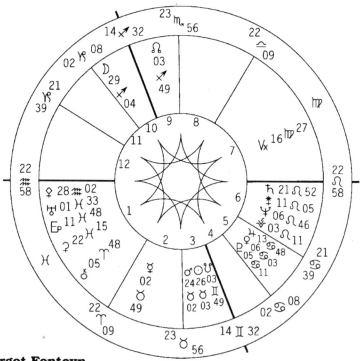

Margot Fonteyn
Source: Quote in *Predictions*, Jan. 1968
Profiles of Women

the marriage asteroid, opposed Pallas and was quincunx P MC, aspects which sometimes lead to separations from relationships, or, as in this case, major changes in them.

Fonteyn met the challenge with courage and strength, living up to the potential of her emphasis in fixed signs and the faith of her first house Pisces. Her natal Sun-Mars conjunction indicates immense personal power, which was further emphasized by P Mars semisextile the Sun and P Jupiter sextile Mars. Aspects between fire planets, Mars, Sun, Jupiter, are the strongest indications of the natural confidence of fire. The Vesta-Saturn conjunction, in contrast, though in the sign of Leo which does add confidence and strength, is mostly earth, with the nature of the

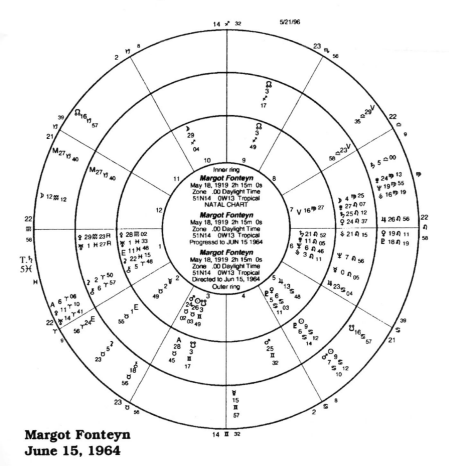

Margot Fonteyn
June 15, 1964

two factors and the sixth house emphasizing the practicality to cope with the material world. Of our twelve sides of life symbolized by astrology, the three "obsessive-compulsive" ones are Vesta, Pluto, and Saturn (Letters Six, Eight, and Ten). When they aspect each other, especially with a conjunction as part of the configuration since it is the strongest aspect, we know that all details will be under control or the individual will die trying.

Fonteyn's Solar Arc Saturn was in 5 Libra square Pluto and opposite Chiron when Arias was shot. The combination of a cardinal T-square in the arcs and fixed sign squares and oppositions in the progressions is a power struggle pattern. T Saturn was also dramatic — opposite her P Moon, square the lunar nodes and quincunx Vesta and Neptune, but trine to Pluto/Venus. Fonteyn had been using her power struggle potential in appropriate and healthy ways in her competition as a star in the entertainment world. The injury to her husband brought out her immense strength and stamina in new ways as her husband became a "career" in the sense that she took personal responsibility for helping him survive and recover. Saturn in the seventh house can be a problem if one partner is playing parent and the other is forced to play the role of child in what is theoretically a peer relationship. As a temporary role in an emergency, a partner becoming a caring parent can be very constructive, as Fonteyn demonstrated.

Into Orbit

When it comes to Saturn conjunct angles, the MC seems to be the favorite among prominent politicians in my collection. I turned up six in a brief scan, including a range from very conservative to very liberal. As has been said repeatedly, it is necessary to consider the whole chart and even then, the details still depend on the person. The early family and surroundings are obviously vital in understanding a person. But people can also grow and change. Three of the six have been lifetime Democrats, two were Republicans, and one started as a Democrat and changed parties.

Long before he went into politics, John Glenn was famous as the first American astronaut to orbit the earth in a space capsule. Glenn was born on July 18, 1921 at 4 PM EST in Cambridge, OH.

He was a naval aviation cadet, went through flight school, served as a Marine in the Pacific in World War II and also served in Korea in 1953. He served with NASA from 1959 to 1964, and made his famous orbital flight on February 7, 1962.

Glenn's Saturn and Jupiter were both conjunct his MC, sextile his Mars, trine his Antivertex and, more widely, forming a grand trine to Vesta and the Moon. The grand trine in earth signs and houses indicates a very competent person. When we add his stellium in Cancer in the eighth house, it is not surprising that he is a political conservative. It is more surprising that his early life included so many risk-taking activities, but Glenn also had some strong trines involving fire signs and houses. His fourth house Chiron in Aries has held a progressed trine to Neptune in the ninth house for most of his life, demonstrating a very secure faith, which included the subconscious level since Neptune is a water planet

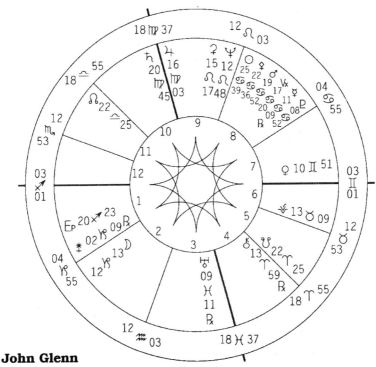

John Glenn
Source: Birth Certificate
[Lois] Rodden-ISAR Database

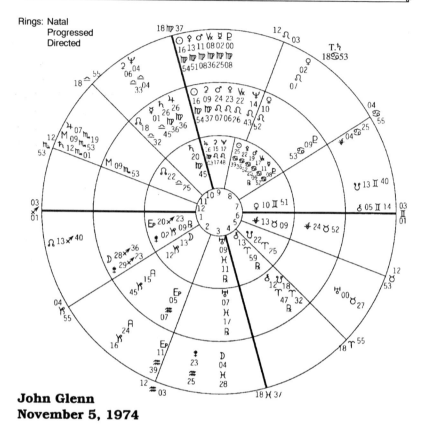

John Glenn
November 5, 1974

and Chiron is in a water house. Sagittarius rising and its ruler, Jupiter, in its own house with strong trines and sextiles, are keys to conscious faith.

Throughout his NASA period and beyond it, Glenn had his P Saturn sextile his natal Sun, a very positive indication of the ability to achieve his ambitions. In February 1962, when he was a space pioneer, T Saturn was sextile his Ascendant from Aquarius and trioctile natal Saturn and MC. His P Venus was conjunct his Sun and sextile Saturn. D Saturn (in 29 Libra) did not have any traditional aspects to the standard factors, but D Neptune was conjunct natal Saturn.

Glenn was elected as a U.S. Senator from Ohio in 1974. He had a business career between NASA and his entry into politics. T

Saturn was in 18 Cancer in 1974 conjunct Mars and closely sextile his MC, which is at the midpoint of Jupiter and Saturn, giving extra strength. P Jupiter and P Saturn were holding a long conjunction as Jupiter gradually passed the slower planet. Glenn also had his P MC in a grand trine to Pluto and Uranus, but P East Point was trioctile Saturn. D Saturn was square Neptune and trine Mercury. By the time he took on the office, D Saturn was opposite Vesta for the job change and about to sextile the Moon.

Football and Politics

Jack Kemp is like Glenn in being a lifetime moderately conservative Republican who came into politics from a different field than the usual law background. Kemp was born on July 13, 1935 at 3:15 AM PST in Los Angeles, California.

He went into professional football after graduating from college and was especially successful in 1964 and 1965. He helped the Buffalo Bills win three consecutive Eastern Division titles and two AFL championships. In 1965 he was named the AFL player of the year and the most valuable player in the Bills. But he had a series of injuries after that, including two broken ankles, two broken shoulders, a broken knee and eleven concussions. By 1969 he was forced to retire from football and he worked for a bank in Buffalo. He had previously been a special assistant for Ronald Reagan, who was then governor of California. In 1970 he was asked to run for Congress in New York's thirty-ninth district, and he won in November. He was reelected in 1972, 1974 and 1976 with huge margins. In 1978 the Democrats did not even field a candidate against him.

Kemp's Saturn was precisely on his MC at birth, but it retrograded back into the ninth house. It was closely trioctile Pluto and more widely octile-trioctile the lunar nodes and Mars and square East Point, Chiron, and the Moon. Its only harmony aspects were a wide trine to Jupiter and a sextile to Uranus, but the latter aspect became exact in progressions and has lasted for years, showing Kemp's capacity for success in public service work, with the planets and houses all connected to the transpersonal area.

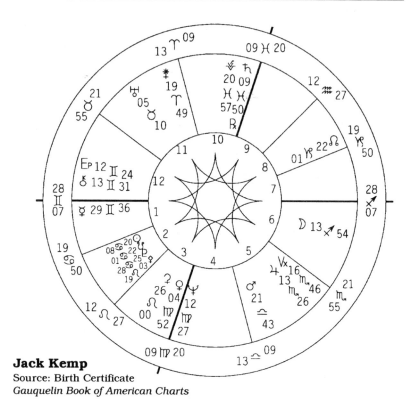

Jack Kemp
Source: Birth Certificate
Gauquelin Book of American Charts

Another key to success in his later adult life was Kemp's P Jupiter moving into sextile-trines to the mean or average P lunar nodes. There are two ways to calculate the lunar nodes: their average position, which moves approximately three minutes a day retrograde, and the "true" node, which is irregular, sometimes retrograde and sometimes direct. Both seem to be meaningful, so I look at both positions. Charts like Kemp's are important since they demonstrate the potential for success despite major conflict aspects.

Other than the general potential for a power struggle life suggested by the conflict aspects to the dominant Saturn, the main keys to a possible attraction to sports are shown by Chiron. If we take it as similar to Jupiter, we can note its close conjunction to the East Point, which is like having it on the Ascendant, and its long progressed opposition to the Moon in Sagittarius in the house of work, plus its quincunx to Jupiter. Mars and Jupiter in the fifth house, fire planets in a fire house, add to the fire emphasis. Activities which require physical energy and/or personal risks are usually associated with fire in some form.

Kemp had a T Saturn return on his natal Saturn and MC during the last few months of 1965 when he was especially honored. Despite the conflict aspects to Saturn, he had obviously worked hard and successfully to attain his ambitions. But he also had his P Ascendant on the P south lunar node, which is often a lesson not too dissimilar to Saturn, and the angle aspect lasted for some years during which he was experiencing multiple injuries. Note that the nodes formed a grand cross with Mars and Juno in cardinal signs in fixed houses. The cardinal-fixed mixture is

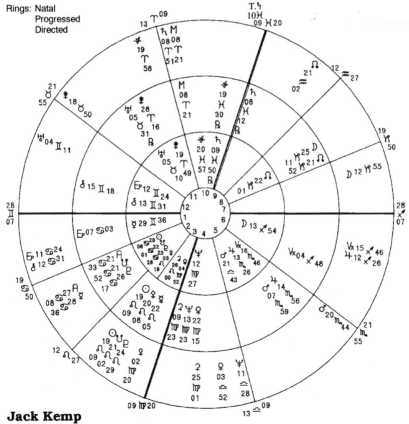

Jack Kemp
November 15, 1965

especially likely to be involved in power struggles, and we can't expect to win them all.

By 1969, when Kemp left football, his P Ascendant had reached a conjunction with Pluto, one of the keys to joint resources, including banking. By November 1970, when he entered politics, Kemp's P Moon was in 9 Aries semisextile his Saturn-MC. His P Ascendant was trioctile MC-Saturn and T Saturn was octile P MC. Despite the conflict aspects involving Saturn and the MC, Kemp won. When he assumed the new office in January 1971, his P Moon was crossing his P MC, a highly appropriate aspect for a change in his work and his home, with P Moon opposite the IC at the same time. P Saturn was not helpful, since for years it stayed in an octile-trioctile to the lunar nodes and Mars, but P Sun did have a trine to Kemp's MC in Washington D.C. and P MC was trine the Moon, quincunx Jupiter, and sextile Chiron. D Saturn was, of course, right there with the MC since Directions move the whole chart the same amount.

Dixiecrat

Jesse Helms is the former Democrat who turned Republican during Richard Nixon's first term as president even though he was concerned about Nixon's appeasement of China and friendship with Tito in Yugoslavia. Helms was a rabid anti-Communist and defense hawk. He had been involved in media work on a newspaper and as a radio commentator in North Carolina before entering politics.

Helms was born on October 18, 1921 at 11 AM EST in Monroe, North Carolina. Like Glenn, who was born the same year, Helms had Jupiter conjunct Saturn, but they were in early Libra with both in the ninth house, making a stellium in Libra versus Glenn's in Cancer. However, his power drive was at least equally strong with a tenth house Sun and Capricorn in the first house. Also, his P Jupiter and Saturn moved into his tenth house, with Saturn holding a conjunction with the MC for years that is still exact within one degree. Helms' grand cross is in cardinal signs and houses and politics is an appropriate arena for the power struggle. His chart suggests that he lacks the secure faith of Glenn. Though

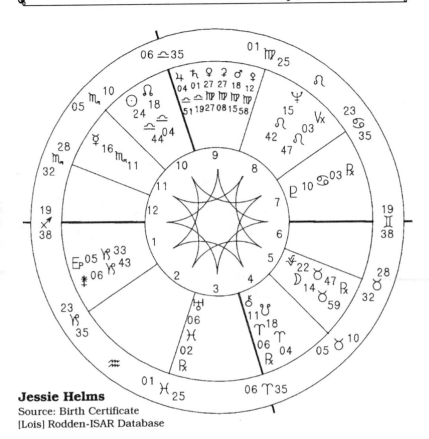

Jessie Helms
Source: Birth Certificate
[Lois] Rodden-ISAR Database

Chiron and Neptune were trine at birth, the aspect was never exact. Instead, Helms has P Neptune square the Moon for his whole life, showing problems with subconscious faith. P Jupiter, a primary key to conscious faith, squared the East Point, then Juno, then his East Point in Washington D.C. and then Pluto, pointing to continuing issues involving beliefs, faith, and ethics in some way. In addition to his support of the military-industrial complex, Helms is noted for his support of tobacco, a major crop in North Carolina, and for his recent campaign for reelection which played on racial tensions.

Helms was first elected to the U.S. Senate from North Carolina in November 1972. P Saturn had already reached his MC by early 1964 if his birth time is accurate. Astrologers always worry about even hour birth times. P Saturn was quincunx Uranus, so Helms was probably in a perpetual state of discontent. His P Ascendant added a quincunx to Pluto as a further support for changes in his associates, but he also had several very harmonious progressions. Inner harmony does not guarantee success, but it supports it since it shows that we know what we want and think we should have it. Helms' P MC was sextile Venus and trine the P Moon, while P Venus was sextile Saturn. T Saturn had very mixed aspects. It was on the Descendant square Mars, but trine P Mars, which was on P Ceres. D Saturn opposed Vesta, an appropriate aspect for a change of work. By the time Helms was sworn into the office in January 1973, his P Moon was opposite Saturn for the change and T Saturn was back to 14 Gemini sextile-trine the P lunar nodes.

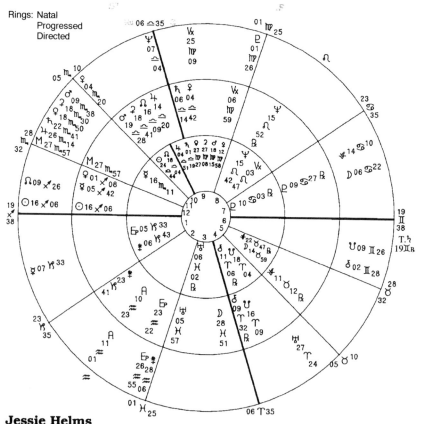

Jessie Helms
November 7, 1972

Texan

Lloyd Bentsen is one more well-known politician born in the same year as Glenn and Helms, but earlier than Helms so his Jupiter-Saturn conjunction is in Virgo like Glenn. Bentsen was born on February 11, 1921 at 2:30 AM CST in Mission, Texas.

He traveled a more typical route into politics, getting a law degree in 1942, practicing law briefly, serving as a judge for a couple of years, then in the Texas Congress, and being elected as Senator from Texas in November 1970.

Bentsen has remained a Democrat, but he is a fairly conservative one, with P Saturn holding a conjunction with his MC like Helms, though in a different sign. In contrast to Glenn and Helms, Bentsen has fewer factors in the top half of his chart, but all three

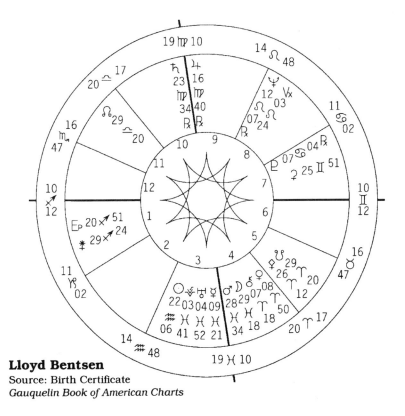

Lloyd Bentsen
Source: Birth Certificate
Gauquelin Book of American Charts

men have Sagittarius rising. Bentsen has an additional strong focus on idealism with five factors in Pisces: three planets, the Moon, and the asteroid Vesta. Of course an emphasis on idealism and faith does not tell us how the individual will express it. We have to watch the life to know that. An identification with "God" can be manifested as a desire to only do the right and perfect thing or as the feeling that we "are God" and have the right to do anything we please. Bentsen's public image is untarnished, but less well-known material poses troubling questions about his and George Bush's involvement with the Savings and Loan debacle in Texas which might make Whitewater look like minor league.

When Bentsen was elected Senator in November 1970, T Saturn was in 19 Taurus with a very positive trine to his MC and a conjunction to progressed Pallas, our political asteroid. By the time he took office the next January, T Saturn had retrograded

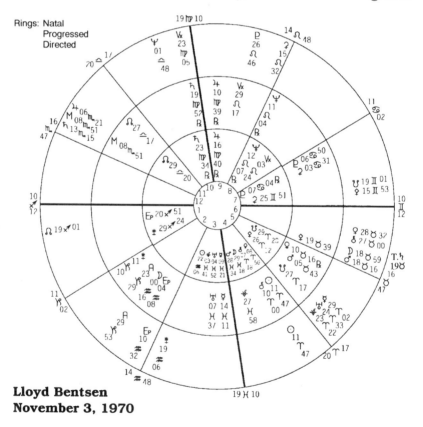

Lloyd Bentsen
November 3, 1970

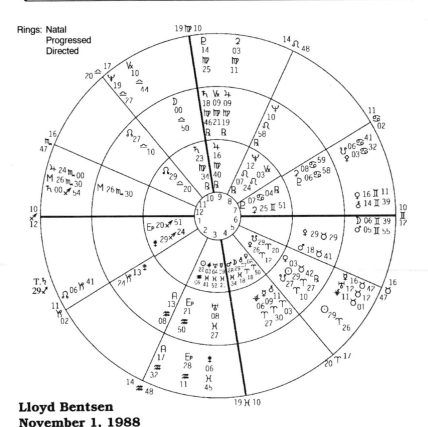

Lloyd Bentsen
November 1, 1988

back into a trine to Jupiter. His progressed angles also showed the potential for a major change of career and power in the world. P Ascendant was trine natal Saturn and P East Point was trioctile P Saturn. P MC was trine Mercury and had recently ended a trine to P Uranus, which was holding a long P trine to Pluto. P MC was also quincunx Venus in the fourth house for the change of residence as well as career when he moved to Washington, D.C. P Venus was trine P Jupiter and P Juno, forming a grand trine in earth signs and fire houses — a successful steamroller combination. P Sun was trine P Neptune and P Mars was sextile Uranus, about to start a sextile to P Pluto. P Vesta was on natal Mars. Few astrologers would have any doubt about Bentsen's ability to win that election.

In contrast to the very harmonious progressions, D Saturn was just coming to an octile to Juno and a trioctile to the Moon. I wonder whether his wife was less than thrilled about the move?

Bentsen left his Senate post to campaign with Michael Dukakis in 1988, running as the potential Vice President. At the election, T Saturn was on his Juno with mixed aspects. It was sextile-trine the lunar nodes and trine the P Sun, but square Mars and the Moon. P Ascendant was also in conflict with Mars with an octile. Conflict aspects between Mars and the angles which share the meaning of Mars are keys to some kind of ambivalence over what we want to do or can do, yet P Mars trine the MC and P Saturn showed that on some level he wanted the new power role. P MC quincunx one P node and semisextile the other can signify some kind of change, and P Venus trioctile the MC and P Saturn repeated the mixed message. D Saturn entering a new sign and quincunx the south node and semisextile the north repeated the message. Dukakis and Bentsen lost, and the two men retired to their respective home states.

Minnesota Morals

It is intriguing to note how many of our recent candidates for the top executive offices have had Saturn conjunct an angle. Walter Mondale was in the U.S. Senate for years, but he was also Vice President under Jimmy Carter. Mondale was born on January 5, 1928 at 10:30 AM CST in Ceylon, Minnesota. Like Helms, Mondale had Saturn at birth on the ninth house side of the MC and it progressed onto the angle to stay there for years. But the resemblance between the two men ends there. Mondale was a deeply ethical man, the son of a minister and married to the daughter of a minister. Over the years, it has been fascinating to watch the unusually high moral caliber of many of the politicians in and from Minnesota. Some commentators have called the state the conscience of our nation. That does not mean that all of their people in power are embryo saints, but many seem to have escaped the common consequences of power, when its temptations for abuse lead to a fall.

Mondale's potential for idealism shouts from the chart, with a stellium in Pisces in the first house that includes Jupiter, its co-ruler, and Mars in Sagittarius repeats the identification with the search for perfection. Every one of the ten male power people considered in this section had some kind of combination of Letter One (identity) with Letter Nine and/or Twelve (faith and ideals), but it is much stronger in some of them. Plus, we still do not know how individuals will select and manifest their ideals until we observe their lives. These men are all bright and articulate. They have all been successful in the world, some in several careers. They have all used their power to change the world, though we, the public, will put different values on their differing results.

Mondale, like his running mate Carter, is a liberal, though not an extremist. Democrats tend to believe that the government can and should help ordinary people. Republicans tend to believe that

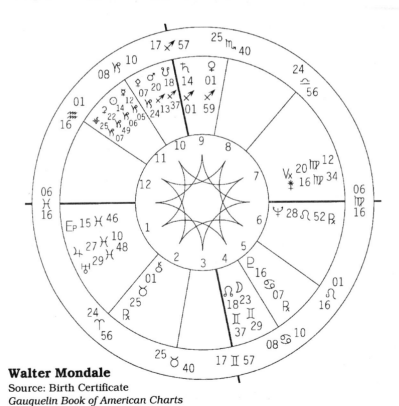

Walter Mondale
Source: Birth Certificate
Gauquelin Book of American Charts

the government is a threat and should only defend us against criminals and other countries.

Mondale was initially appointed to the U.S. Senate to finish the term of Hubert Humphrey, and he took over the office on January 4, 1965. He won a full six-year term as senator in November 1966. He was the Vice President under Carter from January 1977 to 1981. He toured the U.S. campaigning for the presidency for some months in 1974, and tried again in 1984, but lost.

It is easy to see the feeling Mondale must have had that he should use his personal power to make a better world. With Mars in Sagittarius in the tenth house close to the MC and P Saturn in Sagittarius moving from the ninth house to stay on the MC for years, with Neptune in the sixth house and the rising Pisces, he must have felt an urgent need to work to save the world. His strong Capricorn, added to factors in all the earth houses, shows the potential for realism, but that often leaves the individual feeling that no matter what has been accomplished, it is never enough, as he contrasts what is with what ought to be. When I talk to clients with this type of chart, I tell them that it is ok to be human, to do the best they can but also to enjoy the journey.

The two sides of perfectionism are the ideals of Letters Nine and Twelve and the awareness of flaws of Letters Six and Ten. In addition to the emphasis already described, Mondale has also had P south lunar node conjunct Saturn and Chiron trioctile P Saturn for years. When he took his seat in the Senate in 1965, T Saturn was in 1 Pisces square Venus in double Sagittarius (the sign and the house), trioctile Pluto, octile the Sun, but with at least one harmonious aspect, a sextile to Chiron.

Mondale's P MC in his Washington D.C. chart was in the same degree when he lost his race for the presidency in 1984. One of the fascinating exercises available in astrology is the way you can see repeated patterns at different stages in life and become aware of the repeated issues being faced.

Other aspects at the time of the 1984 loss included P Moon opposite Vesta, P East Point quincunx Mars, P Ascendant square P Sun, P Mercury opposite Neptune, P MC quincunx Pluto, and P Mars octile-trioctile the MC and the lunar nodes. There were some harmonious aspects, but it looked like a losing game. Conflict aspects are not just indicative of outer circumstances beyond our

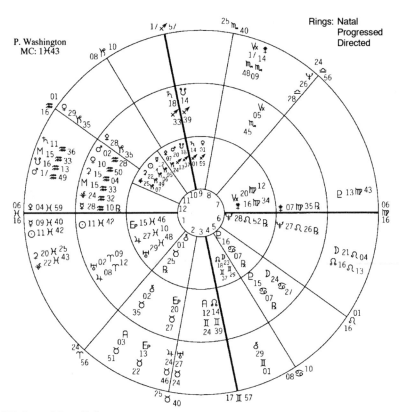

Walter Mondale
November 6, 1984

control. They describe deep inner ambivalence about our ability to handle a situation. In idealists, they often indicate the subconscious feeling that they just can't ever do enough.

Mondale was appointed Ambassador to Japan by President Clinton, so perhaps he is currently expressing his Sagittarian nature more through experiences in another country and less in wishing he could do more to save the world.

Born to Power

As examples of women born with Saturn on the MC, I chose two who were born to power, one who earned it professionally, and one who failed to use it effectively and had it used against her. The two women who were born to power are Queen Elizabeth II of England and her sister, Princess Margaret. Obviously, there are many differences between their charts, but Saturn provides a clue to the one with the greater power. The Saturn-MC conjunction for Elizabeth was just over one degree from exact and Saturn was sextile her Ascendant. Margaret had Saturn in the tenth house, but it was nearly four degrees from the MC and it was exactly square her Ascendant.

Elizabeth was born on April 21, 1926, at 2:40 AM UT in London, England. Margaret was born on August 21, 1930 at 9:22 PM GDT in Glamis, Scotland. George VI, the father of the sisters, was the second son of the king and not expected to inherit the throne. But Edward VIII, the oldest son, abdicated his right to be King on December 11, 1936 in order to marry a divorced American woman named Wallis Simpson. So George inherited the title and his oldest daughter, Elizabeth became the next in line for it.

We can see major power issues in Margaret's chart with her strong Aries, including all three angles, the Ascendant, East Point, and Antivertex, square her tenth house Saturn and MC. The aspects describe a confrontation between personal will and the limits of personal will. Margaret also has Uranus in the first house in Aries square Jupiter in Cancer in the fourth house, and opposite Venus in Libra in the seventh house. The lunar nodes in Aries-Libra complete a cardinal grand cross with Pluto, Pallas, and the Moon in Cancer and Juno in Capricorn. With a cardinal cross, we want to express our personal will as we choose, while also being dependent or nurturing, while also maintaining close peer relationships, while also having power in the world. Life should be big enough to include personal interests, a home and family, a mate, and a career, but it does take awareness and compromise to make room in our lives for everything.

When the cardinal dilemma is not handled effectively, we may repress one or more of our basic desires, or project them into other

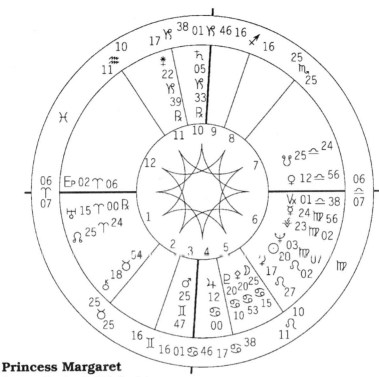

Princess Margaret
Source: Quotes *British Register*
[Lois] Rodden-ISAR Database

people, or displace them, trying to satisfy them where they do not work well. For example, we may compete in relationships which should be cooperative, against our own "team." Most individuals with strong conflict aspects involving cardinal or fixed factors are competitive and need a socially acceptable outlet for this. Healthy, defined as "game-playing," power struggles are possible in sports, games, competitive businesses, and fighting for causes. None of these are easily available to a young princess, though the family did raise prize race horses and loved riding. Margaret's power struggle was displaced into relationship issues and finally into defying the rigid rules of proper action for an English princess. She first fell in love with a divorced man who could not make a legitimate husband according to the rules of the official Anglican Church of England. Margaret's marriage to a photographer eventually ended in divorce, and finally she formed a liaison with a man much younger than herself. None of this seems remarkable in our divorce-prone society, but it was contrary to the protocol for a member of the royal family of England.

Margaret was only six years old when her father inherited the throne of England and dramatically altered her life. Her new power role was played out in London, where her local MC shifted to four Capricorn, barely over one degree from her natal Saturn, to match the pattern in her sister's natal chart. In fact, Margaret's P Saturn had retrograded to one degree and one minute from her London MC when the change came and her P Sun was trine her local MC and still within the one-degree orb of a conjunction with P

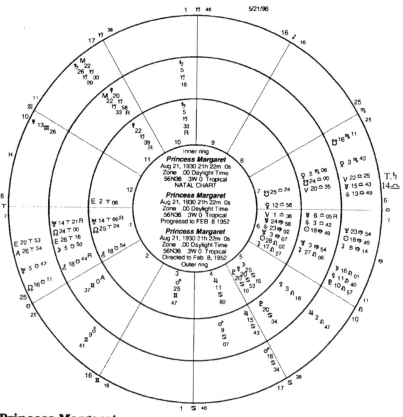

Princess Margaret
February 8, 1952

Neptune. In one way, the new role invited an inflated ego, a hazard with Sun-Neptune, but with its restrictions and obligations, it was not an easy adjustment for a lively, emotionally expressive, fun-loving child. Solar Arc Saturn reinforced the pressure in the new situation with an exact square to Margaret's London Ascendant. T Saturn was less impressive in 16 Pisces, quincunx Ceres and more widely semisextile Uranus and sextile Chiron.

Margaret was twenty-one years old when her father died on February 6, 1952, and her sister inherited the throne. Saturn was strongly aspected at the time, having continuously held a conjunction with Margaret's London MC and a square to her natal Ascendant during the interval in which her father was King of England. At the time of his death, P Venus had reached a sextile to Saturn, P Moon trined it, and P Mercury squared it and opposed the Ascendant. Solar Arc Saturn squared the mean lunar nodes and was quincunx Mars, highly appropriate aspects for stress involving and/or a separation from an authority figure. T Saturn gave the same message with an opposition to Uranus and a square to P Jupiter, pointing to major developments affecting personal action and home and family. P MC in London opposed the Moon and squared the true lunar nodes. Many other aspects could be mentioned, but it was certainly a time of major change for Margaret.

As with many of the examples presented in this book, Margaret's chart demonstrates the psychological issues which she faced, but she did not suffer the doom and gloom crisis events which would be predicted by traditional astrology. She continues an active social life among the world's elite, with financial security and the pleasures which money can buy.

While Margaret's chart was dominated by conflict aspects in cardinal signs and houses, Elizabeth was born with a powerful T-square in fixed signs but partly in cardinal houses, with one corner sharing the cardinality since it was formed by the MC and Saturn, a cardinal planet in its own nature. Most individuals with a cardinal grand cross or T-square will make major changes in their lives from time to time. They may change any or all of the corners — personal action including health, home and family matters, partnerships, or careers. The fixed sides of life are characterized by "enduring self-will." They are **not** unchanging, but they show the determination to change when the individual chooses and to resist being pressured into changing by outside forces. The fixed instinct is to keep going until we get "there," wherever we have defined as "there." Long-term progressed squares between fixed factors are typically experienced as a kind of impasse or stalemate. So the life may remain quite stable for long periods despite an inner sense of tension and a constant effort to stay in control of oneself and/or the situation.

If a genuine inner compromise has not been worked out which allows some satisfaction for all of the desires involved in the configuration, any of the standard defense mechanisms may occur. Repression can lead to personal illness. Projection can lead to others manifesting some of the personal desires for one, usually in excessive ways. Displacement can lead to some desires being sought in inappropriate places or ways.

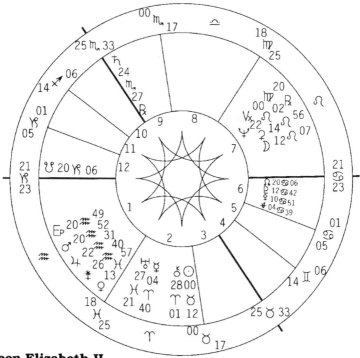

Queen Elizabeth II
Source: Fagin in *American Astrology*
says "recorded", *Profiles of Women*

Queen Elizabeth's chart provides a classical illustration of the central issue of both the cardinal and fixed sides of life: the handling of power in dealing with other people, the need to integrate personal rights and power with the rights and power of others, to make room for both. When we look at the earth and water factors in the Queen's chart, we see the capacity for enormous self-discipline and self-control. Capricorn rising and Saturn, the ruler of the sign, on the MC, which is like Saturn conjunct itself, show an identification with the **LAW**. My will is Law. I am responsible. If I don't make sure everything is done correctly, I will be guilty. My conscience will get me or the world will put me down. Traditional astrology saw the south lunar node as very similar to another Saturn, describing an area of life where we first had to learn something and then to give something to life. (The north lunar node, in contrast, was described as more like Jupiter, where things came easily. Some modern astrologers have muddled these interpretations and told people to ignore their south nodes. Believe me, it is as unsafe to ignore the south node as to ignore Saturn.)

Saturn's placement in Scorpio adds to the inner compulsion to gain self-control. Its position just inside the ninth house shows an identification with the "Absolute" in some form. Depending on the person, we may seek final truth, feel we have it and be a guru or judge or teacher, or try to make the world conform to our vision of how it ought to be. Elizabeth's identification with the Absolute is repeated by the first house Jupiter and factors in Pisces, including the Antivertex as an auxiliary Ascendant. Since Uranus rules the Aquarius in the first house, its position in Pisces reinforces the theme. The two extremes of such patterns, of a personal identification with the Absolute, range from feeling we "ought to be god" and trying very hard to be perfect, to feeling that we "are god" so we have a right to anything we want. God should give it to us or we can take it. Obviously, the latter attitude produces con-artists and psychopaths. The safe place, as usual, is in the middle — accepting our humanness, but continuing to try to live up to our ideals while enjoying the journey.

The Queen's strongly occupied second and sixth houses add to the earth tendency to take life seriously. Chiron conjunct the Sun, holding a progressed conjunction for years, connects ideal-

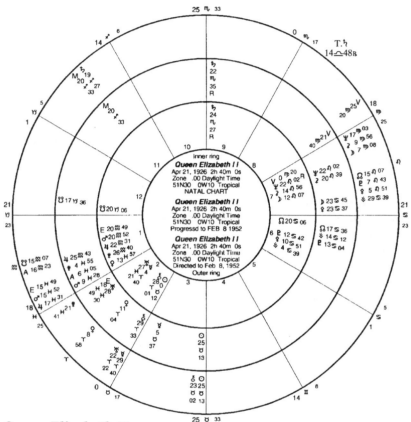

Queen Elizabeth II
February 8, 1952

ism to the ego. She is not only identified with the Absolute from birth, she is driven by the desire to do more, to keep expanding and be recognized for it. Where our Sun is placed, we need to shine, to create life, and to be admired. In double Taurus, both the sign and house, this could be expressed through making money, collecting possessions, indulging the appetites, creating beauty, etc. Though her personal wealth is not public knowledge, Elizabeth may be the wealthiest woman on earth. She owns extensive property in addition to receiving income from the government, and only recently has begun paying taxes on some of her wealth. She also carries heavy responsibilities, including financially supporting many relatives in the minor nobility. In general, she has reportedly been a prudent caretaker of her wealth, and she has carried out her royal duties with dignity and devotion.

When we look at Elizabeth's public life, the earth and water in her chart are obvious. The fire and air are not obvious, so we have to suspect some projection has been occurring. Her sister, Margaret, is an obvious target for some of the Aquarius and Aries. As noted above, Margaret is strongly identified with her rising Uranus in Aries. Elizabeth's children and their spouses are also suspects. Mercury, ruling Elizabeth's fifth house, is in Aries in the Taurus house and widely conjunct Uranus. The combination fits the strong-willed and indulgent nature of some of her children. Jupiter rules Elizabeth's eleventh house as a key to the spouses of her children, and its position conjunct Mars in Aquarius in the Aries house certainly fits Fergie, Andrew's former wife. It also describes the media circus around Diana, wife of Charles, the heir to the throne, and the personal disruption this has produced in Elizabeth's formerly carefully controlled and "proper" life. The parts of a chart which are most commonly projected are the partnership houses. Prince Philip is undoubtedly doing some of Elizabeth's Leo, but with two water factors there, Moon and Neptune, and Ceres which carries many qualities similar to the Moon, he does it discreetly. The rumors of his private pleasures remain rumors, while the next generation has their activities and their photographs in the daily scandal tabloids.

As indicated above, Elizabeth's father died on February 6, 1952. She was proclaimed Queen two days later, but the official coronation took place on June 2, 1953 with magnificent pomp and ceremony. When she became legally the queen of England, Elizabeth's P Moon was conjunct P Pallas in the seventh house for her new public political role and trine Saturn for her increased status. Her P Sun was crossing the IC, opposite the MC, for the loss of her parent and her change of career. P Sun was also square P Jupiter for the challenge to her faith as she took on the responsibility of the new role. As is typical in astrology, a single factor can carry many meanings. Jupiter is always a key to one's beliefs, values, and ultimate goals. In Elizabeth's chart, its first house position makes it part of her identity and instinctive action. It rules part of her tenth house since part of Sagittarius is placed there, so it is also a key to her role in the society and ability to handle power realistically. It also rules part of her eleventh house to add to the Aquarian tendencies shown by its sign. Elizabeth has not been a scholar — the Mars-Jupiter conjunction fits her love of the country, dogs, and horses — but the royal family is known to consult alternative health practitioners, including homeopaths. P Jupiter's long square to Elizabeth's Saturn and then MC show her struggle to control her Aquarian instincts to properly play her royal role.

Other aspects when Elizabeth became Queen included a long square from P Neptune to P Saturn and an opposition to natal Jupiter, again showing the challenge to her faith from the heavy responsibilities of the royal role. P Ceres, which is like a Virgo-Cancer mixture, opposed the East Point and Mars as she changed her job and became a surrogate parent of her country. P MC was trine P Ceres and sextile the East Point and Mars as she took on the new power. Many other aspects could be listed that fit the major change in Elizabeth's life, but interested readers can spot them for themselves.

Solar Arc Saturn was, of course, just over a degree earlier than the P MC since the MC is directed by the amount of the solar arc, so the relative positions of the two will remain constant. Solar Arc Saturn had not yet reached the aspects to P Ceres and East Point and Mars, but they were in orb by the next year when the coronation took place. At the time she became legally the Queen, Solar Arc Saturn was semisextile and quincunx the lunar nodes, a common configuration when we have changes in relationships which affect our emotional security. Transiting Saturn was retrograding just under fifteen Libra, moving into squares to P Vesta and Pluto and quincunx Venus. The aspect to Venus which rules the fourth house fits the separation from a parent, and a square to Pluto is commonly present with a death, when we are learning to let go. Vesta had been progressing over N and P Pluto for several years as George VI had been in failing health since 1948.

As her children and their "significant others" continue to make headlines in the tabloid newspapers of the world, Elizabeth remains a bulwark of propriety, now struggling against the possible dissolution of the monarchy. Like her sister, she has financial security and a life that many in the world would envy. But she faces her own challenges and the challenges of life are also its opportunities for growth.

Battered by Others' Power

Our third woman with Saturn on the MC, instead of being born into a power role, became a victim of someone else's power. There is always the danger that if we are not expressing major emotions voluntarily in the world in some way, they may backfire against us. MC conjunct Saturn shows an inner drive to be in a power position in the world. Properly expressed, we do this through a career. If this desire is repressed, there is a danger of illness. If it is displaced, we may try to use power in inappropriate ways. If it is projected, others may use power against us.

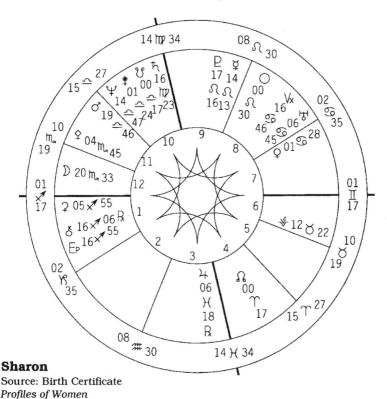

Sharon
Source: Birth Certificate
Profiles of Women

Sharon was born on July 23, 1950 at 4:08 PM PDT in San Mateo, CA. Her data is given in Lois Rodden's *Profiles of Women*. Sharon was an artist, which fits her creative Sagittarius and Leo, her Libra emphasis, her Jupiter in Pisces and Moon in the Pisces house. The Venus sides of life seek pleasure, and artistic activities are positive outlets for this. The Neptune side of life is seeking infinite love and beauty. Fire is the truly creative element, symbolizing the urge to do our new and unique thing in the world. Venus may just rearrange things to make them more esthetically satisfying, but Sharon had Venus on Uranus, which, like fire, is driven by the urge to break new ground. Sharon's Vesta in Taurus in its own Virgo house shows the potential for craftsmanship, for practical skill with details in her work. Its trine to Saturn in Virgo is an emphatic reinforcement of that potential.

In addition to the indications of artistic talent, Sharon's chart points to the freedom-closeness dilemma which is so common in our western world. Factors in the sign and house of Sagittarius, Mars in the Aquarian house, and a lunar node in Aries describe the freedom desires. Factors in the sign and house of Libra and Scorpio emphasize the desire for a mate, while Cancer and Leo add to the hunger for close relationships. A compromise is needed to allow room in the life for both. But the need to be in control of her own life and/or the fear of being controlled can make it more difficult to manage a comfortable peer relationship. Leo-Scorpio mixtures are usually an indication of strong sensual drives, and Sharon had her Leo Sun in the natural house of Scorpio, while the Moon, ruler of Cancer on the eighth cusp, was in the sign of Scorpio. If this natural desire is not being satisfied and the need to use power is blocked, there can be a real danger of attracting someone else with excessive sensuality and power drives.

Sharon was raped on March 1, 1977. She had been painting in front of her window in a ground-floor apartment when a young man broke in about one AM. Lois Rodden pointed out in her discussion of the chart that 4,033 women were raped in Los Angeles in 1977, so it is a shockingly common form of males using their superior physical strength against females. If astrology is finally recognized as a valuable tool by science, we may learn to understand and handle more effectively the psychological tensions in both the predator and the victim which permit such violence.

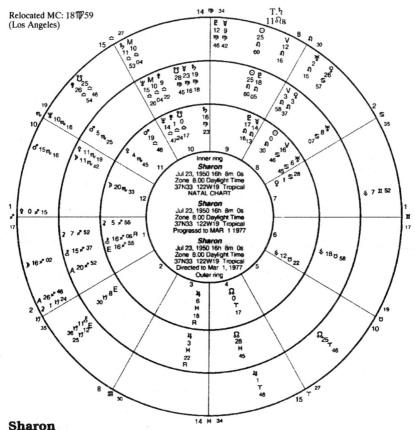

Relocated MC: 18♏59
(Los Angeles)

Inner ring
Sharon
Jul 23, 1950 16h 8m 0s
Zone 8.00 Daylight Time
37N33 122W19 Tropical
NATAL CHART

Sharon
Jul 23, 1950 16h 8m 0s
Zone 8.00 Daylight Time
37N33 122W19 Tropical
Progressd to MAR 1 1977

Sharon
Jul 23, 1950 16h 8m 0s
Zone 8.00 Daylight Time
37N33 122W19 Tropical
Directed to Mar 1, 1977
Outer ring

**Sharon
March 1, 1977**

Sharon's aspects at the time included an even more intense Saturn than her natal chart, since her move to Los Angeles put P Saturn on her local MC within one degree. P Chiron was square natal Saturn, pointing to the issue of faith versus practicality. Sharon acknowledged her lack of common sense in exposing herself as she had. Plus, any conflict aspects between the first house and the tenth show a confrontation between personal will and power versus the limits of personal power, so they call for realism. Sharon's subconscious desire for a mate but ambivalence around the issues of power and freedom versus closeness was suggested by her P Antivertex opposite P Venus—an aspect similar to having Venus on the Descendant. P Saturn and the local MC were octile-trioctile the opposition, to repeat the theme. The same issue of mate and power was shown by P MC conjunct P Juno, the Scorpio asteroid, and the P Sun was octile P MC. P Mars in Scorpio was conjunct Pallas, another asteroid connected to relationships, to repeat the message, and P Moon was conjunct P Pallas in Scorpio with an opposition to Vesta. P Vesta squared P Pluto. The conflict aspects involving fixed planets and signs and houses pointed to some type of power issue, which, of course, could have involved money, or material possessions, or any number of variations on the ability to share the material world with others for mutual pleasure.

Directed Saturn was quincunx Vesta and transiting Saturn squared Vesta. I have not seen many cases involving rape, but I would expect aspects to Vesta in any event which included sexual problems. Vesta seems to be the "ultimate" Virgo, with great potential skill in handling a job but often difficulties in close personal relationships, especially where sex is involved. Vesta was the vestal virgin, totally dedicated to her job. It is also frequently prominent in healers or when there are health problems.

Sharon handled the traumatic experience and was able to move on.

Cosmo "Girl"

Our last woman with Saturn on the MC is Helen Gurley Brown who was born on February 18, 1922 at 3 AM CST in Green Forest, AR. Like Collette, Brown is a professional writer who discovered her talent early in life. Though she said in an interview that she was terrified from the day she was born, her fear did not stop her from writing stories and poems as a child, from putting on school programs and giving dancing lessons to other children, and from being the class valedictorian when she graduated from high school in 1939. Brown attended two colleges but did not complete a degree. Her father had died when she was ten years old and she was a "depression" baby. She is described as having gone through 18 secretarial-type jobs, including working as a copy-writer and account executive for advertising companies in Hollywood, but

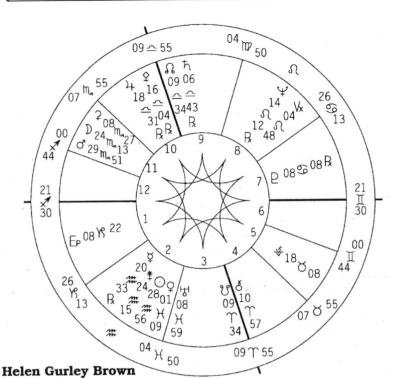

Helen Gurley Brown
Source: Birth Certificate
Profiles of Women

realized that she did not like office work. At that point, her husband suggested that she write a book about single women in a permissive society, and Brown hit the big time. Her book, *Sex and the Single Girl,* was published in 1962, became a best seller, and was made into a movie. She was made Editor-in-Chief of *Cosmopolitan* Magazine in March 1965 and reduced its emphasis on fiction to focus on young women. One critic called her initial May 1965 issue an antifeminist equivalent of *Playboy.* Brown is still writing. She published books in 1965, 1966, 1969, 1982, and in 1993 at the age of seventy-one she produced a book on survival by women over fifty.

Brown's identification with the quest for knowledge and the urge to pass it on to others is shown by her Sagittarian Ascendant and by Saturn, which rules the Capricorn in the first house, being placed in the natural house of Sagittarius. Though I usually interpret ninth house factors as future-oriented, any keys to Letter One, including the rulers of all signs in the first house, provide information about what the individual is doing from the beginning of life. The placement of first house rulers in the fifth, ninth, or eleventh houses suggests that their talents from the past will be carried farther. Saturn's conjunction with the north lunar node also suggests talents from the past, while the sign of Libra points to artistic ability. Brown's chart is strongly air, with its emphasis on Libra and Aquarius, including factors in the natural house of Aquarius. She is clearly a highly articulate and verbally fluent person. The *U.S. World Almanac* from 1976 to 1981 named Brown as one out of the twenty-five most influential women in the United States.

Though secondary progressions are my preferred system for current issues and projecting into the future, solar arc directions can also be useful and often provide especially strong indications of drastic events in the early life. The arcs are very easy to calculate and can be done mentally for early events, since everything is moved about one degree per year. When we add ten degrees to Brown's natal positions to see the aspects in the year her father died, we can see that the Sun would conjunct Uranus and quincunx the north lunar node for a possible relationship change. Vesta would square the Sun. Neptune would square the Moon. Uranus would quincunx Jupiter. Pluto and the East Point would square Jupiter. Saturn would conjunct Pallas. Ceres would oppose Vesta. Clearly, any astrologer working with solar arcs would expect age ten to be important.

When Brown married on September 25, 1959, her P Sun opposed Saturn. Her progressed Sun squared Pluto and the East Point and then conjuncted the P south lunar node while she was writing her best-selling book. Obviously, she was handling her cardinal cross well, successfully managing to stay married, hold down a job, and still do her own creative writing at the same time. Instead of her marriage interfering with her job, it was her husband's suggestion which led to her success, though it was her own talent and hard work which accomplished it. Brown's P lunar nodes held squares to her East Point axis and Pluto for many years of her life, and P Pallas, one of the relationship asteroids, was also in the cardinal cross when she married. Other aspects at the time included P MC opposite Vesta for her change of work, and P Juno,

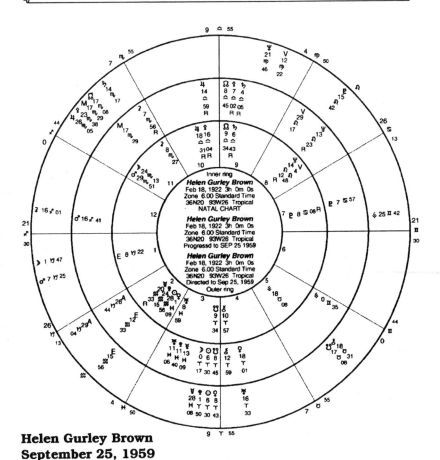

Helen Gurley Brown
September 25, 1959

the marriage asteroid, conjunct P Uranus. P Venus opposed Jupiter and was quincunx P MC. P Moon had just entered Aries and formed a P New Moon a few months after the marriage, with the lights still opposing Saturn. The New Moon marks a new thirty-year cycle in the life—in Brown's case, as a successful writer. Saturn does not offer "something for nothing," but it can signal success if we realistically work for it.

Iron Lady

Though a majority of the men in my collection who had Saturn on the angles turned out to be politicians, dealing with government power, I found almost no women in that field. We do have one prominent example in Margaret Thatcher, the first woman Prime Minister of England. "Maggie" Thatcher was born on October 13, 1925 at 9 AM UT in Grantham, England. Her birth time comes from her thanks to British astrologer Charles Harvey.

Thatcher was born with Saturn in the sign of Scorpio conjunct her Ascendant within less than two degrees. As additional emphasis on her Scorpionic nature, Pluto, the Ascendant ruler, was in its own house in a station, about to go retrograde. A planet in a station is given extra weight, whether it is changing to direct or retrograde motion as seen from earth. Pluto's trine to Saturn and

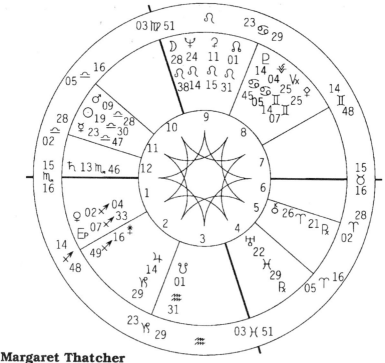

Margaret Thatcher
Source: Charles Harvey quotes her
[Lois] Rodden-ISAR Database

the Ascendant which it rules is a sign of inner harmony. Also, because of the water emphasis, it shows the potential for security coming partly from others, whether from a partner or inheritance or return on investments, etc. Water is the element of the subconscious, so trines with water planets or houses or signs show inner harmony at the subconscious level, the faith that the world will meet our needs. A wide trine from Uranus in Pisces in the fourth house reinforces the message. However, there is also plenty of conflict in the chart. P Pluto has remained opposite Jupiter all of Thatcher's life, while P Jupiter moved through a square to the Sun and then a square to Mercury and P Chiron. The conflict aspects in cardinal signs in fixed houses added to squares in the fixed signs of Leo and Scorpio show power-struggle tendencies in the character. These can be handled successfully in sports and business; Thatcher chose politics — a highly appropriate outlet.

Libra is one of the most common signs associated with the law and politics, so Thatcher's Mars, Sun, and Mercury in that sign also made it a good choice. Venus or the Moon in Libra are more likely to be peacemakers, willing to compromise. Mars and the Sun, as fire factors which seek personal power, are more likely to compete. Mercury in Libra can be a good "devil's advocate," willing to argue on either side of an issue to make sure both sides are represented. But Thatcher had strong convictions, with her Sagittarius identification shown by the sign in the first house and both auxiliary Ascendants, the East Point and the Antivertex, in the sign. Leo in the ninth house is also usually a sign of personal ego investment in one's own "truth." With three keys to "mothering" there, the Moon, Ceres, and a lunar node, Thatcher might be sure that her beliefs were for the good of the people, regardless of how the people felt about it. Neptune in the configuration adds to the emotional subconscious commitment to personal beliefs. Chiron in Aries repeats the identification with the Absolute and "final truth", while Jupiter in Capricorn in the Taurus house shows someone likely to put her beliefs into tangible form, to make a career out of them.

Thatcher first became Prime Minister on May 3, 1979 as the leader of the Conservative Party in England. Unlike the system in the U.S., when a majority of one of the Political Parties is elected to Parliament, the Party leader becomes the Prime Minister. At that time, Thatcher's P MC had just started a sextile to her Moon, though her local P MC in London had started the aspect about six months earlier. P Sun had just started a quincunx to P Pluto for the change in personal action and power, and it was also octile-trioctile the mean positions of the P lunar nodes. I use both the "true" and "mean" methods for calculating the nodes since both seem to work. P Mercury was on the Antivertex opposite Pallas for the change in Thatcher's political power and media attention. P Mercury also held a grand fire trine to Chiron and P Ceres and P Neptune. Other aspects included P East Point on P Jupiter square Mercury and P Chiron and quincunx Neptune. This T-square in

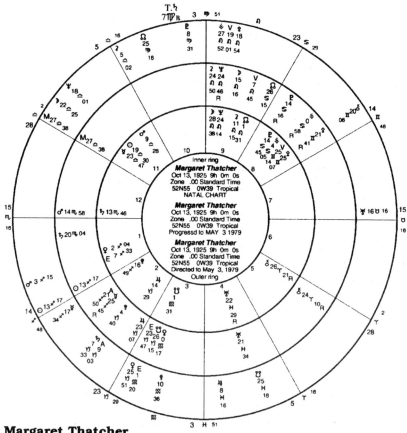

Margaret Thatcher
May 3, 1979

cardinal signs in fixed houses is a classic picture of a power struggle, which Thatcher won, but I'm not sure how many astrologers would have predicted the outcome. P Ascendant opposed P Pallas to reinforce the change in personal political action.

Transiting Saturn at the time was in 7 Virgo, making Thatcher an example of Grant Lewi's theory that individuals reach a peak of power as Saturn reaches their MCs. However, T Saturn was octile-trioctile the progressed cardinal T-square described above and square the East Point axis, signaling the continuous power struggles to come. Solar Arc Saturn was in 7 Capricorn trine T Saturn and on the midpoint of two angles, the East Point and P

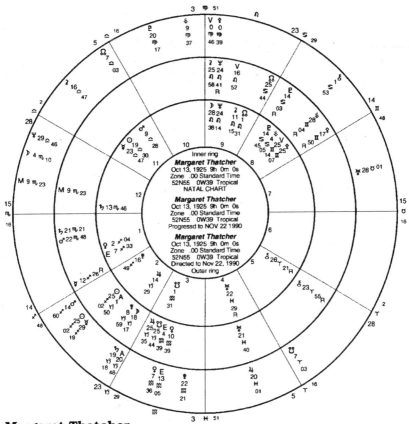

Margaret Thatcher
November 22, 1990

Antivertex, holding semisextiles to both. Perhaps that was a hint of Thatcher's continued success in putting into effect her conservative program to reduce taxes and social programs, which increased the disparity between the rich and the poor.

The network of aspects centered on P Mercury when Thatcher first became Prime Minister is fascinating because when Thatcher's P Sun moved into the same degree she was forced to resign on November 22, 1990. She had been reelected twice and had held power for eleven and a half years—the longest period of any Prime Minister of England in this century. Her P Moon when she left the post was in 18 Capricorn trioctile her MC, square her Sun, and quincunx P Pallas. P Venus opposed Ceres, one of our keys to work. Thatcher's P Ascendant in London opposed Vesta, our primary Virgo asteroid. P Juno squared Mars as she battled for her principles. Thatcher was given a title afterwards, in appreciation of her assistance to the elite of England. She has written a book and done lecture tours in the U.S. The "Iron Lady," as she was known for years, is still speaking out for her convictions, living up to that Saturn on the Ascendant.

Massachusetts Miracle?

Our last Saturn-MC male leader is Michael Dukakis, who campaigned for the presidency in 1988 and lost to George Bush. As already mentioned, Bentsen was the Vice Presidential candidate with Dukakis, so both members of that ticket had the power signature. Dukakis was born on November 3, 1933 at 5:50 PM EST in Boston, Massachusetts.

Mondale's Saturn and MC in Sagittarius fit his minister father. Aquarius was there for Dukakis, whose father was an obstetrician. You will remember that the Gauquelin research found Saturn in the ninth house for famous doctors and scientists. P Saturn was on the MC for a number of years for Dukakis, but it had moved beyond it before he ran for a national office. He earlier had served in the Massachusetts House of Representatives for eight years while Saturn was conjunct his MC. During this period, he showed his liberal potential, sponsoring legislation for the

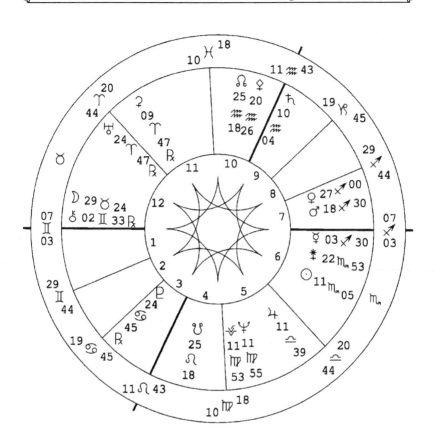

Michael Dukakis

Source: Fran McEvoy quotes hospital records
[Lois] Rodden-ISAR Database

protection of consumers and the environment, including the first no-fault insurance law.

Dukakis was elected governor of Massachusetts on November 5, 1974 and took over the office on January 2, 1975. Most astrologers allow a wider orb of up to three degrees for transits, while progressions and directions are limited to one-degree orbs. T Saturn was in 18 Cancer for the election, with a quincunx to Mars and his tenth house Pallas, a yod pointing to a major change of activity. As another of those fascinating repetitions of patterns, when Dukakis lost the presidential election in November 1988, his

Michael Dukakis
November 5, 1974

P Ascendant in Washington D.C. was in the same 18 Cancer degree, holding a yod to Mars in 18 Sagittarius and P Venus in 18 Aquarius. How much was it the cosmos and how much was it his own nature saying "You can handle the governorship, but the presidency is an overreach"?

Other aspects when Dukakis won the Massachusetts governorship were mixed, as usual. Among others were P Sun sextile/trine the lunar nodes and P East Point trine Pallas while P MC was trine Pluto. At the same time, P Moon squared its P nodes, P MC was octile Saturn, and P Ascendant was octile Chiron. The aspect mixture fits the situation: enough confidence and skill to win the office and enough challenges in the office to give him a hard time. Dukakis had P Jupiter sextile Mars from just after he began his career in the state legislature through his single term as Governor. His career to that point had tilted toward the liberal side and he was widely admired. When he became governor, he found the state in a financial crisis, and he alienated many of his liberal supporters by cutting services and raising taxes to restore the state to financial solvency.

The aspects in 1988, as in 1974, were mixed, but they did not seem insurmountable. There were several progressed quincunxes, including P Sun to the Ascendant, P Mercury to Pluto, P Pallas to P Vesta, P Ceres to the Sun, though it was also sextile Saturn. P Ascendant, which was conjunct Pluto, was also quincunx the north lunar node, and P Uranus was holding a long quincunx to Juno in addition to a long square to Pluto. As we have seen, the quincunx can be present when the politician wins and moves into

Michael Dukakis
November 1, 1988

a new job and home, or when he loses and is separated from his goal. Dukakis also had harmony aspects, including a grand trine between P Mars, P Vesta, and P Chiron. P Chiron was in a long conjunction with the Moon which brought it into the configuration, though Mars had moved beyond the one-degree orb to the Moon which is allowed in progressions and directions. P Juno squared a tight natal Vesta-Neptune conjunction, but it was sextile the MC. It was indeed a mixed picture.

If we simply concentrated on the various positions of Saturn, we would see T Saturn on the eighth house cusp with an octile to P Saturn and a quincunx to the Moon. That is not a positive augury. But D Saturn was just under 6 Aries, coming to a sextile to the Ascendant. The outcome still seems uncertain using traditional astrological factors and techniques.

I was told to omit the new asteroids when writing this book, but perhaps a brief look is permissible in this last example chart. Few astrologers are aware that there are now over 5,000 of these small planets whose orbits have been calculated and who have been given a variety of names. Of the hundreds with which I have worked so far, the names have fit the situation when the asteroids were added to horoscopes. It is impossible to work with the asteroids and to still believe in chance. The personal name asteroids have been among the most amazing when they consistently appear in prominent positions in the charts of people with those names, but the asteroids named for mythical figures and geographical areas have also been meaningful.

We can start by noting that when Michael Dukakis was born, Michel, the French version of his first name, was conjunct his Sun within less than one degree. P Michel opposed his Chiron when he was separated from his goal of becoming president. It was also octile his natal George in 16 Libra 53, the first name of his opponent for the office. P George and P Herberta, two names of Bush, were conjunct and both opposed the natal East Point of Dukakis, one of the keys to his basic identity. P Georgia, another version of George, was in 24 Libra conjunct natal Herberta, again joining two names of his opponent, and they squared Pluto and P Ascendant and opposed Uranus. Natal Georgia was on Barbara, Bush's wife's name, and the P MC of Dukakis opposed both of them. How does the universe manage that? What are the statistical odds that two political opponents would have their personal names all involved in conflict aspects at the time they are in a contest? Remember, we are looking at the sky one day after birth for each year of life—symbolism piled on symbolism. All aspects mentioned are exact within one degree.

There is more. The asteroid Washingtonia had an "ia" added to it to "feminize" it — a policy no longer followed — but it stands for our nation's capital which was the power goal for both Dukakis and Bush. (Herberta and Georgia also were named for men, but the asteroid name was "feminized" because they had "ordinary" orbits. Only asteroids with unusual orbits could be given "masculine" names prior to recent protests by feminists which produced a change in the policy.)

Dukakis had P Washingtonia on his MC square his natal Sun and Michel. His P Mars was on his natal America in the ninth house as he fought for the trust of the country, but P America was square natal Moon and P Chiron as the people dashed his hopes. It was also quincunx P Victoria. I am watching Ganesa, which was named for the Hindu god with the head of an elephant, to see whether it will "work" for the Republican Party. Dukakis had P Ganesa on his eighth house cusp, and the Republicans as the Party of the rich always outspend the Democrats.

There is always more that might be said, but time and space run out in this corner of the cosmos. If we needed any more evidence that the universe is meaningful and that the sky offers us symbolic ways to decipher the meaning, these tiny asteroids would provide it. The physical universe studied by materialistic science is a part of it — perhaps equivalent to what you could see of a city by looking through a keyhole. Every religion has its own keyhole, too. And every school of astrology is diligently pursuing its individual insights through its own keyhole. But the cosmos is an "and," not an "either-or." Perhaps each of us is a bubble of self-consciousness rooted in the sea of universal consciousness which is totally connected and open. Perhaps we are all participating, connected parts of the Absolute as it seeks to manifest as yet unrealized potentials.

CHAPTER NINE

ASTROLOGY
AND HEALTH

A basic concept being discussed in this book is the view that astrology is a psychological system, that the nature of ultimate reality is more like mind than matter. Obviously, life as we experience it in this physical world is a mixture of consciousness (including the subconscious) and physical forces which are theoretically interchangeable energy/matter. It is pointless to argue which comes first, the chicken or the egg. In the physical world, our experience is circular. Our bodies, our emotions, our ideas, our beliefs, and our actions are in a constant state of flux in the process of living, interacting with and influencing each other.

Modern science in recent years has been amassing evidence for the "mind-body" connection, demonstrating the degree to which our emotions affect our body functions. Hans Selye demonstrated the effects of stress, including both physical and emotional stress, showing how it could lead to the breakdown of the immune system. The relatively new field of psychoneuroimmunology is exploring the connections between emotions and body reactions. Yet, many, perhaps most, medical doctors still function as if the body was a machine which they have to repair when it stops functioning properly. Fortunately, an increasing number, often calling themselves "holistic" doctors, are open to complementary methods of healing, and are recognizing that there is a person in the body who is playing a vital role in determining its state of health or illness.

One of these modern MDs is Christiane Northrup in Maine, who publishes a monthly newsletter called "Women's Health." She says flatly that toxic emotions are frequently the cause of the bodily symptoms we call illness and that more positive emotions hold the key to sudden and inexplicable remissions of illness. Dr. Northrup has also written a book called *Women's Bodies, Women's Wisdom* offering her ideas on how to create physical and emotional health.

Andrew Weil, MD is a professor at the University of Arizona Medical School in Tucson. He is the author of several books and a firm believer in the power of the mind to influence the body. Dr. Weil's latest book is called *Spontaneous Healing* and is devoted to ways to enhance our bodies' natural ability to maintain health and to heal themselves.

Martin Rush, MD is a psychiatrist in Ohio who called his book *Decoding the Secret Language of Your Body*. He describes the "many ways our bodies send us messages" with our symptoms, starting with whispers, moving to louder calls, and finally to screams with more serious illnesses.

Henry Dreher is not an MD, but he has been studying and writing about health and medicine for years. His book, *The Immune Power Personality*, describes a variety of research that provides evidence for seven personality traits which can be developed to help us stay healthy. His seven traits have considerable overlap, but each is based on a body of research carried out by a different individual or a group of individuals.

Many more references could be cited, including the quarterly journal *Advances* that is produced by the Institute for the Advancement of Health, which has been publishing studies on mind-body interrelationships since its inception in 1984. The Institute was originally spearheaded and funded by Eileen Rockefeller Growald, but more recently it was taken over by the Fetzer Foundation in Kalamazoo, Michigan.

The clinical psychologist Lawrence Le Shan, Ph.D. has published several books about his work, especially concerning the role of the personality in getting and recovering from cancer. The use of mental visualization as an aid in recovering from cancer was publicized by Carl Simonton, MD and his former wife Stephanie. Lawrence Dossey, MD has documented the healing effects of prayer in a recent book. The use of biofeedback for the healing of both psychological and physical problems is expanding in many areas, spearheaded by Dr. Elmer Green, who directed the research department of the Menninger Clinic in Topeka, Kansas until his recent retirement. The evidence is monumental, yet the pervasive belief that ultimate reality is meaningless energy/matter, that consciousness is only an "epiphenomenon" produced by the physical brain, still prevents most people from making full use of their potential mind-power. Dr. Deepak Chopra has become a media star in recent years with his books, cassette tapes, magazine and TV interviews, all challenging the pervasive materialism which sees people as helpless victims subject to "bad luck" or "bad genes" when they are ill, and dependent on a medical mechanic to fix their ailing bodies.

Of course, the metaphysicians have been telling us for over one hundred years that our minds create our bodies and our lives. Mary Baker Eddy, who founded Christian Science, the Fillmores, who founded Unity, Ernest Holmes, who founded Religious Science, Norman Vincent Peale, who stayed in a traditional Christian denomination but popularized the "power of positive thinking," and countless others have emphasized the power of the mind. But there is a major problem with much of the metaphysical preaching. The standard approach is almost entirely focused on "negative thinking", which is blamed for every variety of life problem from illness to unfulfilling relationships to poverty. In my experience, **emotions rather than thoughts are the power that creates life**. Repeating mantrams like Coue's "every day in every way I am getting better and better" may help **if** the individual starts feeling more positive. But if the subconscious feelings are unchanged, the life will remain unchanged. In fact, it may get worse if people add guilt to the rest of their destructive emotions, being assured by the metaphysical gurus that they would not have problems if they just changed their "thinking."

A helpful metaphor pictures our thoughts as similar to the rudder in a boat. The rudder can help to steer the boat, but the boat's power comes from an engine, or oars pulled by a person, or the wind in the sails. The emotions are the power, and the intellect can influence them **if** we can move the angle of the rudder or of the sails or of the oars. If the subconscious emotional habits are too set to be altered by the intellect, we are not in control of the boat. Our emotional habits are the basis of our character and they create our destiny. I believe that these emotional habits evolved during past experiences, that they are operating from the beginning of each new life, and that they are symbolized in the patterns in the horoscope, the map of the sky at birth. To the extent that we can change our **emotional habits**, and only to that extent, can we change our destiny, our physical and psychological health and the events in our lives.

The subconscious aspect of the mind, which is most of it, controls our bodies and our lives. It keeps us breathing while we sleep, digests our food, repairs minor damage like bruises, cuts, and burns to the skin, copes with marauding germs and bacteria, etc. Obviously, our bodies need adequate nutrition, exercise, rest, shelter, etc., to continue to function. Given those physical necessities, I think that most illness stems from negative emotions. These can be fear, anger, guilt, depression, self-pity, resentment, etc., etc. If we consciously acknowledge the painful feelings, assure the subconscious side of the mind that we can and will deal with the problem, do what is within our power to change the situation, and then can trust that a Higher Power will help what is beyond our personal power, bodily symptoms will usually clear spontaneously. I truly believe that the body can be self-healing if its physical necessities are provided and its manager, the subconscious, is reasonably happy and basically confident about the future. The confidence should include some faith in one's personal ability to handle things and some faith in a Higher Power which will help when we have done the best we can.

Fire is the element of such faith. Mars and the Sun and their signs and houses symbolize our personal self-confidence that we have the right and the power to be ourselves. Jupiter and its signs and houses symbolize our faith in a power beyond human beings. If we put our faith in a fragment of life: money, a job, another human (such as a parent or a mate or a child or a friend), or even in a "narrow" exclusive religious dogma that masquerades as

Final Truth, it is a kind of idolatry. The substitute for the Absolute will let us down. Often, we will lose our idol to force us to find a bigger God. The Absolute is beyond our comprehension at this stage of life. All we can know with certainty is that it must be more life-enhancing than life-destructive, for otherwise everything would already be destroyed. So we can trust "IT" to enhance our lives after we have done our best. Confidence, faith, hope are symbolized in astrology by fire plus Letter Twelve, and they are the keys to the immune system. When they are blocked by negative emotions as listed above, fear, depression, self-pity, inadequacy, guilt, anger, resentment, etc., we shut down the immune system and the recuperative power of life itself.

Conscious positive thoughts can actually make matters worse when they become a form of denial of the subconscious miserable feelings that are intensifying the problems. The subconscious uses body symptoms to get our attention, to get us to deal with the destructive emotions. The body symptom can be a whisper or a scream as Dr. Rush suggests, but it is saying "I am not happy. Do something." When we consciously deny the painful feelings, chanting that they are unreal, error, etc., without dealing with the feelings or the life situations, the subconscious gets more desperate and the symptoms often get worse. Babies and small children have not yet developed the conscious awareness to be able to do anything about their situation, so they need help, and serious physical problems also call for medical assistance. But activity which builds one's self-esteem and strengthens one's faith in general can help to start us on the road to improved health. Happiness and health are partners, reinforcing each other.

I am not a medical doctor, and **I do not make physical diagnoses from a horoscope**. I think that many details are possible with each of the psychological principles in astrology, so when astrologers are trying to specify details, whether in the body or in the life events, they are guessing from many possibilities. If the astrologer's psychic ability is functioning well at that time and/or with that client, the guesses may be quite accurate. But I have seen many examples of inaccurate guesses which needlessly alarmed and misled the client. Basically, I think it is bad psychology, bad metaphysics, and bad astrology to tell people they are going to be sick. I stay with the psychological issues shown in the horoscope, with the belief that if we successfully integrate the emotional conflicts which we all have, we are not likely to be sick. Integration involves staying conscious of conflicts and looking for ways to compromise so no part of us is totally blocked and denied.

What astrology **can** do is to move from the life detail back to the psychological principle which lies behind it. So, if the client has a problem with part of the body and provides this information to the astrologer, **it is often possible to clarify the emotional roots of the problem**. Then the client can let the MD or alternative healer work with the physical level and the client can use the psychological insight to work on that level, and hopefully also to draw on spiritual resources as well.

Traditional astrology spelled out the general outline of corre-lations between the physical body and the twelve sides of life. Everyone has seen the diagram of the "grand man of the zodiac" with Aries at the head and Pisces at the feet. This ancient insight seems to be accurate, but it is obviously only a small part of the picture. The physical body is complex almost beyond imagining, and we need research to support and clarify even the limited number of correlations which we have between body areas and psychological principles. The need for caution is obvious when we examine the conflicting claims made by different schools of astrology. Western astrology, up to and including Vedic astrology in India, uses four elements and classes two as "positive" and two as "negative." These words are not to be construed as "good" and "bad", though there is a tilt in that direction in light of our cultural bias which favors males, with fire and air called masculine and positive and earth and water called feminine and negative. Chi-nese astrology uses five elements, omitting air and including wood and metal. When you analyze the association of the major body organs with the elements, there is almost an exact reversal between the two systems. The organs called positive in China are mostly connected with zodiacal signs called negative in the west. If the correlations were exactly reversed, it would just be a matter of semantics, but there are some discrepancies, so it is not possible to exactly match the two systems. Obviously, such major issues will only be settled by systematic research.

The principles presented in this chapter are from western astrology and should not be mixed with theories from Chinese or other oriental astrology. The concepts have not been validated by research. They are based on anecdotal experience and logic. **They should not be used to attempt physical diagnosis from a horoscope, but only to move from known physical symptoms to theoretical emotions** which may be contributing to problems on any level of the life.

Individuals seeking to improve their health should work on all levels, including the physical level with diet, rest, exercise, and medical help when needed, along with dealing with the emotional habits and the spiritual beliefs. We need to first become conscious of the emotions, and then to try to change the painful habits. Self-pity is the quickest way I know to become a victim! It shuts down the fire. We need to become conscious of our subconscious beliefs about the nature of life and the Absolute, and to change fear into faith. Changing subconscious habits and firmly held beliefs is not easy! We can read about the research of parapsychology which demolishes the dogma of materialism. Astrology shows us a world of meaning, not chance. Associating with people who have faith can help. Emotions are contagious. We are connected at the subconscious level, open to all emotions which resonate with our own. So if we are feeling fear, we are reinforced by being connected to fear everywhere and everywhen. Time and space are the parameters in which we live in the physical world, but they are quite different in the subconscious Whole.

As has been written repeatedly, I think the sky shows the cosmic order but it does not create it. I think we are born where our habits fit the state of the cosmos, we do what comes naturally, get the consequences, and eventually learn to change the emotional habits which are inviting unpleasant consequences. The horoscope just helps us to become consciously aware of what in us is producing our lives, so we can use the rudder to steer the boat. When the mirror in the sky is highlighting Saturn, we know it is time for feedback on how we have been handling the rules of the game.

We can react with fear of our report card and attract more fear from the universe and believe that Saturn is doing something to us. Sensitive people do experience an increase of the relevant emotion as they resonate with its expression everywhere and everywhen. The mistake is in believing that Saturn is causing or even just influencing our experience. The clock offers an alternate form of information to the experience of a growling stomach to confirm that it is lunch time. The clock does not make us hungry. Hunger is part of our own internal rhythm.

Alternately, instead of reacting with fear when Saturn is prominent in current patterns in the sky, we can react with a realistic analysis of what personal habits and past actions have permitted the current consequences in the life. If we have been ignoring the rules, ignorance does not excuse us. If we have been fighting the rules, they are bigger than our personal wills. If we have been trying to run away, the rules are there, wherever we run. As long as we live in this physical world, we have to deal with them realistically. When we do that, we get great results! An important reason for offering this chapter in this book is that dealing with one's physical body is a significant part of handling the rules and responsibilities which Saturn represents. Thus, we are presenting some practical guidelines for assisting health maintenance. Good health, in turn, allows a person to do more of what s/he wants to do.

We can only change our own attitudes and actions. We can't change anyone else. So there will be many times when we can't change outer circumstances in our lives, but we can change our attitudes. Our experience is always based on our evaluation of what happens. Different individuals can have what seem to others to be identical events in their lives, but their inner experiences and reactions can be totally different. The vital, paramount importance of our beliefs is partly due to the fact that our evaluations are determined by our beliefs. Our belief system or world view determines what we consider real versus imaginary, what we rate as important, what we class as ethical or moral, what we see as desirable and as possible.

The most striking healings from supposedly incurable illnesses are usually seen when an individual has a religious conversion experience which truly changes the basic beliefs. Faith may not move mountains without the aid of some muscles, but it can heal the body. Just accepting our own humanness and the humanness of others so we stop expecting more perfection than is possible can be incredibly healing. Consciously acknowledging frustrations but also making sure that every day we do some things just for pleasure can be truly healing. Liking ourselves and our lives along with faith in the Infinite Whole of which we are a part helps to keep our immune systems fully functional.

We **can** change past emotional habits if we keep substituting the optimistic potentials of evolving life to replace the pain of the past. Pain is a warning signal. It calls for attention and changing what we are doing. We learn through pain, but if we simply go on suffering without changing our attitudes and actions, we have flunked the lesson. We need to look for what we can do and do it.

Psychological - Astrological - Physical Associations

Letter One in our astrological alphabet includes Mars, all factors in or ruling the first house, and all factors in Aries. Psychologically, Letter One shows our sense of our personal identity at birth, our sense of our right and our power to be ourselves and to do what we want. Physical associations include a major role in the immune system which resists attacks from pollution, bacteria, viruses, etc. Low energy is one of the first signs that we are blocking ourselves, whether we feel we can't do what we want due to lack of personal power or due to our conscience and the rights of other people. Alternately, we may feel we have to do activities we don't want to do.

Usually, the Mars principle will be in conflict with other drives in the nature such as the desire for pleasant relationships with other people, or practical limits in job opportunities and the need to pay the bills, or responsibilities for a family, etc. Life always calls for compromise between our different and inherently conflicting desires. No one can do everything he or she desires at all times. Those who try, like Charles Stewart, are classed as psychopaths and eventually they hit the limits of personal will and power in some form. (Stewart murdered his wife to collect on her insurance and tried to blame a black man for the murder.)

Other physical problems associated with the Mars principle include anything which breaks the skin and leads to bloodshed, from minor cuts to major surgery. Mars is also associated with burns and fever, including inflammation anywhere in the body. Any diagnostic term which ends in "itis" such as appendicitis is partly connected to our right and power to do what we want. Formerly, doctors tried to reduce any elevation in the temperature of patients until they realized the higher-than-normal temperature was an effort by the body to fight off infections. It should only be lowered when it is so high that it becomes life-threatening.

Mars is also associated with iron, so anemia points to a blocked Mars. With its association with the head, headaches are common reactions to a blocked Mars. Blocked sinuses and other symptoms of colds include Mars and when fluid is involved, we know that one of our water desires is also implicated. The latter could be Letter Four if home and family issues are the problem, or Letter Eight if peer relationships are primary, or Letter Twelve if lack of faith in a Higher Power is the source of the blockage. Aneurysms, which are blood clots which block arteries or veins, and strokes when cells break, and hemorrhage internally are also probably the Mars principle in conflict with one of the water or earth desires for security.

If we assign the five visible planets to the five traditional senses, Mars would logically be connected to taste, which requires immediate contact and is theoretically subject to one's control in deciding to take something into the mouth. Mars rules the muscles, so muscle problems call for us to work to develop our physical strength. Accidents are frequently connected to Letter One. Minor accidents may be due to an excess of Mars overconfidence. Major accidents more typically let us escape from having to do something we did not want to do but felt we had to force ourselves to do. Violence generally involves the Mars principle. When we are the subject of violence, attacked by others, it is usually a sign that we are failing to use our own power in constructive ways.

Mars was feared in the ancient world, which saw the destructive consequences when power was abused and which failed to realize that Mars represented one's personal rights and power and was destructive only when blocked or manifested excessively. If we sit down and stop using our muscles in our later years, we lose our self-confidence along with our physical strength and open ourselves to many illnesses which are not the inevitable result of aging but are an abandonment of our Mars action. No one can do everything they want, but we had better do some things that we want.

Letter Two includes Venus, all factors in or ruling the signs in the second house, and all factors in Taurus. There are far fewer problems associated with Letter Two than with Letter One. Venus is the pleasure principle. As Letter Two, it indicates our capacity to enjoy the material world even when it is not perfect. Think of Ferdinand sitting in the field smelling the flowers. Of course, if you put a fire planet in Taurus or conjunct Venus, or a fire planet or sign in the second house, the combination will be much more energetic.

Taurus rules the throat in the grand man of the zodiac, and as the key to our pleasure, Venus is also associated with sugar, so it is implicated in diabetes. I think that Venus is also a key to the skin, but this is an area of controversy in astrology, with some astrologers connecting the skin to Cancer and some to Capricorn. We make contact with others with the skin, so the Libra side of Venus is a logical association, and it will be discussed again when we look at Libra. If we assign the five visible planets to the five traditional senses, Venus seems closer to the sense of touch, with the Taurus love of texture.

The first two sides of life are totally focused on personal desires, with the connotation of youth, naiveté, and a kind of spontaneous immediacy. By Letter Three, we are starting to take the needs and rights of others into account, seeing beyond ourselves.

Though physical problems can be due to excesses, most are due to inner conflicts between different desires. We can assume that throat problems signal a lack of pleasure in the life, but something has to be blocking the pleasure. Often, sore throats are due to drainage from the sinuses, signaling some sort of Mars block when we can't do what we want to do. The inhibition is usually a water issue, but it can also involve earth since both elements seek security. Infections always involve a water principle when negative emotions have been denied recognition and resolution. So the Letter Two problems mostly just point to a denial of pleasure, but other factors will provide the key to the reason for the denial. Overweight is possible with Letter Two, but since its basic desire is pleasure, usually the individual will avoid serious obesity, which leads to major discomfort.

Letter Three includes Mercury, all factors in or ruling the signs in the third house, and all factors in Gemini. The basic desire here is the development of the conscious side of the mind, the ability to learn and to communicate. We develop these skills by observing life and interacting with people around us who are peers, including siblings, other collateral relatives who are not authority figures, and neighbors. The basic drive of Letter Three is insatiable curiosity, which is satisfied through activity involving eye-mind-hand coordination. Of the five traditional senses, vision fits best here. We are learning here to be detached, objective, with air, space, between us and the world so we are spectators and commentators. Perspective is an air word, the capacity to see both the good and the bad, to gain conscious understanding, to talk about the situation, and then to accept it without having to do anything about it.

Physically, this side of life is associated with the lungs for breathing and speech, with the nervous system which conveys information from the senses to the mind and instructions back from the mind to the muscles, and with the arms and hands which are used to investigate the world around us. Problems can include breathing difficulty such as asthma, emphysema, and tuberculosis. These normally are indicated by conflict between some form of Letter Three and one of the water sides of life. The water need for security or simply subconscious habits from the past are the most common blocks to the air ability to take things lightly as a spectator who is separated from possible threats literally by space and metaphorically by understanding which provides the ability to handle things. Difficulty in breathing is sometimes correlated with holding back on speech for fear of alienating others or saying something inaccurate.

Problems with the nervous system are likely to have a Letter Three component, but can include much more. Electricity carries the information along the nerves, which brings Uranus into the picture. It is carried in the myelin sheath, a fatty outer layer of the nerves, and fat brings in Jupiter. When the nerve impulse has to cross the space between one nerve and the next, it is carried across this synapse by a fluid, which brings in a water principle—probably Letter Four, which is very involved in running the body. Mercury, Uranus, and Jupiter are all associated with intelligence and the Moon is the major key to the personal subconscious.

Most Mercury problems can be helped by developing conscious awareness and understanding of the situation and developing the detachment of a broad perspective. It is always possible to have problems due to excesses in one area of life, but more often, the Mercury motto is helpful: "If it is not going to be important in one hundred years, don't worry about it." A relatively new psychotherapy technique (called EMDR or Eye Movement Desensitization and Reprocessing) developed in California has been found to be helpful for work with post-traumatic stress disorder. Francine Shapiro is the woman who developed the system. The technique works, but the therapists mostly don't know why it works. The traditional technique for such problems calls for the former victim of rape or war trauma or whatever to repeatedly visualize the experience. Theoretically, eventually the traumatic memories would diminish in intensity, but this does not always happen. The new action added to such re-experiencing of the past trauma involves the therapist moving his or her fingers in front of the client while the latter follows the moving hand with the eyes. Somehow, this simple action seemed to lessen the emotional charge of the painful memories. Francine Shapiro has just published a handbook for clinicians, *Eye Movement Desensitization and Reprocessing: Basic Principles and Procedures* (Guilford Press, 1996). Note, the hand and the eyes are both Mercury. Somehow, this action helps clients to gain more objectivity and perspective, to distance themselves from the emotional pain and to start to let it go.

Letter Four includes the Moon, all factors in or ruling the signs in the fourth house, and all factors in Cancer. Letter Four symbolizes our emotional security needs, our baby side which we never totally outgrow and our capacity to be a parent and nurture others. It includes the home and family, both the family we are born into and one of the parents, and the family we produce ourselves as adults. Letter Five is our ability to procreate offspring, as one form of creativity, but Letter Four is our ability to take care of them after we get them.

As a key to one's personal subconscious mind, Letter Four is involved in many body functions, including the stomach and the breasts of women which provide food for their infants. Digestion starts in the stomach, though it continues through Letters Six, Seven, and Eight. These are all part of the interpersonal area where we are learning what is ours and what is not ours in relationships with other people. In a metaphorically similar way, the digestive process discriminates and retains what is personally useful, rightfully ours, in our food, and it relinquishes what is not appropriately ours so it is discarded as waste.

Water symbolizes the subconscious side of the mind, as has been said repeatedly, so it is the repository of habits from the past. It is also the psychic element open to, connecting us to, the Whole, so there is always a sense of vulnerability with water. Its role is to absorb and assimilate the results of the experiences of the other three elements. Assimilated experiences become habits, responses carried out automatically at the subconscious level without the need for conscious attention and decision. Habits free us to let us explore new options, to keep learning and growing while routine subsistence activity is handled by the subconscious.

Since the water instinct is always to hold on and hold in, to maintain the familiar past, it is often in conflict with the fire and air urges to let go and to move on. Constructive, life-enhancing habits are highly valuable, as indicated, to permit new growth. But it is also possible for the subconscious to become mired in painful, self-defeating emotional habits. When we repress our negative emotions, which means we ignore them and keep them out of conscious awareness, the subconscious gets our attention with body symptoms. One physical result can be the production of tumors, encapsulated fluid. These may be benign where minor issues are involved or malignant with more intense, destructive emotions. Becoming conscious of the emotional pain is a positive first step toward healing, but it is also necessary to take action to deal with the life problems and then to replace the self-defeating attitudes with more constructive emotional habits. Lawrence LeShan and others have helped people with supposedly terminal cancer to recover by first uncovering the pain but then focusing on positive things that were within the client's power, rather than just dwelling on what was making them miserable as is sometimes done in psychotherapy. Excitement, zest, enthusiasm carried into action can rekindle and release the blocked fire.

Serious obesity is often a Letter Four problem. When one's emotional security is threatened, the last security may be our ability to eat and prevent starvation. Letter Two eats for pleasure which is lost with serious overweight, so the tendency is to stop short of extreme excesses. Food may be temporarily reassuring, but it cannot provide total security, so there is no natural stopping place for Letter Four. Lack of exercise is also usually involved in obesity. Both Letters Two and Four tend to be more passive or indolent unless, of course, they are connected to fire or to the work ethic of Letters Six and Ten. There is increasing evidence that the currently popular low fat, high carbohydrate diet only helps people who are physically active. Many very heavy people have developed insulin resistance so their bodies release excessive insulin when they eat even "healthy" carbohydrates such as grains and potatoes. As long as there is insulin in the system, it will not burn fat. If inadequate protein is being eaten with a very low calorie diet and the person is mostly sedentary, the body will burn the muscles rather than the stored fat. Since it is the muscles which are able to burn the fat, the consequences leave them worse off than they were before the diet. When they eat mostly vegetables as their carbohydrates, avoiding the foods which used to be called starches, and they eat more protein and fat, their bodies learn to burn fat so they not only burn up the fat being eaten but also the stored fat, and they can lose weight relatively easily without being hungry. Since everyone is an individual, some experimentation may be needed to find the food mix which works best, but the current belief in "one diet fits all" is not working, as the numbers of overweight people in the U.S. keep increasing.

I have seen some cases of serious illness in people who were unable to let themselves be dependent. They had to be sick to let themselves be cared for. Ulcers used to be a male illness when men carried the total responsibility for the security of their families and could not let themselves acknowledge their own emotional needs. In recent years, the majority of ulcer cases are occurring among women who are forced to carry responsibility with little support from others. The true believers in materialism, who think that illness is solely due to physical causes, have been rejoicing since a bacterium was discovered as the cause of many cases of ulcers. However, this does not exonerate the emotions, since they enhance or impair the immune system which is supposed to handle such threats as bacteria, viruses, parasites, etc. Life is interdependent. If we lack a support system from a family, we need to build friendships, and sometimes pets are helpful. Studies have shown that people with pets live longer and stay more healthy than those who are isolated.

Letter Five includes the Sun, all factors in or ruling the signs in the fifth house, and all factors in Leo. Letter Five represents our ego, our self-esteem, our need to do more than we have done before and to be admired for it. This includes loving and being loved, procreating children we hope to be proud of, persuading others to do what we want, winning applause, etc.

Physically, Letter Five is connected to the heart, the biggest muscle in the body and the only one which has to burn fat because carbohydrates do not provide the sustained energy it requires. In the past, most men had heart problems when their career ambitions were not satisfied. Fewer women had heart problems, and they tended to be associated with frustrations in their love relationships. It is possible that more men are currently lacking in love as their wives have had to go to work to help support the family, and more women may have shifted their ambitions into their careers. It is also possible that reduced exercise is a factor, as many more people are in sedentary careers, with few left on the farm and machines taking over much of the heavy labor. It is likely that diet is also a major factor in the increased heart problems which developed in this century. The current scapegoat is saturated fat, but we ate much more fat meat and cream and butter in the last century. Some modern nutritionists are accumulating evidence that the harmful fat is the hydrogenated vegetable oils with their transfatty acids. Margarine may be far more harmful than butter. These oils are chemically treated to be able to stay on the shelf without getting rancid, and the great increase in heart problems coincided with their coming into general use in the U.S. At least there is some agreement that monounsaturated olive oil is probably the most healthy form of fat. There are some essential fatty acids which are necessary to assimilate vitamins A and E. There are essential amino acids which we get in protein. There are no essential carbohydrates, though we need the vitamins found in vegetables and fruits.

Though diet and exercise may be a major part of the picture, I would also always look at the self-esteem needs of anyone with heart problems. As with Mars, which is associated with the rest of our muscles, exercise increases our muscles and with them, our strength and our confidence in our ability to cope with the world. When we feel good about ourselves, we can still love and enjoy others but have less need for their approval.

Letter Six includes Mercury as a ruler of Virgo as well as Gemini, and I think that the asteroid Vesta is the "ultimate Virgo." Also part of the picture are all factors in or ruling the signs in the sixth house and all factors in Virgo. The psychological drive of Letter Six is the urge to do something worth doing and to do it well. This includes being able to function effectively in a job and in the body, so health is general is part of Letter Six. Money is part of the Taurus pleasure. The Virgo goal is a sense of accomplishment, being able to handle details, to take things apart and put them together so they work better, to get tangible results.

In the body, Virgo is associated with most of the intestines where we take our food apart, select what is functional for us, and discard what we can't use. A basic component of the work ethic is the critical attitude that can spot flaws and figure out how to do it better. One of the main dangers with Letter Six is displacement, looking for flaws in everything our life touches and thinking we should be able to fix it all. This attitude can be quite destructive in personal relationships, and too much self-criticism can be very hard on the health. We need to notice our assets, not just our flaws. I have seen cases of diverticulitis, an inflammation of the intestines, which were connected to the effort to do everything perfectly. The intestines recovered when the individual was able to accept human limits and not feel responsible for everything in their lives. We can do one or two things really well to satisfy our Virgo/Vesta drive, but trying to do everything well is hard on both the health and the people around us.

The asteroid Ceres seems to be partly Virgo and partly Cancer. It offers clues to one's experiences with an original mother-figure and also the ability to mother others, so it is the nurturing side of Virgo which does its job to help people. Vesta, in contrast, seeks to do a good job for the sake of doing a good job. If other people get in the way, the attitude may be that the job is more important than the people. Both Ceres and Vesta are sometimes clues to health issues, but I have seen this much more often with Vesta. Both asteroids can also indicate the capacity and the urge to be healers.

Many health problems as well as accidents are related to work frustrations. When we are in jobs which deny our personal needs and aspirations, but security needs prevent just walking off the job, illness is a way to get out of it without personal guilt and sometimes with financial aid from the society. It is a painful way to quit a job, but, of course, no one does this consciously, deliberately. If we get frustrated enough, the subconscious says "I can fix that if you are not going to do anything about it." Any weak link in the body can be used by the subconscious to escape the misery of a hated job.

Letter Seven includes Venus as a ruler of Libra as well as Taurus, and the asteroid Pallas seems to be mostly like Libra. Also part of the picture are all factors in and rulers of the signs in the seventh house and all factors in Libra. The primary drive of Libra is the need for close, lasting peer relationships. This includes marriage but is not limited to that. It can be expressed also through business associates and counseling relationships. Letter Seven is typically emphasized in lawyers and politicians, in people in personnel work, labor arbitration, etc., associated with a strong desire for harmony, balance, fair play and social justice. Talent in the graphic arts is also common. I have sometimes seen Pallas and other forms of Letter Seven associated with problems in seeing patterns, in dyslexia, mirror vision, left-right handed confusion, etc.

The Venus association with pleasure is shared with Taurus, but in Libra the pleasure is sought from human relationships rather than from the physical world. The ability of the body to handle sugar remains Venusian, so diabetes is one possible problem stemming from relationship conflicts. When other forms of pleasure are denied, there is a danger of eating more sweets as a substitute. I think the skin is also associated with Venus. The most common time for skin problems is in the teens when young people are starting dating and afraid of being rejected. The anxiety produces excess hormones which cannot all be eliminated through the kidneys and some of them escape through the skin. The kidneys are traditionally associated with Libra. They continue the digestive process which is largely done by the Virgo intestines as we discriminate between what is ours and what is not ours and release the latter. The kidneys extract the last needed fluid from our food as its unused part is on its way out of the system.

Life is always a juggling act. Protein is essential to feed our Mars muscles, but too much protein is hard on the Venus kidneys. We are constantly trying to balance the seesaw of our personal needs versus the rights and needs of others. Compromise remains the name of the game. Letter Seven needs other people, but "healthy" competition as well as cooperation can provide an outlet. Competition is "healthy" when we know it is a game; when we can win sometimes, lose sometimes, and keep on playing with mutual pleasure for the opponents. Individuals with a major emphasis on Letters Seven and Eight are usually helped by having a variety of peer relationships, including some which are cooperative, some which are competitive, and some in which they help other people. It is important to avoid displacing the competitive instinct into relationships which should be cooperative, in effect, fighting members of our own team.

Letter Eight involves Pluto as its primary ruler, with Mars remaining a traditional co-ruler. I think that the asteroid Juno is another key to Letter Eight, along with all factors in or ruling the signs in the eighth house plus all factors in Scorpio. Like Letter Seven, Letter Eight deals with close, lasting peer relationships. Where the one-seven polarity in astrology describes the confrontation between personal will and the wills of others expressed in open speech and action, the elements air and fire, the two-eight polarity describes the ability to share money, possessions, and sensuality with a mate. Both polarities deal with power, but the fixed quality is associated with enduring self-will, so compromise may be harder.

As fixed water, Letter Eight is especially intense, driven by the compulsion to go to whatever has been defined as the end. I consider this side of life to be one of the most difficult of the twelve, with its combination of the need to be in control of oneself but also the need for a mate. It has the water urge to absorb and assimilate, but is theoretically supposed to allow equality in peer relationships. Where Taurus is free to indulge the appetites, Scorpio is seeking to master them. If we handle Letter Eight successfully, we achieve self-insight partly through the mirror of the mate and we achieve self-mastery partly out of respect for the rights of the mate.

At the physical level, Letter Eight represents the last stage in the digestive process, the bowels and the bladder. It may also be involved in the lower colon. As previously indicated, research is badly needed to clarify many of our astrological associations at the physical level. One obvious health problem connected to Letter Eight is constipation, which can lead to hemorrhoids and surgery. A primary emotional and physical challenge for Letter Eight involves learning when is enough and how to let go. As discussed with Letter Four, when negative emotions are repressed, they can lead to pus in the system, whether in the form of cysts or tumors or infections of all kinds. Metaphorically, the blocked, festering emotions are like the Dead Sea. Without an outlet, the emotions become poisonous and deadly.

It is possible that sexual organs are also connected to Letter Eight. Where Letter Five describes sex as an expression of love and for procreation, though sometimes abused for personal power and self-esteem, Letter Eight includes sex for shared pleasure with a mate. We may share money, possessions, and many other forms of pleasure, but sex is one of the most intense of these experiences. Individuals who have not developed sufficient self-confidence to share pleasure with others and who lack empathy, the ability to feel with others, may express the Letter Eight desires in destructive ways. As had been said repeatedly, life is a balancing act. All of the Letter Seven alternatives are also possible here: "healthy" competition, cooperation, and helping others. Depth psychotherapy is especially connected to Letter Eight and is recommended for any physical problems which involve the digestive system in general and/or the sex organs.

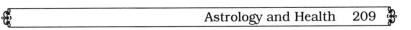

It seems strongly possible that one of our newer illnesses, AIDS, is a Letter Eight phenomenon. A study by Lois Rodden of planetary aspects in over two hundred individuals diagnosed with AIDS found many more conflict aspects to Pluto than to any other planet. This seems appropriate since the HIV infection is transmitted much of the time through sex. However, additional research may also discover a Letter Twelve component, since the use of contaminated needles by drug addicts is another frequent source of the infection. As previously indicated, infections in general are associated with the water principle in astrology. More air, conscious awareness and detachment, and more fire, genuine self-liking, with a variety of ways to actively enjoy life, might help.

Letter Nine includes Jupiter, all factors in or ruling the signs in the ninth house, and all factors in Sagittarius. In my experience, the small planet (or comet?) Chiron also carries the meaning of Jupiter. Chiron can be expressed as the Letter Nine search for Truth or as the Letter Twelve mystic who can be an artist, a savior, or a victim. With Letter Nine, we are dealing with the belief system which directs our lives. Whether we look to science, to philosophy, to conventional religion, to metaphysics, or create our own unique world view, our faith determines what we trust, where and how we look for meaning, our value hierarchy, choices, and goals.

Though the thighs are traditionally given to Jupiter, its most important physical association is with the liver. The liver is an incredibly complex chemical factory in the body which transmutes potentially poisonous chemicals into forms which the body can use or into harmless forms which can be eliminated. The potentially harmful chemicals may come from outside in our food, drink, the air we breathe, etc., or they may be created by the body in the form of excessive hormones produced by negative emotions. In either case, the liver copes and can even restore itself when it is partially destroyed by excesses such as too much alcohol. Metaphorically, our faith in a benign Higher Power plays the same role in our lives. It helps us handle the stresses which are an inevitable part of life.

Despite its primary focus on physical forces, modern science is gradually accumulating evidence for the power of faith in facilitating healing. The medical establishment in England has actually passed laws which permit an MD to refer a patient to a spiritual healer or another alternate form of healing in which the patient has faith. Most scientists still see the placebo effect as a nuisance which interferes with their efforts to test the efficacy of different drugs or other forms of treatment.

The placebo effect is simply the result of patients having faith in the doctor or in the treatment, even though in a double-blind research study they may be getting a sugar pill. Often, the placebo effect is as strong as the physical treatment, but the belief in materialism prevents it being a subject of research. If any physical treatment produced the results achieved by placebos, it would be the subject of multiple studies trying to find out what is happening, under what circumstances, and what we can do to strengthen the effect.

We can gain faith in ourselves by any kind of successful action. Of course, we have to define what we consider successful to be able to achieve it. If our expectations are too high, we may never feel successful. It is much harder to acquire faith in a higher power, especially if we have been well educated in modern science. Even if we are just logical, most of the conventional religions seem dubious, to put it mildly. How could a universal god be as parochial, as exclusive, as unloving and even cruel as the one described in most conventional religions? Astrology, as usually presented, is equally illogical. There are contradictory claims by different systems, but also there are just so many ways to say the same thing, and so many possible life details which can be manifested in connection with the same principle. Physical forces just don't cut it when we get the message with Mars in one chart, with Aries in another, with the first house in another, etc. We can get the message in transits, in secondary and tertiary and minor progressions, in solar and lunar and planetary returns, in a variety of arcs of directions, etc. As computers have increased our scope in recent years, we have been able to explore still more new techniques, to demonstrate that no matter how we manipulate the sky, we still see the same order in a slightly different way.

So, for me, parapsychology research supported early experiences with a psychic mother who demonstrated that materialism explained only a very limited part of reality. Personal spiritual experiences were helpful. But astrology especially showed me a vaster world than any formal belief system with which I was familiar, including the standard belief systems of astrology. Truth is a goal we never reach, but we can know that the Infinite Whole is more inclusive than any limited human conception. We can trust it, keep searching for more truth, and enjoy the journey.

As a minor afterthought, the physical sense left for Jupiter is the sense of smell. Like hearing, which belongs to Saturn, odors come from a distance, so they fit the larger, transpersonal area of life. Sight also involves distance, but we have more personal control of our vision through our ability to voluntarily close our eyes. Scent and hearing cannot be shut out without extra effort. One other small clue exists in the strong interrelationship between smell and taste, which interact and reinforce each other as Mars and Jupiter aspects intensify each other's fire. Of course, as with the nervous system, it is quite possible that the senses may involve several different primary principles rather than being limited to one.

Letter Ten, the primary subject of this book, includes Saturn, all factors in and ruling the signs in the tenth house, and all factors in Capricorn. As readers know by now, Letter Ten indicates the rules of the game of life in this physical world. When we know the necessary rules and live within them voluntarily, we are successful. When we ignore or fight or try to run away from the rules, eventually we get the consequences and they are usually painful.

At the physical level, Letter Ten is connected to all of the crystallized parts of the body, teeth and bones, including the sense of hearing through the bones of the inner ear. In the grand man of the zodiac, Saturn is especially related to the knees. It is also associated with falls. When we overreach and try to do more than we can do, we fall (fail). We are metaphorically brought to our knees. Many physical problems are associated with this principle, especially those which become more common in one's later years. With osteoporosis in our bones and cavities in our teeth, we lose crystallization where we need it. Bones and teeth crumble or break. With gout, arthritis, rheumatism, stones in the body, etc., we get crystals where we do not want them, in the joints, muscles, or organs such as the kidneys and gall bladder. Arteriosclerosis may be involved, or any other form of obstruction which interferes with normal flexibility and flow. We need some capacity for rigid structure. An internal backbone is essential for large animals living in an air environment, in contrast to large invertebrates which can live in the sea. But we are constantly balancing rigid strength against flexibility.

The prototype of this issue is pictured in the confrontation between Mars and Saturn. It is now known that muscle action (Mars) is a primary source of bone strength (Saturn) which helps to prevent osteoporosis and the many varieties of arthritic/ rheumatoid problems. Many back problems stem from muscles which are too weak to properly hold the spinal bones in place. Personal will and power have to work cooperatively with the limits of personal will to survive in this physical world. What a lack of understanding it demonstrates when the planets which symbolize these two essential parts of life are feared as malefics. But because beliefs are so hard to change, astrologers who have bought into the traditional beliefs may never be able to grasp this view of the cosmos. For most people, their belief system is the foundation of their world. They react to a threat to their beliefs as they react to an earthquake—with terror. If their personal self-esteem has been invested in the traditional beliefs, they may react with outrage. In the end, it may be easier for professional psychologists who have managed to see beyond materialism to understand and value astrology as a psychological system.

The obvious physical antidote to these "old-age" problems is to stay active. Since our bodies, emotions, intellects, and spiritual essences are totally intertwined and interacting, improvement in any area is likely to bring improvement in the others. As we strengthen our muscles with physical activity, we strengthen our emotional self-confidence and our physical competence. As we learn intellectually to understand the laws of the physical world and work with them, we also gain in self-confidence and effectiveness in the world. As we open to guidance from the Infinite, we are encouraged to do what will benefit us and others and will help us reach our full potential.

Letter Eleven includes Uranus, and Saturn is still considered a co-ruler of this part of life. Also included are all factors in and ruling the signs in the eleventh house and all factors in Aquarius.

The primary urge of Letter Eleven is to resist any limits, to go beyond all limits. Since Saturn is the key to realistic limits, its rulership of Aquarius seems strange to the astrologers who fear Saturn and love Aquarius as the sign most associated with astrology. But the obvious answer is that once we have internalized the necessary limits of Saturn in the form of practical knowledge and a conscience, we are free to do whatever we want. And, when Letter Eleven is properly expressed, we want the same freedom for everyone that we want for ourselves.

Aquarius is related to the ankles in the grand man of the zodiac, but its more significant association is probably to electricity. Not knowing about electricity, the ancient world called Uranus the water-bearer, but he was correctly seen as a sky god and Aquarius as an air sign. The wavy lines which symbolize Aquarius are now interpreted as moving electricity. As mentioned in the discussion of Letter Three, the nervous system transports its information with electricity. I do not know of any systematic research in the area, but I would expect epilepsy to be involved with Letter Eleven, among other principles related to the mind and the brain. In view of its passionate pursuit of freedom, Letter Eleven may also be connected to body systems involving free circulation. Blockages may stem from an unresolved conflict between Letter Ten and Letter Eleven. In the limited number of cases of paralysis I have seen, the charts of the individuals had such conflicts. As one of the three sides of life which demand freedom, Letter Eleven can also be involved in accidents when we insist on doing what we please, sometimes against our better judgment. More serious accidents are normally managed by the subconscious to get us out of some kind of bind. But when Uranus builds on the solid base of Saturn, the sky is not a limit. We can ride a rocket into space.

Letter Twelve includes Neptune as well as Jupiter, its traditional ruler, plus all factors in or ruling the signs in the twelfth house and all factors in Pisces. This last side of life as symbolized by astrology seeks to bring it all together. It represents the mystic's hunger for infinite love and beauty and oneness with the Whole. This desire may lead into artistic expression, or into efforts to heal the world, to make it more ideal, or we may become victims if we simply wish the world were more ideal without doing anything to make it happen.

Neptune owns the feet in the grand man of the zodiac, but it can be involved in many more problems in the body. Like all the water sides of life, there is the potential for cysts, tumors, and infections, which, with Letter Twelve, are connected to a lack of faith in a Higher Power at the subconscious level. It is also implicated in allergies, which are due to being overly sensitive. As indicated earlier, water is the psychic element, since we are open to the cosmos through the subconscious. Psychic ability is a form of sensitivity which can be painful when overdone. Things which are harmless to others can be poison to someone who is overly sensitive. Letter Twelve is also associated with the immune system, probably the lymph system among others. Letter Six, the polar partner of Letter Twelve, shows our capacity to take things apart, to discriminate. Letter Twelve puts it all together and believes that it all is or should be perfect.

Astrologers who expect analysis and discrimination everywhere and all the time may have trouble handling Letter Twelve. They often write it off as deception, self-deception, confusion, and see only its victim potential. It is true that Letter Twelve is implicated in many forms of escapism, including addictions to drugs and alcohol, psychoses, and chronic illness as a way of escaping from the world or in those who have simply given up. But there is a place for everything. Letter Twelve is less effective on the job unless it is a job which requires empathy and compassion, where it is splendid. It is not a good idea to cross a busy street while in the state of samadhi. But the potential of Letter Twelve to heal bodies and relationships and the world is pulling at us as we move through the Piscean Age. For over two thousand years, humanity has been seeking to develop the empathy and compassion, the ability to feel what others are feeling and to care, which could make this physical world into paradise. Obviously, we are a long way from the goal of Letter Twelve as too many leaders worship competition and greed and promote the law of the jungle. But we have eternity. We are participating parts of the Infinite Whole, sharing its evolution to reach as yet unimaginable potentials.

HEALING WITH THE HORSOCOPE

by **Maritha Pottenger**

THE BASICS

The evidence from research is fairly clear at this point. To remain healthiest throughout our lives, we need pure **food**, **water**, and **air**. Just as importantly, we need **love** (supportive relationships with others)—to both give and receive love. We need adequate **exercise, sleep, relaxation**, and **challenging activities** (such as work). We need faith or a sense of **meaning and purpose**. Healthy functioning starts from these basics and builds.

For **General Vitality/Recuperative Strength**: build Letters 1, 5, and 9 (**fire**). Thus, astrology reflects the paramount importance of **physical exercise (Letter 1**--building the muscles)—now known to be the best overall curative for many conditions and the best way to retard aging. Astrology reflects the vital significance of **faith, hope, and a positive attitude (Letter 9**). The "placebo effect" (belief in the efficacy of a substance that does "nothing" in reality) is powerful! People who have a more positive attitude live longer and healthier lives. Astrology shows us how truly essential **positive self-esteem** is (**Letter 5**: the ability to love oneself and others, to feel proud of who we are). Many lifestyle difficulties which threaten people's health (domestic violence, overeating, smoking, drinking) have all or part of their roots in low self-esteem. So, **keep the basics in your life and feed your fire!**

	Physical	Mental	Emotional	Spiritual
To Strengthen Letter 1	body building sports, exercise movement	identifying personal desires analyze anger	assertiveness training saying "no" to impositions pioneering, courageous acts	Spiritual Warrior Self-directed path Personal philosophy

To Balance (too much) Letter 1: Build Letters 4, 7, and 10 (or 6, 8).

	Physical	Mental	Emotional	Spiritual
To Strengthen Letter 2	indulging appetites e.g., backrubs, food, hot tubs...	thinking/talking about pleasures, resources	enjoying beauty, relaxing, accepting life, being comfortable	prosperity consciousness, increasing self-worth

To Balance (too much) Letter 2: Build Letters 5, 8, and 11 (or 7, 9).

	Physical	Mental	Emotional	Spiritual
To Strengthen Letter 3	flexibility exercises stretches anything with fingers	reading; classes communication mental exercises	humor, cultivating lightheartedness casual "airy" attitude	opening up to many different experiences Religious Science

To Balance (too much) Letter 3: Build Letters 6, 9, and 12 (or 8, 10).

	Physical	Mental	Emotional	Spiritual
To Strengthen Letter 4	hugs, carresses nourishing food deep, "belly" breaths	reparenting literature analyzing one's family patterns	asking for small favors loving pets home-centered activities	faith in Universe's nurturing/ caretaking Goddess religions

To Balance (too much) Letter 4: Build Letters 1, 7, and 10 (or 9, 11).

	Physical	Mental	Emotional	Spiritual
To Strengthen Letter 5	exciting sports, games healthy heart diet, exercise.	getting/giving compliments list noteworthy acts	charades, drama generosity, gifts Type B behavior	visualizing connection to infinite energy religious spectacles

To Balance (too much) Letter 5: Build Letters 2, 8, and 11 (or 10, 12).

	Physical	Mental	Emotional	Spiritual
To Strengthen Letter 6	pure food, air, water handicrafts, models fixing anything	analysis, repairs class on organizing making lists	feeling competent feeling healthy, fit; noticing improvements	visualizing Universe as efficient, right Science of Mind

To Balance (too much) Letter 6: Build Letters 3, 9, and 12 (or 11, 1).

	Physical	Mental	Emotional	Spiritual
To Strengthen Letter 7	balance beam polarity therapy graceful movement	mediator training relationship analysis art classes	cooperative ventures practicing empathy enjoying aesthetics	Universal Beauty Taoist philosophy affirming sharing

To Balance (too much) Letter 7: Build Letters 1, 4, and 10 (or 2, 12).

To Strengthen Letter 8	endurance training Iron Man/Woman making love	research detective work looking at Shadow	depth psycho- therapy sex therapy, grief therapy releasing, forgiving (self/ others) Tantric yoga	Cathartic philosophies Kahuna rituals

To Balance (too much) Letter 8: Build Letters 2, 5, and 11 (or 1, 3).

To Strengthen Letter 9	hiking, marathons thigh exercises faith/trust circle	values clarification philosophical discussions	taking adventur- ous trips; fighting for truth/justice risking for greater gain	trying many different churches, spiritual paths, beliefs.

To Balance (too much) Letter 9: Build Letters 3, 6, 12 (or 2, 4).

To Strengthen Letter 10	calcium, bone-building clarifying real limits sensible back care; proper rest, diet, etc.	exercising expertise, authority apprenticeships Reality Therapy	traditional paths note tangible accomplishments practice internal locus of control	traditional Father religions, structured beliefs

To Balance (too much) Letter 10: Build Letters 1, 4, and 7 (or 3, 5).

To Strengthen Letter 11	yoga (flexibility) enhance circulation freestyle dancing	invention (paper play) brainstorming networking	acts of rebellion humanitarian acts appreciating individuality	unusual beliefs faith in future exotic religions

To Balance (too much) Letter 11: Build Letters 2, 5, and 8 (or 4 and 6)

To Strengthen Letter 12	dancing, move to music right brain exercises graceful sports with/near/in/by water	transcendence through art guided imagery dream journal	Cosmic consciousness feeling one with Nature compassion, healing	Cosmic con- sciousness meditation Ecstatic religious experiences

To Balance (too much) Letter 12: Build Letters 3, 6, and 9 (or 5, 7).

CHAPTER TEN

WHERE DO WE GO FROM HERE?

As we approach the end of both a century and a millennium, the pace of change and its accompanying emotional intensity are escalating. Many individuals are threatened and responding by clinging to and trying to defend familiar dogmas. Some of the dogmas are classed as religion and some are called science, but concepts are still dogmas if they are believed to be final truth and reality and thus beyond question.

The June 8, 1996 issue of *Science News* has an article which illustrates the point. Author Janet Raloff in an article called "When Science and Beliefs Collide" describes a study by Raymond Eve, a social psychologist at the University of Texas at Arlington. Eve and his coworkers administered questionnaires to two different groups of people who were both classed as "believers." One group attended a creationism fair in the summer of 1995 and the other group was made up of Wiccans (defined as white witches), pagans, and adherents of other goddess sects who attended a magical-arts fair.

Only a minority of the creationists were fundamentalist Christians. Their common thread seemed to be respect for tradition and authority. Naturally, a preponderant majority of over eighty percent rejected the scientific claim that the earth is at least four billion years old. But Eve was apparently surprised to find that about sixty percent of the Wiccan-pagans also rejected the age of the earth, though they did not call themselves creationists. In the areas of traditional family values and social issues, the two groups were almost polar opposites. The Wiccans were classed as postmodernists, which included a deep respect for nature, a rejection of Christianity and other patriarchal religions, and a tendency to see "reality" as individual, personal, and subjective. The implication, though not clearly stated, is that the Wiccan-pagans rejected the view of reality as objective, universal, and materialistic as it is defined by western science. Many of the Wiccan-pagans polled by Eve were very well educated, so he held that their attitudes could not be ascribed to ignorance. Eve's conclusion was that they were actually more anti-science than the creationists in holding, for example, "that astrology accurately predicts personality and behavior." p. 360

Do you see a hint of scientific dogma in such a conclusion? Science has rejected astrology, mostly without examining it. Science defines truth as what science says is true. So anyone who questions any of the statements of science is an anti-science believer, denying "truth."

The day is coming, and I think it is coming soon, when the evidence from astrological research will be very hard for science to ignore. Sara Klein carried out a research project for her Ph.D. in psychology at a California Institute, and got stunning, significant statistical results. She obtained the birth dates and the accident dates of over 1,000 individuals who applied for workman's compensation following work-related accidents which kept them off the job for three months or more. The accidents happened significantly often within a few days of the birthdate, or three, six or nine months after the birthdate. Astrologically, the transiting Sun was conjunct, square, or opposite the natal Sun, with odds in the millions against this occurring by chance. Some of the chi squares had eight and nine zeros, which is unheard of in research dealing with human beings.

Ever since Sara completed her degree in 1992, she and I have been trying to get additional data to replicate her study. Though we think of the United States as a scientifically advanced country, we have not found anyone in an official position who had the courage to give us more data. There is no reason to worry about privacy, since all we need is the date of birth and the date of the accident, and, if possible, the sex of the injured worker. But the power of the religious fundamentalists and the dogmatic materialistic scientists, plus perhaps the threat of law suits in our litigious society for anything outside of conventional activities, has kept even people who were open to astrology from risking any association with such a project. After nearly four years of effort, we have finally found a source of data in a western European country where the authorities are less afraid to investigate a heretical idea. Note that astrology is a heresy, a major threat, to both fundamentalist western religions and official science. Heresy, the refusal to believe what your "group" pronounces to be the truth, gets you excommunicated from the group. The Wiccan-pagans and eastern religions have no problem with astrology. Their world-views are big enough to include the possibility that meaning is an inherent part of the cosmos.

The first very preliminary results are in from the new data which we obtained from Sweden. The dates of 2,865 serious work-related accidents were checked against the birthdates of the victims, and they did NOT support the results observed in the California data. One of my sons, Mark Pottenger, wrote a computer program to test a variety of orbs: whole signs, 15 degrees, 10 degrees, 5 degrees, and 1 degree. He checked the whole group, all the males, and all the females. He also removed the individuals born on a date when the Sun might have changed signs and the accidents on those cuspal dates, and analyzed the smaller groups in the same way. The resulting chi-squares were totally non-significant.

Of course, the work has barely begun. We will be checking aspects from all of the transiting planets at the time of the accidents to the birth charts of the victims. In over 2400 accidents, we have the time of the accident. In the other approximately 400 we will not be able to use the Moon's position. We do not have the birth time or place of the accident victims, but we can still do a lot with what we have. This will, of course, take time, but if any results are available before this book goes to the printer, we will include them.

My current thinking is that the different results in these two studies indicate the importance of cultural differences. The Sun symbolizes ego, self-esteem, self-confidence, etc. in any country, but cultures vary widely in the way they encourage or disparage a full expression of these feelings.

California, the "golden" state, is particularly associated with the Sun principle, from the days of the gold rush to the heyday of Hollywood. Sweden is noted for its social safety net, for cradle to grave protection of its citizens, but also for pervasive depression and a high number of suicides. We may find very different patterns emphasizing Moon-Saturn for the Swedish victims rather than the ego-fire observed in California.

As an example of such cultural differences, a Hindu astrologer who moved to California kept being surprised when women failed to marry during periods when there were aspects in their charts which would have indicated marriage in India. After some years, he realized that the emphasis on personal independence in California meant that individuals needed much stronger aspects showing a much more intense desire for marriage before it was likely to happen.

Another interesting discrepancy between the California and Swedish figures was the tendency in Sweden for older individual to have a larger number of the critical accidents when the serious accidents were analyzed as a percentage of the total accidents for the different age groups. In California, the age seemed irrelevant. Since coordination and general fitness do tend to decline in the later years, and healing tends to take longer, it seems logical to expect the results seen in Sweden. One wonders whether some of the claims by younger workers in California might have been fraudulent. Also, California does not have cradle to grave protection. Individuals have to have enough fire self-confidence to file a claim to receive help. The preceding are tentative and very preliminary ideas. Only much more research will settle some of the questions.

Although highly significant results in the Swedish data would have been very exciting, I was not actually surprised by what we found. When the California data produced such extreme results, I was actually puzzled. If such a simple pattern as T Sun conjunct, square, or opposite N Sun for accidents had actually been a universal one, it seemed likely to me that astrologers would have noticed it centuries ago. Sara Klein's search of the astrological literature did not find it. Life and humans are more complex. The psychological climates in different cultures at different times are part of the picture, highlighting some of the life drives and downplaying others. And, in the end, we are all individuals with the potential for learning and growth.

As Eve discovered in his Texas study, some educated people have found that astrology is a fact of life. He apparently knows nothing of the research which has already been done by the Gauquelins and others. Eventually, we will produce the evidence needed to clarify the controversies, to support the valuable insights and to discard a lot of overly simplistic theories. It will be fascinating to watch the reactions of materialistic "scientists" when they have to face major results in astrology research. Most will, of course, ignore them or denounce them as fraud when the statistics are too overwhelming for the results to be called coincidence. Most people are too attached to their foundation beliefs about the world to be able to change. Naturally, the same can be said of most astrologers, who are also human. Astrology would have demonstrated its validity long ago if it were really physical forces producing specific events, permitting precise, detailed predictions. I think that it is because astrology is a psychological system, because it shows a "state of mind" which can be manifested in many different details, that it has proved so hard to "prove." It shows "issues" in the life, not details, and this makes it truly helpful because when we understand the emotional desires/drives which form our basic characters, we can seek to satisfy them in more effective ways. We can change the details in our lives.

We can change the details **if** we can change our basic emotional reactions! The evidence of research in parapsychology supports the theory that at the subconscious level of the mind, we are all connected. Consider as a theory to be tested the possibility that ultimate reality is made of emotion (desire/aversion) and information. Emotion is the driving power. Information can influence and direct it to a limited extent. When we experience anxiety during a Saturn aspect, or pleasure when Venus is prominent, or energy with Mars, or optimism with Jupiter, or whatever, it **might** be that the sky is just a mirror, letting us see our likely emotional state at that time because we were born when we matched the state of the cosmos so our own evolving habits parallel the evolving cosmos and are visible in the mirror in the sky. And, since at that subconscious level, we are connected as participating parts of the evolving whole, any emotion we feel connects us to the same emotion everywhere and everywhen. The materialistic assumption is that Saturn or whatever "made" us feel that way, and we **do** feel influenced. But what if the emotion is really our own nature being expressed and the "influence" is really our resonance with that same emotion everywhere and everywhen??? What if what we receive from the cosmos is not an influence affecting an innocent victim, but an **echo** reinforcing our own habits?

The only way to check the accuracy of a theory is to test it. You can test this theory by doing something that will change your emotional state and then seeing what happens. It is vital that emotions be really changed, not just consciously denied, repressed and ignored! Saying mantrams may help, but it is rarely enough. We usually have to **do** something that lets us identify ourselves in new ways. Habits don't just go away even when we have recognized that they are producing painful results. We have to replace them with new habits.

I have been experimenting with this for years, but everyone has to find his or her own reality. I am in agreement with the Wiccan-pagans. I think we each live in our personal subjective reality, experiencing the results of our emotional habits. Astrology can help us understand our emotional desires/drives **if** we are willing to test that idea. If we prefer to blame the planets (or our parents or our society or other manifestations of the Whole which are outside of our control), so be it. Life is growth and I trust it. We are learning to manifest new and greater potentials. Hopefully, we can also learn to enjoy the journey.

NOTES

1   The Astrological Ages are based on a "wobble" in the Earth's movements which results in the equinoxes and solstices turning in front of the background of the constellations or "fixed" stars. At the spring and fall equinoxes, the day and night are equally long. At one solstice, the day reaches its greatest length and the night is shortest, and the reverse is true at the other solstice. In the western or tropical zodiac, the four cardinal signs start at these turning points in the year when the relative lengths of day and night change. The Sun is at zero Aries for the spring equinox in the northern hemisphere and the tropical or seasonal zodiac signs are 30-degree divisions of the Earth's path (the ecliptic) which start at that point. The movement of zero Aries (and the rest of the zodiac) in front of the constellations is called the "Precession of the Equinoxes," and it takes about 26,000 years for the complete circuit. The period during which zero Aries is passing in front of each of the constellations or groups of stars is called the "Age" of that constellation. Different astrologers have suggested very different dates for the end of our current Piscean Age and the beginning of the coming Aquarian Age, but that is an argument for another time.

2   Astrology works with four elements — fire, earth, air and water, which are discussed in detail on page 17.

3   All of the planets have nodes where their orbits intersect the plane of the Earth's orbit, which is like an imaginary floor extended to infinity. North nodes are located where planets or the Moon cross into the northern hemisphere; south nodes where they return to the southern hemisphere. The nodes carry the meaning of the planet which forms them. The Moon's nodes are similar in meaning to two more Moons in the chart, showing where we seek emotional security. At the nodes of Mars, we tend to be personally identified and active. Most individuals who are playing power roles in the world have prominent Saturn and/or Pluto nodes, and the rest of the planetary nodes can be similarly read as another form of the astrological alphabet — the twelve sides of life.

4   The nickname of "dwad" refers to *dwadasamsas* which are divisions of each zodiacal sign into twelve equal sections of two and one half degrees each. The dwads carry a subtle overtone of the twelve signs, like a whole zodiac, within each sign. The system I have found most reliable starts each sign with the dwad of that sign, and the rest of the zodiacal signs follow in order. For example, zero to two and a half Gemini is the Gemini dwad. The Cancer dwad is from two and a half Gemini to five Gemini. The Leo dwad is from five Gemini to seven and a half Gemini, etc.

5   There are many systems of "Directions", but all of them add the same amount to every factor in the chart: all planets, angles, nodes, or whatever is being used. The most commonly used system of Directions moves all factors the distance traveled by the Secondary Progressed Sun, which is called the "solar arc." The Sun is slightly faster in the winter and slower in he summer, but its movement is approximately one degree a day, which is equal to a year in the life of an individual in this system. For a forty-year-old individual, everything in the chart will have moved about forty degrees.

    For additional information, see my book *Progressions, Directions, and Rectification*.

6   There are several systems of "Progressions", but the most commonly used one equates one day in the sky with one year of life. So, for the potentials at the age of forty, we look at the patterns in the sky forty days after birth. The progressed Sun will be about forty degrees later than the natal Sun, and my preferred method for the MC is to progress it the same distance as the Sun, but every other factor in the chart will have its own unique motion.

    For additional information, see my book *Progressions, Directions, and Rectification*.

REFERENCES

Dobyns, Zipporah, *The Asteroid Ephemeris*, TIA Publications, 1973.

Dobyns, Zipporah, *Expanding Astrology's Universe*, ACS, 1985.

Dobyns, Zipporah, *The Node Book*, TIA Publications, 1973

Dobyns, Zipporah, *Planets on the Move*, ACS Publications, 1994.

Dobyns, Zipporah, *Progressions, Directions, and Rectification*, TIA Publications, 1975.

Dreher, Henry, *The Immune Power Personality*, Dutton, NY, 1995.

Friedman, Howard S. PhD, *The Self-Healing Personality*, Henry Holt & Co, NY, 1991.

Northrup,Christiane MD, *Women's Bodies, Women's Wisdom*, Bantam Books, 1994.

Pottenger, Maritha, *Complete Horoscope Interpretation*, ACS Publications, 1986.

Pottenger, Maritha, *Easy Astrology Guide*, ACS Publications, 1996.

Pottenger, Maritha, *Encounter Astrology*, TIA Publications, 1978.

Pottenger Maritha, *Healing with the Horoscope*, ACS Publications, 1982.

Pottenger, Maritha, *Your Starway to Love* (2nd edition), ACS Publications, 1996.

Rodden, Lois, *American Book of Charts* (out of print), ACS Publications, 1980. (Reprinted as *Astro-Data II* by AFA, 1988)

Rodden, Lois, *Profiles of Women*, AFA, 1979

Rush, Martin MD, *Decoding the Secret Language of Your Body*, Simon & Schuster, NY, 1994.

Trager, James, *The Women's Chronology*, Henry Holt & Co, NY, 1994.

Weil, Andrew MD, *Spontaneous Healing*, Alfred A. Knopf, NY, 1995.

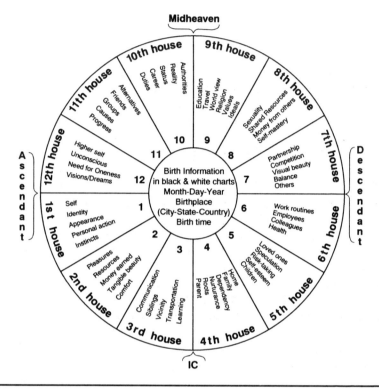

Keywords for Signs

Aries: assertive, brave, first, impetuous, energetic, self-oriented.

Taurus: comfortable, deliberate, dependable, placid, possessive, sensual.

Gemini: fluent, versatile, curious, intermittent, clever, nimble.

Cancer: nurturing, warm, dependent, sympathetic, protective, security-oriented.

Leo: creative, risk-taking, charismatic, fun-loving, generous, exciting.

Virgo: work-oriented, painstaking, efficient, pragmatic, exacting, discreet.

Libra: cooperative, diplomatic, fence-sitting, competitive, aesthetic.

Scorpio: penetrating, intense, resourceful, powerful, compulsive.

Sagittarius: benevolent, optimistic, extravagant, enthusiastic, idealistic.

Capricorn: responsible, formal, traditional, authoritative, career-oriented.

Aquarius: unique, rebellious, futuristic, independent, inventive, objective.

Pisces: compassionate, mystical, illusory, sensitive, spiritual, dreamy.

Aspect	Symbol	Fraction of Circle	Degrees
Conjunction	☌	1/1	0°
Square	□	1/4	90°
Trine	△	1/3	120°
Opposition	☍	1/2	180°

Aspect	Symbol	Fraction of Circle	Degrees
Sextile	✳	1/6	60°
Sesquiquadrate (tri-octile)	⚼	3/8	135°
Semisquare (octile)	∠	1/8	45°
Semisextile	⎵	1/12	30°
Quincunx (or Inconjunct)	⚻	5/12	150°

Keywords for Aspects

conjunction is (are) tied to/mixed with
sextile support(s), aids, assists
square conflict(s) or compete(s) with (∠ and ⚼ similar)
trine reinforce(s), amplifies, exaggerates, harmonizes
quincunx seem(s) at odds with/feels incompatible with
opposition one side could be overdone at the expense of the other
or projected, seesaw swings

Astrological Alphabet

Letter	Planet	Glyph	House	Sign	Glyph	Quality	Element
1	Mars	♂	1	Aries	♈	Cardinal	Fire
2	Venus	♀	2	Taurus	♉	Fixed	Earth
3	Mercury	☿	3	Gemini	♊	Mutable	Air
4	Moon	☽	4	Cancer	♋	Cardinal	Water
5	Sun	☉	5	Leo	♌	Fixed	Fire
6	Mercury	☿	6	Virgo	♍	Mutable	Earth
	Ceres	⚳					
	Vesta	⚶					
7	Venus	♀	7	Libra	♎	Cardinal	Air
	Pallas	⚴					
8	Pluto	♀ or ♇	8	Scorpio	♏	Fixed	Water
	Juno	⚵					
9	Jupiter	♃	9	Sagittarius	♐	Mutable	Fire
	Chiron	⚷					
10	Saturn	♄	10	Capricorn	♑	Cardinal	Earth
11	Uranus	♅	11	Aquarius	♒	Fixed	Air
12	Neptune	♆	12	Pisces	♓	Mutable	Water

PLANETS

Sun: ☉ self-esteem, life force/vitality, creativity, risk-taking instincts, pride, star quality, fun-loving spirit, inner child, drive for excitement, need for recreation, speculative side, sexual passion, need to shine

Moon: ☽ emotions, security needs, caretaking instincts, dependency needs, drive to nurture, vulnerabilities, homing instincts, receptivity, moods, habit patterns, women (including mother)

Mercury: ☿ urge to communicate, thinking, listening/talking, capacity to learn, adaptability/flexibility, information-gathering skills, casual contacts, logic, awareness, dexterity, perception

Venus: ♀ desire for pleasure, sensuality, urge for comfort/ease, need for tangible beauty, drive for stability/predictability, sweetness, affection, relating needs, material assets

Mars: ♂ assertion, self-expression, independence, personal power, desires, spontaneous instincts, immediate needs, anger, sexual drive, early identity, doing one's thing

Jupiter: ♃ ideals and goals, beliefs, values, morality/ethics, faith, optimism, quest for the truth, philosophy/religion, drive for expanded horizons, high expectations, seeking the best/highest

Saturn: ♄ reality quotient; authority instincts, practicality, capacity to deal with limits, career drives, sense of responsibility, discipline/effort, status ambitions, urge to solidify/contract, wisdom of experience

Uranus: ♅ individuality, freedom drives, inventiveness, originality, humanitarian instincts, detachment, pull toward the future, eccentricity, innovation, sudden changes

Neptune: ♆ quest for Oneness/Union/transcendence, idealism, quest for infinite love and beauty, intuition, savior/victim potentials, compassion, imagination/fantasy, mysticism, escapism

Pluto: ♇ or ♀̇ intensity, drive for self-mastery, intimacy instincts, sexual needs, drive for transformation, elimination/completion urges, resentment/forgiveness, probing, complicated motives, compulsions

Ascendant: A personal identity, personal action, appearance, physical body, natural self-expression

Midheaven: M sense of authority, career aspirations, power drives and power figures, status

EXTRA BODIES

Halley's Comet: ☄ limelight, high focus, rise to power and fall

Chiron: ⚷ drive for knowledge, ideals, maverick, truth-seeking, teacher/healer

THE "BIG FOUR" ASTEROIDS

Ceres: ⚳ earth mother, productivity, health, growing things, health issues, mother figure

Juno: ⚵ marriage, beauty, intimacy, shared resources, giving and receiving

Pallas: ⚴ perception skills, equality, justice, balance, competition, visual aesthetics

Vesta: ⚶ responsibility, efficiency, tunnel vision, alienation, capable, health issues, concentration

Also by ACS Publications

All About Astrology Series of booklets
The American Atlas, Expanded Fifth Edition (Shanks)
The American Ephemeris for the 20th Century [Noon or Midnight] 1900 to 2000, Rev. 5th Ed.
The American Ephemeris for the 21st Century [Noon or Midnight] 2001-2050, Rev. 2nd Ed.
The American Heliocentric Ephemeris 1901-2000
The American Heliocentric Ephemeris 2001-2025
The American Midpoint Ephemeris 1996-2000
The American Sidereal Ephemeris 1976-2000, 2nd Edition
The American Sidereal Ephemeris 2001-2025
Asteroid Goddesses (George & Bloch)
Astro-Alchemy (Negus)
Astrological Insights into Personality (Lundsted)
Astrology for the Light Side of the Brain (Rogers-Gallagher)
Basic Astrology: A Guide for Teachers & Students (Negus)
Basic Astrology: A Workbook for Students (Negus)
The Book of Jupiter (Waram)
The Book of Neptune (Waram)
The Book of Pluto (Forrest)
The Book of Uranus (Negus)
The Changing Sky (Forrest)
Complete Horoscope Interpretation (Pottenger)
Cosmic Combinations (Negus)
Dial Detective (Simms)
Easy Tarot Guide (Masino)
Easy Astrology Guide (Pottenger)
Expanding Astrology's Universe (Dobyns)
Finding our Way Through the Dark (George)
Future Signs (Simms)
Hands That Heal (Burns)
Healing with the Horoscope (Pottenger)
The Inner Sky (Forrest)
The International Atlas, Revised Fourth Edition (Shanks)
The Michelsen Book of Tables (Michelsen)
Midpoints (Munkasey)
New Insights into Astrology (Press)
The Night Speaks (Forrest)
The Only Way to... Learn Astrology, Vols. I-VI (March & McEvers)
        Volume I - Basic Principles
        Volume II - Math & Interpretation Techniques
        Volume III - Horoscope Analysis
        Volume IV- Learn About Tomorrow: Current Patterns
        Volume V - Learn About Relationships: Synastry Techniques
        Volume VI - Learn About Horary and Electional Astrology
Planetary Heredity (M. Gauquelin)
Planets on the Move (Dobyns/Pottenger)
Psychology of the Planets (F. Gauquelin)
Spirit Guides: We Are Not Alone (Belhayes)
Tables of Planetary Phenomena (Michelsen)
Twelve Wings of the Eagle (Simms)
Your Magical Child (Simms)
Your Starway to Love (Pottenger), 2nd Edition

THE PLANETS IN DEPTH

The planets have more complex meanings than a few simple keywords and phrases.

The Book of Uranus
by Joan Negus

This recent volume in the Planets series covers the complex and creative planet Uranus. Joan Negus describes the dichotomies of Uranus — freedom and individuality, humanity and passion — to help you create a positive manifestation of its qualities in your life.

256 pages **BBU-BBS** $15.95

The Book of Pluto
by Steven Forrest

Steven Forrest tackles this planet of intensity with his usual wit, wisdom and compassion. He interprets Pluto through house, sign, and aspect with great sensitivity, incredible honesty and his wonderfully literate style. It's a rich collection of insights!

352 pages **B155X-BBS** $15.95

The Book of Neptune
by Marilyn Waram

A beautifully woven tapestry of warm compassion, acceptance, inspiration and wisdom that touches the heart of Neptune. Marilyn Waram takes you through Neptune in signs, houses and in aspect to the other planets.

256 pages **B121X-BBS** $15.95

The Book of Jupiter
by Marilyn Waram

Marilyn Waram provides a fresh, provocative look at Jupiter, the largest of planets. Through scientific study, Marilyn shows us the traits of "lucky" people and how creating one's own luck or good fortune in your life is possible.

320 pages **B150X-BBS** $15.95

Call Astro Toll-Free Mon-Fri, AM-5PM Pacific Time 1-800-888-9983
Trusted by Professional Astrologers for Over 24 Years
1 Ruffin Rd., San Diego CA 92123. Prices Subject to Change. Shipping and handling will be added.

Your Personal Electronic Astrologers

The Electronic Astrologer Reveals Your Horoscope

Text by Maritha Pottenger — Programmed by Rique Pottenger

"The Electronic Astrologer is the perfect choice for one's first astrology program, as it is effortless to learn and use, and teaches both basic principles and detailed delineations ...this inexpensive report is at least as good as programs costing six times as much!"

- American Astrology Magazine

Astro places the wisdom of astrology and modern technology at your fingertips in *The Electronic Astrologer*.
For Windows IBMWEA-BBS $59.95

The Electronic Astrologer Reveals Your Future

New April '97!

Text by Maritha Pottenger, Maria Kay Simms & Zipporah Dobyns — Programmed by Rique Pottenger

Three great astrologers have collaborated to write the text for this predictive program from **Astro**. The second in *The Electronic Astrologer* series, it promises to be even more popular than the first. *Reveals Your Future* is full of insights, encouragement and suggestions to make the most of any aspect.

The program is incredibly versatile and performs more functions than others at six times the cost.
For Windows IBMWEAF-BBS $59.95

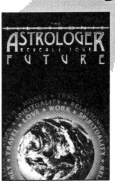

Order Toll Free! 800-888-9983

Trusted by Professional Astrologers for Over 24 Years.

Operators Available 8am to 5pm Pacific Time. 5521 Ruffin Rd., San Diego CA 92123.
Prices subject to change. Shipping and handling will be added.

Personalized Astrology Lessons

Our personalized lessons use your horoscope and offer you an opportunity to master the age-old discipline of astrology. Look deeper into all the issues of your life. Enhance your self-esteem and discover your potential. Maritha Pottenger created these lessons to help curious beginners understand all the tools that astrology has to offer. With an activist approach to astrology, Maritha shows you how to create your future and the life you want! Reinforce these lessons with actual homework assignments that test your knowledge! Ask your representative about specific lesson topics.

Everything Astrological Under the Sun
If you don't see it here, call & ask!

Basic Natal Chart ❖ Heliocentric Chart ❖ 4-Color Student Chart ❖ 8-Color Chart Package ❖ Relocation Chart ❖ Solar Return ❖ Lunar Return ❖ Progressed Chart ❖ Solar Arc Directed Chart ❖ Arabic Parts ❖ Astrodynes ❖ Fixed Stars ❖ Fortune Finder ❖ House Comparisons ❖ Midpoint Structures ❖ Directed Midpoints ❖ Three-Ring Concentric Chart ❖ Chart Comparison List ❖ Composite Chart ❖ Day-by-Day Progressions ❖ Astrolocality Maps ❖ Outer Planet Transits ❖ Calendar Transits ❖ Winning Transits ❖ Horary Chart ❖ Lifetime Lunar Phases ❖ Fertility Report ❖ Vocational Needs Analysis ❖ Hindu Chart ❖ Laminated Dials ❖ Celestial Sphere ❖ Biorhythms ❖ Addey Harmonics ❖ Huber Age Progression ❖ Tertiary Progression ❖ Minor Progressions ❖ Coalescent Chart ❖ Extra Bodies ❖ Dynamic Astrology

Call Astro 800-888-9983
Operators available Mon - Fri, 8AM-5PM Pacific Time
Trusted by professional astrologers for over 24 years

5521 Ruffin Rd., San Diego, CA 92123 Shipping and handling will be added. Prices subject to change.

Notes

Notes

Notes

Notes

Notes

Notes

Notes

Notes

Notes

Notes